The Eberly Library
Waynesburg College
Waynesburg, Pennsylvania

HENRY JAMES'S APPRENTICESHIP

Henry James at Geneva (ca. 1860)

HENRY JAMES'S APPRENTICESHIP
The Tales: 1864-1882

W. R. Martin
and
Warren U. Ober

P.D. Meany Publishers
Toronto

Copyright © 1994
W.R. Martin and Warren U. Ober

Canadian Cataloguing in Publication Data

Martin, W.R. (Walter Rintoul), 1920-
    Henry James's Apprenticeship

Includes bibliographical references and index.
ISBN 0-88835-034-1

1. James, Henry, 1843-1916 - Criticism and
interpretation. I. Ober, Warren U. II. Title

PS2124.M37 1992   813'.4   C92-094355-1

ISBN 0-88835-034-1

*Jacket photo (Henry James at Newport ca. 1863) by permission of the
Houghton Library, Harvard University, and Alexander R. James.*

*Photo on page ii (Henry James at Geneva ca. 1860) by permission of the
Houghton Library, Harvard University, and Alexander R. James.*

Jacket designed and typeset by Glen Patchet.

Printed on acid-free paper in Canada
for
P.D. Meany Publishers
Box 118, Streetsville
Ontario, Canada
L5M 2B7.

TABLE OF CONTENTS

ACKNOWLEDGEMENTS AND ABBREVIATIONS

For most of the tales we comment on we have fortunately been able to refer to the new, most useful, but still incomplete variorum series edited by Maqbool Aziz, *The Tales of Henry James*, 3 Vols. (Oxford: The Clarendon Press, 1973-84); unless otherwise stated, all references to this edition are to the first published versions of the tales, and these appear in parentheses in the text as numerals and without any reference to title. References to works listed below appear in the text with the abbreviations indicated. Dates of reprintings are given in the headings after the title of each tale; square brackets indicate that the reprinting was unrevised.

A	*Henry James: Autobiography*, ed. Frederick W. Dupee (Princeton: Princeton University Press, 1983).
AS	Henry James, *The American Scene*, ed. W.H. Auden (New York: Charles Scribner's Sons, 1946).
ECT	*The Complete Tales of Henry James*, 12 Vols., ed. Leon Edel (Philadelphia: J.B. Lippincott, 1961-64).
EL	Leon Edel, *Henry James: A Life* (New York: Harper & Row, 1985).

JF	F.O. Matthiessen, *The James Family* (New York: Alfred A. Knopf, 1947).
L	*Henry James: Letters*, 4 Vols., ed. Leon Edel (Cambridge, Mass.: Harvard University Press, 1974-84).
LC I	*Henry James, Literary Criticism: Essays on Literature; American Writers; English Writers*, ed. Leon Edel and Mark Wilson (New York: Library of America, 1984).
LC II	*Henry James, Literary Criticism: French Writers; Other European Writers; The Prefaces to the New York Edition*, ed. Leon Edel and Mark Wilson (New York: Library of America, 1984).
LL	*The Letters of Henry James*, 2 vols., ed. Percy Lubbock (New York: Charles Scribner's Sons, 1920).
N	*The Complete Notebooks of Henry James*, ed. Leon Edel and Lyall H. Powers (Oxford: Oxford University Press, 1987).
N 71-80	*Henry James: Novels 1871-1880*, ed. William T. Stafford (New York: Library of America, 1983).
TBW	Adeline R. Tintner, *The Book World of Henry James: Appropriating the Classics* (Ann Arbor, Michigan: UMI Research Press, 1987).
TMW	Adeline R. Tintner, *The Museum World of Henry James* (Ann Arbor, Michigan: UMI Research Press, 1986).

We owe a good deal to all the writers and editors in this list, especially to Leon Edel for his titanic labours and to Adeline Tintner for her painstaking identification of sources, but we do not always agree with their conclusions.

We must record our indebtedness and gratitude to many friends and fellow Jacobites, in particular to our colleague, William R. Macnaughton, whose book on James's later novels appeared while we were at work on this study of his early tales.

We are very grateful to Prof. G.E. Slethaug, Chairman of the Department of English, University of Waterloo, who has been helpful to us in innumerable ways, and to Illona Haus, who has done the word-processing for our book so efficiently and put up with all our revisions and indecisions so cheerfully.

Although our footnotes record our acknowledgements in detail, we want here to record our thanks to editors and publishers for permission to use material that first appeared in essays by us in various journals:

American Literary Realism 1870-1910, 24, 2 (1992): 81-87, "Henry James's 'Longstaff's Marriage' and 'Barbara Allan,'" by W.R. Martin and Warren U. Ober. By permission of McFarland & Company, Inc., Publishers, Jefferson, N.C. Volume 24 of *American Literary Realism* © McFarland & Company, Inc.

ANQ: A Quarterly Journal of Short Articles, Notes, and Reviews, N.S. 2 (1989): 137-38, "*Hamlet* and Henry James's First Fiction," by W.R. Martin.

The Arizona Quarterly, 42 (1986): 305-14, "Refurbishing James's 'A Light Man,'" by W.R. Martin and Warren U. Ober. (Copyright is held by Arizona Board of Regents.)

English Language Notes, 25 (1987): 44-48, "James's 'My Friend Bingham' and Coleridge's 'Ancient Mariner,'" by W.R. Martin and Warren U. Ober.

Studies in Short Fiction, 17 (1980): 497-99, "The Narrator's 'Retreat' in James's 'Four Meetings,' " by W.R. Martin;

22 (1985); 469-71, "Hemingway and James: 'A Canary for One' and 'Daisy Miller,'" by W.R. Martin and Warren U. Ober;

24 (1987); 57-58, "The Provenience of Henry James's First Tale," by W.R. Martin and Warren U. Ober;

25 (1988); 153-55, "'5 M.S. Pages': Henry James's Additions to 'A Day of Days,'" by W.R. Martin and Warren

U. Ober;

     26 (1989): 1-9, "Captain Diamond and Old Hickory: Realities and Ambivalence in Henry James's 'The Ghostly Rental,'" by W.R. Martin and Warren U. Ober;

     27 (1990): 260-63, "Henry James's 'Benvolio' and Milton," by W.R. Martin and Warren U. Ober.

PREFACE

There is an abundance of books on Henry James, and, especially since the appearance of Leon Edel's five-volume biography (1953-72), the spate of publication has been too strong for any but the devoted specialist to make way against. Asked whether there is need for yet another book, our immediate reply is Lear's: reason not the need. Our second is that, preposterous and sententious as it may at first sound, human prosperity--and perhaps even survival--depends on the lively realization in our daily routines and avocations of the finest insights and the highest values we can grasp and hold. We believe with Shelley, a forebear whom James honoured, that we need constantly to peruse and ponder the works of all our great writers because it is in these works of the creative imagination that human potentialities and aspirations are made known as they are nowhere else.

It is true that James did not enter into the circumstances and feelings of the common people, the factory or farm laborer, or the illiterate and incoherent. No longer a mere shy young man, on his second visit to Italy and well able to converse in Italian, he confessed, "I have been nearly a year in Italy and have hardly spoken to an Italian creature save washerwomen and waiters" (L I, 428). He has on occasion even been called a snob. He did enjoy his solitariness and moreover was able to put it to good use: he had extraordinary insight into and sympathy with the experience of cultivated individuals, even when they were separated from him by gulfs of space, time, and culture. ("Cultivation" is a term that many over-sensitive people fight shy of nowadays, but it refers to a reality that we ignore at our peril.) If James did not embrace a Bottom or an Ancient Pistol in his art, he did incorporate visions of the highest consciousness; indeed it has been held against him that his characters "live almost entirely off the tops of their minds" and even that they are "eviscerated" (JF 591, 678). If there is truth in what his older brother told him in 1890 apropos *The Tragic Muse*, "The work is too refined, too elaborate and minute, and requires to be read with too much leisure to appeal to any but the select few," we must not forget that William went on to say, "But you mustn't mind that. It will *always* have its audience" (JF 333). James's intelligence and sensibility will always be precious to some individuals in civilized society.

This book examines individually and seriatim the first 38 tales James wrote. It uses them as a convenient, comparatively narrow, but significant focus to identify James's permanent interests and predispositions as a man and artist, to assess each tale's success as a work of art, and to chart his development from a diffident apprenticeship to the remarkably mature virtuosity of his late thirties, which foreshadows his later mastery. Preparing his life's work for the New York Edition (1907-09), he could, like Prospero or Napoleon, survey his own great empire of the imagination.

The concept of this book has its origin in the notion that James, who (as his frequent quotations show) was saturated in Shakespeare, found his Ur-myth, or an image of it, in the plays, especially in *Hamlet, Othello*, and *The Tempest*, where an Innocent is nearly or actually entrapped by the snares of the World. We believe this notion, naive as it may be, is not altogether wide of the truth, and its shadow is constantly visible throughout the book. James went a long way towards fulfilling the novelist's need for a myth and a rhetoric by developing the agon of the Innocent and by establishing centres of consciousness as prisms for his narratives.

A cognate origin is our series of studies of separate tales in which James clearly imitated, borrowed, or in some ingenious manner derived his plot or theme from great works or writers that he admired, though the borrowing was never slavish, and, even though often long unnoticed, never surreptitious or plagiaristic. This method or process is a feature not merely of his early tales, but is conspicuous even in his last collection, *The Finer Grain* (1910),[1] and is discernible in his deathbed dictations. James's ability to enter into, appropriate, and transform for his own artistic purposes the creations of other writers is an aspect of that ambivalence that was an important element in his greatness, that chameleon quality that Keats described and that James shares with Shakespeare, whom he recognized as a universal genius.

COMPREHENDING CONTRADICTIONS

The literal played in our education as small a part as it ever played in any, and we wholesomely breathed inconsistency and ate and drank contradictions.
(A 123-24)

Our father [said] that we could plead nothing less than the whole privilege of Christendom and that there was no communion, even that of the Catholics, even that of the Jews, even that of the Swedenborgians, from which we need find ourselves excluded.
(A 133-34)

As more or less of [an artist] myself . . . I deal with being, I invoke and evoke, I figure and represent, I seize and fix, as many phases and aspects and conceptions of it as my infirm hand allows me strength for.
(JF 611)

Nothing is my *last word* about anything--I am interminably supersubtle and analytic--and with the blessing of heaven, I shall live to make all sorts of representations of all sorts of things. It will take a much cleverer person than myself to discover my last impression . . . of anything.
Letter of 21 March 1879 to Mrs. F.H. Hill.
(L II, 221)

I am that queer monster the artist . . . an inexhaustible sensibility.
Letter of 21 March 1914 to Henry Adams.
(L IV, 706)

The house of fiction has in short not one window, but a million--a number of possible windows not to be reckoned, rather; every one of which has been pierced, or is still pierceable, in its vast front, by the need of the individual vision and by the pressure of the individual will.
Preface to *The Portrait of a Lady*, 1908.
(LC II, 1075)

xiv

Introduction

THE YOUNG MAN AND THE EARLY TALES

Henry James lived from 1843 to 1916. What kind of person was he? We can probably find in a combination of his personal, physical, family, and cultural circumstances reasons why he did not have the sort of natural ebullience, confidence, and assertiveness of, say, Dickens. In old age James recalled his temperament as a small boy: "up to my twelfth year" he was prone to "dawdle and gape" about New York (A 10, 17), and "gaping," sometimes with "wondering," recurs as an amusing motif throughout his account of his childhood and young manhood.[1] His part in the Civil War, in which his two younger brothers both fought for the North as volunteers, he describes as that of "seeing, sharing, envying, applauding, pitying, all from too far-off" (A 461), but even before he suffered the "horrid even if . . . obscure hurt" (A 415) that he claims prevented his active service, he was not notable for the more obvious kinds of activity and initiative: it is characteristic that, writing to Thomas Sergeant Perry from Geneva at the age of seventeen, he laments that there are "no such fields and meadows and groves as there are near Lily Pond [at Newport, Rhode Island], places where you can halt and lie out on the flat of your back and loll and loaf and reverise (Don't you remember?)" (L I, 20). In 1874, at the age of 30, he confessed: "I have been nearly a year in Italy and have hardly spoken to an Italian creature save washerwomen and waiters" (L I, 428). And yet by the winter of 1878-79 this shy and thoughtful young man "dined out" in London no less than 107--or by another account 140--times.[2] Even as a youth he had social grace and a quiet presence, but his demeanour was marked by a certain submissiveness and passivity. He also had the virtues of these qualities: he was his mother's favourite, having "angelic patience"[3]--indeed "angel" became a teasing and somewhat invidious family name for Henry (see EL 157, 245, 278).

As a child, at least, James felt that his father's unconventional career--he never had a job!--made him "ridiculous" among his fellows (A 278). His father, though often affectionate and always sympathetic, had an expansive and, if not a forceful, at least an effective, personality, and a standing among those interested in intellectual and spiritual speculation that made him a difficult figure for a son as respectful as Henry was to cross, not the less so because of what Robert C. Le Clair refers to as "the parents' looseness of rein."[4] James's mother too was a far from negligible force, and, although, when she died early in 1882, James could say "she was the perfection of a mother--the sweetest, gentlest, most beneficent human being I have ever known" (L II, 379), she was in fact oppressively solicitous, getting her way "not by assertion but by selflessness,"[5] which made her authority harder to withstand. The power of James's parents over their children was exercised with the best intentions, but it was not always benign. James wrote discreetly but no doubt with feeling when he told his mother in a letter of January 1881: "One wishes to be morally united to one's family; but after a certain age, one doesn't wish to be materially united--at least, too closely" (L II, 331). Here he is arguing that his brother William, now 40 and a husband and father, should be independent of and separate from his parents in Cambridge, Mass.; Henry himself had in fact virtually left home, though not until 1875, when he was 32. Moreover, three years later, in the year in which "Daisy Miller" was to make him at last financially independent, he is still having to explain to his father why he has borrowed more on his letter of credit (L II, 175-76); for as long as they lived he would in his letters call them "Daddy" and "Mammy" (L II, 346, 350).

William, only little more than a year older than Henry, was lively, extroverted, and active, and destined to become one of the leading intellects of his time. As Matthiessen puts it, William was "active and participating," while Henry was "passive and observing" (JF 74). Henry felt himself overshadowed by William, accepted his "primogeniture," and "always maintained an attitude of graceful inadequacy."[6] Towards the end of his life James wrote: "I never for all the time of childhood and youth in the least caught up with him or overtook him" (A 7-8), and even then, at the age of 70 and after William had died, James writes autobiographies with titles--*A Small Boy and Others* and *Notes of a Son and Brother*--that appear to divert attention from himself.[7]

James's personal insecurity found some assuagement in the very circumstances that seem to have caused it: to some extent he identified himself with the family in which he felt himself overshadowed. The talents and achievements of (especially) his father and of William and Alice, as well as his own, reflected credit on all involved. Thus in July 1880, for example, he excuses the postponement of a visit home to America by saying it will allow him to complete *The Portrait of a Lady* without haste and also perhaps to write a life of Dickens--he never did!--and thus, "when you see that [these reasons] redound to my profit, glory and general felicity, and therefore, by intimate implication, to yours [his father's and mother's] and my sister's, you will, I think easily accept them" (L II, 295). Edel has justly observed that, when James was the sole survivor and wrote his autobiographies, he "wore the mantle of Family."[8]   The *Autobiography* is certainly a great monument to family pride and solidarity. Here was a notable inconsistency: the diffident boy had a Napoleonic conceit.

There was in addition James's strong feeling, shared almost equally by other members of his family and, indeed, by many cultivated Americans, about history, tradition, and culture, especially in association with Europe, which he often visited with his family as a boy. In a famous passage, James has recorded, for instance, how from boyhood he inhaled "little by little, that is again and again, a general sense of *glory*" (A 196) in the Galerie d'Apollon in the Louvre. It was a feeling of respect, amounting sometimes almost to superstitious reverence, and not altogether without attitudes of excessive humility and abasement. James felt that he must travel in Europe and learn and absorb it before he would be fit to write; he was "the fond observer of the footsteps of genius."[9]   He saw things in a "composite historic light," the absence of which he found so remarkable in Hawthorne's vision (LC I, 309).   James's deference, together with his capacity for gaping, which became the power of passionate observation in the presence of high achievements, contributed to the effect of his self-effacement. As Edel says, James, in his youth at least, "invariably preferred to see rather than to be seen."[10]

James's ever-present ambivalence was evident in the fact that, although his veneration for Europe was nearly obsessive, he was almost complacent in his pride as an American. Writing in 1867 from Boston to T.S. Perry, who was in Europe, he praises "our [American] moral consciousness, our unprecedented spiritual lightness and vigour" (L I, 77); in 1870, writing from England to Boston, he recalls the "intellectual grace" and "moral spontaneity" (L I, 208) in young American women such as Clover Hooper and Minny Temple that is lacking in Englishwomen; in 1879: "All the Americans I meet [in London] . . . strike me as clever--light, bright, quick, keen, etc." (L II, 249). And yet over roughly the same period (the late 1860s and the 1870s) one can also find strong expressions of the opposite feeling: he tells T.S. Perry that even "the female Cambridge [Massachusetts] society" seemed "provincial, common and inelegant" (L I, 72), and his mother that "the Englishmen I have met not only kill, but bury in unfathomable depths, the Americans I have met. A set of people less framed to provoke national self-complacency than the latter it would be hard to imagine. There is but one word to use in regard to them-- vulgar; vulgar, vulgar" (L I, 152); tells Charles Eliot Norton that his patriotism is not "serene"--in fact he is "half ashamed of it" (L I, 362); tells his brother William that Miss Bartlett and Mrs. Sumner, in Rome in 1873, though "both superior and very natural women, and Mrs. Sumner a very charming one," are nevertheless "limited by a kind of characteristic American want of culture" (L I, 364). Five years later Mrs. Sumner, divorced from Charles Sumner, the prominent politician (now deceased), and living under her maiden name, Mason, is "redolent of American civilization. In no other country could such beautiful material have remained so unwrought" (L II, 212); in 1880 he writes that Europe (or London) "is a higher civilization, in literary respects" (L II, 275). James knew very well the embarrassments of being naive and ridiculous, which he portrays often in his "passionate pilgrims," and so achieved a sort of detachment, and it was the interplay of these contrary attitudes in his feelings and imagination that contributed largely to his greatness as an artist. He felt very keenly that "it's a complex fate, being an American, and one of the responsibilities it entails is fighting against a superstitious valuation of Europe" (L I, 274).

Some have said or implied that James's internationalism resulted in a deficiency, making him neither fish nor fowl, robbing him of character and integrity. He himself, with what is less an inconsistency than an extraordinary many-sidedness, was able to say something like this of himself: in April 1899 he could "conjure" William to bring up his sons so that they would be able "to contract local saturations and attachments in respect to their *own* great and glorious country, to learn, and strike roots into, its infinite beauty . . . and variety," and draw "therefrom experiences of a sort that I too miserably lacked . . . in my own too casual youth" (LL I, 316). However, we believe that, for the very reason that he could be, paradoxically, at once detached and sympathetic, and so in a sense both American and European, his art has a unique value. Towards the end of his life, he praised Baltimore's Johns Hopkins University because he saw in it a "reconsecration" of European values and a "continuity" in the process of civilization (AS 320), an instance of what he elsewhere describes as "our national theory of absorption, assimilation and conversion" (A 425). As F.R. Leavis has observed, James "transcends the vindication of one side against the other" and in his fiction "is feeling, creatively, towards an ideal possibility."[11]

As early as at least 1880 James was parrying friendly suggestions that he might marry by saying with characteristically disarming suavity that he was "too good a bachelor to spoil." He was lonely, but that was his deliberate choice. He knew that "one's attitude toward marriage is a part--the most characteristic part, doubtless--of one's general attitude toward life," and that if he married he would be "guilty in my own eyes of an inconsistency" (L II, 323, 314): if he married he would become involved in life in a way that would make impossible the sort of detachment he needed for his writing. In the end, aware of his lack of material success, wide critical acclaim, or influence on great affairs, he perhaps found compensation in embracing a conception of art and of the status of the artist that attributed to himself a function and achievement that had imperial overtones. It was a fruitful and not an altogether delusory concept. Thus, in the last analysis, James *was* consistent--in his devotion to his art.

What sort of an artist, then, was James? He was unlike D.H. Lawrence, whose genius burned with a bright, even fierce spontaneity. James's bush burned brightly too, but it had first to be coaxed into flame with plenty of kindling and a deal of blowing and tending. He did not have as remarkable or as instinctive a mythopoeic faculty as some other great writers have had. As Adeline Tintner says, "Invention was never one of James's strong points" (TBW 125). One might apply to James's creative imagination even in his early work what he himself, late in life, so amusingly said of his intellectual powers at the age of twelve: they were "embalmed . . . in a sort of fatalism of patience, spiritless in a manner, no doubt, yet with an inwardly active, productive and ingenious side" (A 170). Writing of himself as a law student at Harvard a few years later, he puts it more plainly: he was already sure that "on the day . . . when one should cease to live in large measure by one's eyes (with the imagination of course all the while waiting on this) one would have taken the longest step towards not living at all" (A 443).

Rich commentary and reflection became the characteristic mark of James's work, and yet he uses this element to build up to and sometimes to precipitate brief but climactic dramatic encounters in which the latent tensions get sharp focus and definition. His most frequent exhortation to himself in his Prefaces is to "Dramatise!" (LC II 1241, 1244, 1253, 1267, 1269, 1272), and this is usually with regard to his tales. It is an admonition that his reflective native genius seems to have needed. James's *Notebooks*, together with his Prefaces, give perhaps the most illuminating insights available to us about what goes into the making of a work of fiction.

In the early tales we can follow the evolution of the Jamesian protagonist: the sensitive, intelligent, and often innocent observer or participant. James became, as Conrad puts it in his essay, "the historian of fine consciences." Early on we have, for example, Locksley ("A Landscape Painter," 1866), Richard Maule ("Poor Richard," 1867), Euphemia de Mauves and Longmore ("Mme. de Mauves," 1874), and, of course, Daisy Miller (1878), a succession that leads on to the central figures of the later novels: Isabel, Fleda, and Maggie. Together with this we see the scene in which the protagonist--in the early tales usually a man, but later typically a young woman--comes to see clearly the full import of the complex issues involved, and also to achieve self-knowledge. In "Guest's Confession" (1872), for instance, the narrator, "in ardent solitude," lies "motionless" on a "shady streamside" and follows the "logic of [his] meditations" until "an ineffable change stole over [his] spirit" (II, 199-200).

Shakespeare intensified and elevated his plays by writing of kings and others in high places; in Lear, Hamlet, Antony, Macbeth, and Othello the ultimate possibilities of our own lives are writ large. James achieves intensification in an egalitarian age by presenting a different kind of nobility--that of the refined, generous, intelligent, and almost pristinely ingenuous sensibility in which stresses are felt and strains recorded that less sensitive and cultivated natures are only dimly or intermittently conscious of.

James's characters are, if American, often wealthy and, if

European, often both wealthy and aristocratic. But he was sensitive to the dangers of this sort of scenario. He was quick to perceive the by no means obvious weaknesses, such as failure of nerve and sense of purpose, among the English aristocracy at the very time when the British imperium seemed to be at its apogee, and he saw very clearly the demoralization that great wealth can cause. Among his American protagonists in the early tales there are only a few who are conspicuously wealthy. In an 1877 review of a French novelist, Octave Feuillet, he ridicules him because he "relates exclusively the joys and sorrows of the aristocracy; the loves of marquises and countesses alone appear worthy of his attention, and heroes and heroines can hope to make no figure in his pages unless they have an extraordinary number of quarterings" (LC II, 286-87). Of course James was interested not in wealth or rank *per se*, but in cultivated people and in civilized behaviour, and in this imperfect world the qualities he measured will tend, *ceteris paribus*, to be more conspicuous among those who have the means and opportunities to achieve and maintain them.

James Joyce's young Stephen Dedalus proclaims at the end of *A Portrait of the Artist as a Young Man* that he will forge in the smithy of his soul "the uncreated conscience of my race," and one recalls D.H. Lawrence telling an interviewer that "you . . . write from a deep moral sense--for the race, as it were."[12] Though not in any ordinary political or social sense a reformer, James shares with many dedicated artists the deep impulse to promote self-knowledge and help create a new life more refined, intense, and moral, and therefore more delightful, than the one we lead. In a review he published at the age of twenty-one he wrote: "an author's paramount charge is the cure of souls" (LC I, 605); a few months later he spoke of the expectation that a writer "shall contribute to the glory of human nature" (LC I, 1314). It is not irrelevant to remember that James was the son of a man for whom "original sin consisted of self-centered being" and for whom it was to be transcended by shedding "pride in self to find a new sense of self in the divinity within man's nature."[13] To those who complain that the life James creates is unrelated to our own, one can reply that just as James strove for artistic completeness, for a seamless union, for example, of content and form, so did he scrutinize life in the light of the most civilized standards conceived in our culture.

James attached great importance to his tales. He would not have accepted the now widely held prejudice that, volume for volume, they are necessarily less significant than the novels. We can smile at, but we must not dismiss, his youthful, defensive, yet backhandedly proud facetiousness in a letter to his friend T.S. Perry in 1868: "I write little and only tales, which I think it likely I shall continue to manufacture in a hackish manner, for that which is bread. They *cannot* of necessity be very good; but they *shall not* be very bad" (L I, 84). In a letter of January 1871 he told C.E. Norton, one of his mentors, that "to write a series of good little tales I deem ample work for a life-time" (L I, 253). A month before his thirtieth birthday he declared that "to produce some little exemplary works of art is my narrow and lowly dream" (L I, 351), though one should notice that this is in excuse for not having attempted a novel as ambitious as *Middlemarch!* Later in the same month (March 1873) he is telling his mother: "I value none of my early tales enough to bring them forth again, and if I did, should absolutely need to give them an amount of verbal retouching"--he is already an assiduous reviser--but he goes on to say that the work of his last three years is "much better and maturer" (L I, 357). By 1888 he was confiding to Robert Louis Stevenson that he wanted "to leave a multitude of pictures of my time, projecting my small circular frame upon as many different spots as possible" (L III, 240), and in the Preface to *The Lesson of the Master* (1909) he publicly proclaims his affection for and pride in "the beautiful and blest *nouvelle*" (LC II, 1227).

James wrote 112 tales. The short and conclusive answer to those who question their importance is that, of the 24 volumes in the carefully meditated and deliberately planned New York Edition, no less than six are entirely, and three others partly, devoted to a total of 55 tales.[14]

Some readers expect critical studies to launch out boldly into, and to remain sailing among, grand generalizations and high abstractions; they may be disappointed by our approach. One of the great satisfactions in reading James's critical writing is in finding the incisive pronouncements that flowed from his pen throughout his life with curious felicity and authority, and one such, dating from the period of his acknowledged mastership, endorses our method, which is to avoid "doctrine suspended in the void" (LC I, 95) and to concern ourselves with the minute particulars of each of the 38 tales in turn in order to assess it as a work of art. We attempt to arrive at general conclusions by this route. In general we have used the terms, tools, and approach that one finds in James's own reviews of fiction.

In the Preface (1907) to *The American* James wrote: "The

content and the 'importance' of a work of art are . . . wholly dependent on its *being* one: outside of which all prate of its representative character, its meaning and its bearing, its morality and humanity, are an impudent thing" (LC II, 1068). We hope we have avoided prating and impudence! In practical terms our aim is twofold: to offer analyses, based on close reading, of the tales James wrote in the first fifteen years of his career, and then to show how the vision and the faculty that he was refining in these tales prepared him for the writing of his first masterpiece, *The Portrait of a Lady*.

Chapter I

UNPUBLISHED TRANSLATIONS AND THE
FIRST SIX TALES, 1860-67

In considering James's early work one should be on one's guard against the complacency that hindsight sometimes induces, but it is true that one can now see that in his beginnings there are foreshadowings, however faint and tentative, of many features of his mature art. There are translations and frequent "borrowings"; stories of ghosts and the preternatural that are in an established genre; concerns with the embarrassments and pitfalls of the imaginative, the susceptible, and the innocent; techniques involving the point of view; stories about artists and the function of art. All these features and themes recur throughout his career.

After spending his early boyhood in New York and several years in Europe on various trips and sojourns with his family, he lived, still with his family, at Newport for two years. These two years, 1860 to 1862, were important for James, still not 20 years old, because it was while at Newport that he came under crucial influences and tried his hand at translation; one might expect that a youth as diffident and as respectful to seniors, mentors, and predecessors as James was would start in this self-effacing way. He tells us how the painter, John La Farge, seven years his senior, "started me on [Prosper Mérimée's] La Vénus d'Ille; so that nothing would do but that I should translate it, try to render it as lovingly as if it were a classic and old" (A 292). James submitted it for publication, but the New York periodical did him "the honour neither of acknowledging nor printing . . . nor in the least understanding his offering"; this suggests that he valued it as much more than a sensational ghost story; he writes: "Didn't I already see, as I fumbled with a pen, of what the small dense formal garden [of Mérimée's] might be inspiringly symbolic" (A 294). James several times refers to a similar quality in the French writer's work: "zealous artistic conciseness," "selection and concision," "the magic of an edge so fine and a surface so smooth" in "Tamango," "Mateo Falcone," and *"L'Enlèvement de la Redoute"* (LC II, 563, 576, 577), the first two of which he apparently also translated, but with the same lack of success.[1] An additional attraction for James in these stories may have been some Napoleonic associations and a distinctly identified and characterized narrator. He also translated some of La Fontaine's fables, perhaps as a school exercise (A 183), and, according to T.S. Perry, Alfred de Musset's play *Lorenzaccio*, into which he introduced scenes of his own (EL 54-55). In 1877 James said that "Musset always reminds us of Shakespeare" (LC II, 617), and indeed *Lorenzaccio* has often been compared with *Hamlet*, so many echoes of which can be heard in James's fiction, both late and early.

The ghostly or supernatural tales that James wrote throughout his life are not merely gothic and gruesome; there is usually an underlying symbolic meaning or theme, some psychological frame, or some other special effect aimed at. One of these effects is the marriage of romance and realism. As he put it toward the end of his career in the Preface to *The American*, romance deals with "experience liberated, so to speak; experience disengaged, disembroiled, disencumbered, exempt from the conditions that we usually know to attach to it and, if we wish so to put the matter, drag upon it. . . . The balloon of experience is in fact of course tied to the earth, and under that necessity we swing, thanks to a rope of remarkable length, in the more or less commodious car of the imagination; but it is by the rope we know where we are, and from the moment that cable is cut we are at large and unrelated. . . . The art of the romancer is, 'for the fun of it,' insidiously to cut the cable, to cut it without our detecting him." He puts it more succinctly and less equivocally in another Preface-- to *The Spoils of Poynton*--where fiction is said to be experience freed from the "stupid work" of "clumsy Life" (LC II, 1064, 1140). James wants us ensconced in our armchair so that he can waft us and our chair off on a carpet without our noticing that we are no longer imprisoned by the obdurate iron bars of life, but feel imaginatively freed to envisage experience's fullest and finest, without altogether forgetting its basest and most appalling, possibilities. In all James's fiction there is this kind of liberation rather than what is often deprecated as "escape"; in his ghostly tales the liberation is only more patent than in the others. Thus, in a review of February 1874, James says of Mérimée: "Some of his best stories are those in which a fantastic or supernatural element is thrown into startling relief against a background of hard, smooth realism. An admirable success in this line is the 'Venus d'Ille'--a version of the old legend of a love-pledge between a mortal and an effigy of the goddess" (LC II, 564). Cornelia Pulsifer Kelley, noticing that the statue of the goddess claims the young man "as its own" and smothers him "in its nuptial bed embrace,"[2] seems to suggest that the goddess's motive is ordinary sexual jealousy, and other commentators apparently follow her (see EL 85 and TMW xix). We believe, however, that Mérimée's story appealed to James because Mérimée's version of the legend has a more interesting and profound theme. The goddess is moved to revenge not because she is jealous in the common personal manner; her vengeance is more philosophic and springs from a deeper source. She is exacting retribution for the young man's--and his family's--casual and even mercenary attitude to the sacred mystery of love and the consecration of that love in marriage. Mérimée's story carefully indicates the steady accumulation of offered slights, which amount to insult and blasphemy and make the dreadful punishment condign. We suggest that the formal and symbolic element that James admired is in the vindication, by the copper statue of Venus, of fundamental or natural human law, morality, and decency.[3] In following Mérimée, who is himself following perhaps Euripides' *Hippolytus* or *The Bacchae*, James is in a role that is characteristic at this stage: he is an acolyte treading in the footsteps of a figure like T.S. Eliot's compound ghost. Incidentally, it is worth noticing that a few years later, in 1868, in reviewing William Morris's *The Earthly Paradise,* James found "most impressive the terrible hostility of Venus" (LC I, 1189), and that in 1868 and 1874 he was to publish "The Romance of Certain Old Clothes" and other tales that are in some ways similar to *"La Vénus d'Ille"* and derive from Hawthorne, another adept at the mesmerist's sleight, which is described by Miles Coverdale at the beginning of *The Blithedale Romance* as that of extending over his "preternatural conquests" the "laws of our actual life."

After Newport, James went to Harvard in 1862 to study law. He was separated from his family for the first time, but, following a now familiar pattern, William was ahead of him at the university, "on the scene and already at a stage of possession of its contents that I was resigned in advance never to reach" (A 418). James did not take to the law, but it was while at Harvard that he wrote the first things that he published. By 1864 he was writing reviews for the *North American Review* and in 1865 tales for the *Atlantic Monthly*, both prominent Boston publications; in New York his reviews were appearing in the *Nation* in 1865, and in the following year his tales were being published in the *Galaxy*. As far as we know, however, the firstling of his pen was published in a more obscure journal.

"A TRAGEDY OF ERROR"　(*Continental Monthly*, February 1864)

This tale was never acknowledged by James and indeed was not known to be by him until discovered by Leon Edel. It is a grim tale of perfidy between spouses and lovers, of cold-blooded murder and mistaken identity, like one of Balzac's *Contes Drôlatiques*, but chilling, the heinous behaviour being recounted with a sort of sardonic detachment. There is a recurrent device in the narrative ("Such persons as were looking on at the moment saw . . ."; "to a third person, it would have appeared . . ."; "A wayfarer might have taken him for a ravisher . . ." I, 1, 3, 4) which does not reflect the later Jamesian concern with point of view but is a stock and rather clumsy device of Victorian fiction to raise suspicion or create mystery or tension; one finds it in Hawthorne, for instance: "Had a wanderer, bewildered in the melancholy forest, heard their mirth . . ." ("The Maypole of Merry Mount"), and "Some affirm that the lady of the governor was there" ("Young Goodman Brown").
The title is an additional sardonic touch, a nod in the direction of Shakespeare's *The Comedy of Errors*, itself also an early work and a borrowing (from Plautus). James's tale is a borrowing from Chaucer's Franklin's Tale in *The Canterbury Tales*: the location of the tale and the name of the ship, the *Armorique*, recall Chaucer's tale, and then James proceeds to turn the original upside down and inside out, but so systematically that the borrowing is unmistakable. He changes the Franklin's *exemplum* of true love, faith, trust, openness and "gentillesse" into a nightmarish maze of deceit, infidelity, failure to communicate, lies, treachery, and assassination.[4]
We can assume that James was interested in the full range of English literature from Chaucer onwards, but it is interesting to note that, when James attended the Harvard Law School in 1862, "at meals three times a day" he sat opposite "Harvard's Chaucerian and collector of ballads," Francis J. Child, who was "filled with dis-

course about the conduct of the [Civil] war," his talk a "darting flame" on Chaucer too, no doubt (EL 65; A 427-28); his *Observations on the Language of Chaucer* had just appeared.[5] In any event, James shows in his 1867-68 reviews of Morris's *The Life and Death of Jason* and *The Earthly Paradise* that he knew his Chaucer well (LC I, 1177, 1185, 1191).

Interesting questions arise. In his *Autobiography* and some-times in his Prefaces James has a lot to say about his admirations and the influences upon him, and with special reference to his youth he writes of the "admirable commerce of borrowing and lending, taking and giving, not to say stealing and keeping" (A 493). James had no unnecessary "anxiety of influence" (TBW xxii), and T.S. Eliot, in his essay "Philip Massinger," has assured us that "mature poets steal,"[6] so it is not a question of honesty but of whether the writer has appropriated the material thoroughly enough--which may involve transmutation--for artistic purposes that are his own.[7] In any case, James leaves plain clues to his bor-rowings, even if readers and critics have not always recognized them; it seems he sometimes assumed greater sharpness or attention and more familiarity with literature in his readers than they in fact possessed. The naive reader of "A Tragedy of Error" will presumably be sufficiently satisfied with the plot involving lust, sordid intrigue, and murder, but the better-equipped reader, who will be looking for more in any case, can have the added pleasure of recognizing the sources, appreciating the extra resonance that these give the tale, and admiring the neatness with which James has "subverted" Chaucer's tale. The question of different and even divergent readings of the same text involving various levels of insight is worked out fully and brilliantly by James in the much later tale, "The Birthplace."[8]

Chaucer's tale is subverted but not contradicted; there does not seem to be any implication that the Franklin's Tale is false or sentimental. James has performed no more than a pleasant and slightly mischievous trick; his is a readable tale, not to be compared with Chaucer's, which has, moreover, an extra significance: it is told by a particular character, and it takes its place in a series of tales that develop contrasting attitudes to love, marriage, life, and the human condition, whereas James's has no special appropriateness and belongs to no such comprehensive scheme.

Is this sort of borrowing in James's early tales a sign of an inability to build his own structures, evidence of his characteristic diffidence and deference? He was not yet twenty-one when "A

Tragedy of Error" was published, and one could hardly expect that at this stage he would have an attitude or world-view that would require a new myth for its expression.

"THE STORY OF A YEAR" (*Atlantic Monthly*, March 1865)

Henry James did not need the lively conversation of Francis J. Child to bring the Civil War urgently to his mind. His younger brother Wilky, severely wounded in the assault on Fort Wagner, was brought home on a stretcher in August 1863, much as Lieutenant John Ford is in this tale. Though Wilky arrived "almost as one dead" (EL 62), he recovered, but Ford dies, like James's cousin Vernon King, whose death in the war makes so moving the portrait of him in *A Small Boy and Others* (A 219-22). The effect of the war on James was made all the more intense by his "depressingly prolonged" relation to it (A 460-62): he was fully involved emotionally but inactive physically on account of "a horrid even if an obscure hurt" (A 415).

At the centre of "The Story of a Year" is Lizzie, who becomes engaged to Ford at the beginning of the tale but then is flirtatiously involved with Robert Bruce even before news of Ford's misfortune arrives. The story is about her unfaithfulness. Again there are lineaments borrowed from a classic; the tale mirrors "The Mousetrap," which the players perform at Hamlet's behest, and it in turn of course reflects the story of the King, Gertrude, and Claudius in *Hamlet*.[9]

Unlike Hortense in "A Tragedy of Error," Lizzie is far from being a simple villainess; her weakness is merely that she is too susceptible to liking and being liked, too responsive to the amenities of the moment. The story is successful precisely because it is not melodrama. There is a passage of pleasant irony at Lizzie's expense (I, 30-31) but later a good deal of sympathetic insight into her consciousness (I, 39, 41-44). Moreover, Ford's mother, Lizzie's guardian, a formidable character convincingly drawn, is hostile to the girl and seems eager that her engagement to her son should be broken off: after her son's departure for the front, "it suited [his mother's] purpose . . . that her young charge should now go forth into society and pick up acquaintances" (I, 34), which makes us a little less severe toward Lizzie. On the other hand, lest we should condone Lizzie's conduct, lights are cast on it by her correspondence to the Player Queen and thus also to Queen Gertrude. In this way James in this early tale already presents a situation that is complex, denying us the luxury of easy moral judgement.   Also, by bringing his classical model to bear so decisively in the moral scale, James shows that his borrowing is being put to his own legitimate and significant artistic purpose. Looking particularly at French influences, Philip Grover remarks that generally James "greatly changed the original work to fit his own purposes."[10]   This is true; looking ahead to later effects from his borrowings, however, we must agree with Adeline Tintner: in his early attempts there is "frequently a one-to-one compressed correspondence," while James's "later, more mature reworkings . . . show a freer, more subtle, and more generalized" attitude to the source (TBW 4).   We shall find this greater subtlety even as early as 1869 when James published his brilliant "A Light Man"; in his very last tale, "A Round of Visits" (1910), by adapting and, for his own purposes, rewriting Dante's *Inferno*, he offers a bravura demonstration of consummate mastery in his borrowings.   James's mind "tended at all times to create in analogues" (TBW 201), but these did not constrict his own creative powers; at first the borrowing was a trellis, but in the end it was often a launching pad for his highest flights.

Lizzie is portrayed with insight and sympathy, but she is not a heroine, nor was she meant to be.   Thus the difference between her and, say, Isabel, Fleda, or Maggie is that she does not have a fine conscience and high intelligence--or even ingenuity--and the result is that she is less interesting than they are.   She is not self-critical or self-questioning--the "scorn of her own conscience" (I, 55), to which she might have hearkened, does not press her hard enough in the end (as John Marcher's does in "The Beast in the Jungle") to redeem her, and it is this intense inner and spiritualized drama that goes into the making of James's greatest fiction.   Lizzie is weak.

Lastly, one may notice the beginnings of James's wit: "People are apt to think that they may temper the penalties of misconduct by self-commiseration, just as they season the long after-taste of beneficence by a little spice of self-applause" (I, 41-42); the aphorisms of the later James would be a little more urbane and elegant, and a lot less long-winded, sententious, and sardonic.

"A LANDSCAPE PAINTER" (*Atlantic Monthly*, February 1866; 1885)

This tale has technical flaws, but it is more interesting than the two earlier stories if only because it is a more distinctly Jamesian fiction, and we shall frequently refer back to it because it is a sort of forerunner. The narrator, who introduces the tale and whom we have no reason to disbelieve, tells us that young Locksley, the protagonist, is cultivated and wealthy, and Locksley's diary, which tells the story, confirms that he is sophisticated and sensitive. He also tells us that Locksley, who "died seven years ago," was a man of "what are called elegant tastes: that is, he was seriously interested in arts and letters. He wrote some very bad poetry, but he produced a number of remarkable paintings . . . . He had in him the stuff of a great painter" (I, 58). So Locksley is not only the first Jamesian sensitive but also his first artist. Being an artist, young, imaginative, trusting, and wealthy, he is prone to generous error and therefore vulnerable--and liable to suffer. Here we are close to what became probably James's central myth: the sensitive and ingenuous Innocent is confronted by the wiles and wickedness of the World. In general it is not until James's later fiction that the innocent artist and his like are successful in this agon, not until, for example, we meet Gedge ("The Birthplace," 1903), Maggie (*The Golden Bowl,* 1904), and Mark Monteith ("A Round of Visits," 1910); meanwhile we have Locksley, Roderick Hudson (1875), Daisy Miller (1878), and Mark Ambient ("The Author of 'Beltraffio,'" 1884).

James's interest in the theme of the Innocent who is entrapped, especially in its poignant, pathetic, and tragic possibilities, may have determined, and been determined by, some of his most significant admirations. We have already noticed the echoes of Shakespeare in "The Story of a Year"; many aspects of these borrowings from Shakespeare, especially from *Hamlet,* have been documented by Adeline Tintner (TBW 1-50), and Hamlet himself is a prime example of the Innocent caught in the mortal coil: "O cursed spite, / That ever I was born to set it right!" It is remarkable that in "A Landscape Painter" Locksley's diary is larded with locutions associated with Hamlet: the first few lines have "my prophetic soul"; then "the tables of her memory," "there's the rub," and "We could, an we would" (I, 58, 67, 71, 73). Later we shall be commenting again on the frequency with which James quotes from or refers to *Hamlet,* and also, though less often, *The Tempest,* both of which treat the theme of the endangered or victimized Innocent.

One does not of course have to look beyond Genesis to see that the interplay of Innocence and Experience is archetypical in human experience and so informs a great deal of literature, but we believe it is significant that in the novelists whom James particularly admired it is a prominent theme. Even this would not be remarkable if it were not the pathetic and tragic aspects of the encounter that they tend to dwell on. In Balzac we find, almost at random: "It is hard for noble natures to think evil, to believe in ingratitude; only through rough experience do they learn the extent of human corruption."[11]   In Turgenev too we find: "The first disillusionment is painful to anybody, but to a heart which is sincere and anxious to avoid self-deception, which is alien to exaggeration or a frivolous approach, it is almost unbearable."[12]

In an essay on Turgenev, Edmund Wilson discusses the Russian novelist's handling of the theme of innocence with special reference to "The History of Lieutenant Ergunov" (1867), in which the "heavy and clumsy and extremely naive" lieutenant "never discovers that the two girls are prostitutes and that their bully is lurking in the background" even after they have robbed him, bashed in his head, and thrown his body down a ravine. "It is only when we have finished the story that we grasp the whole implication of the triumph of good faith and respect for the innocent. . . . Ergunov is the side of Turgenev himself that never could believe at first that the people who exploited him were not honest."   Wilson goes on to say that this story, enacting the "survival of innocence," is unusual in Turgenev, because generally "the ogresses and devils . . . have the best of it."[13]   Interestingly, the title of one of Turgenev's most haunting tales of hapless Innocence is "The Russian Hamlet" (or "Prince Hamlet of Shchigrovo"), the protagonist of which James, in an 1874 review, calls "a poor gentleman" (LC II, 977). (Years later, in applying the epithet to Marcher of "The Beast in the Jungle" and Stransom of "The Altar of the Dead," James ruefully admits that "my attested predilection for poor sensitive gentlemen almost embarrasses me," LC II, 1250). Turgenev's Hamlet, in capitulating to "the ogresses and devils," describes himself to the narrator as "empty, insignificant, useless, unoriginal. . . . " Forced to submit to "every trivial humiliation," he is even denied the "bitter-sweets of irony. . . . What's the good of irony in solitude!"[14]   "The Russian Hamlet," according to James, "strikes the deep moral note that was to reverberate" through Turgenev's novels (LC II, 977).

"A Landscape Painter" reflects a contemporary work, as well as *Hamlet*. Miriam Allott has shown its distinct relation to Tennyson's "The Lord of Burleigh."[15]   James does not give us a plain likeness of his source, as he does in "The Story of a Year," nor a methodically topsy-turvy image, as in "A Tragedy of Error," but a reflection that is a critical commentary--even a satire--on Tennyson's poem. As Miriam Allott says: "Obviously the naiveté of this Tennysonian fable was too much for James, and he reconstructed it with a youthfully dry sophistication." James is now borrowing constructively to make something quite different.[16]

In James's tale, Locksley, the landscape painter, repairs to a remote coastal village to recover from the rupture of his engagement to a "mercenary" (I, 57) young woman--he idealizes women as well as landscapes--and becomes attached to his landlord's daughter, an attractively candid and resourceful young woman, who is also, paradoxically, a gold-digger; she wants to escape from rusticity and spend money in city shops. Locksley tries to maintain his incognito, but Esther Blunt seizes the opportunity of his illness to peruse his diary (which the reader has followed), discovers he is wealthy, and soon entraps him. Locksley's innocent deception has been overtaken by deceit of a different order, and we gather that his early death at the age of thirty-five (I, 58) is the result of this second crushing disaster in the affairs of his heart, brought on by his generous but rash enthusiasm.

That this is the earliest of James's tales to be revised and republished by him suggests that he set some store by it. In the revision he made some meanings less obtrusive; he changed the surname of landlord and daughter from Blunt to Quarterman. It is more difficult to see why Esther becomes Miriam. Is it possible that James decided that Miriam, who by insisting upon honour equal to Moses' appeared headstrong and wilful, was a more appropriate namesake for this fictional character than Esther, who delivered her people from destruction?

It is the critical and intellectual attitudes that come into play in the tale that give it substance and significance, and that they involved questions that James himself was concerned with at the time is made clear by a passage in a review of his that appeared a year before the tale: "What manner of writing is it which lends itself so frankly to aberrations of taste [such as are to be found in *Azarian: an Episode*, by Harriet Elizabeth (Prescott) Spofford]? It is that literary fashion which, to speak historically, was brought into our literature by Tennyson's poetry. The best name for it, as a literary style, is the ideal descriptive style. Like all founders of schools, Tennyson has been far exceeded by his disciples. The style in question reposes not so much upon the observation of the objects of external nature as the projection of one's fancy upon them"; in contrast to the disciples of Tennyson, James holds up the examples of Mérimée and especially of Balzac (LC I, 603, 607-08).

The point that James wants to make in the tale presents him with a technical problem that is not solved. An omniscient narrator would perhaps make the meaning too clear and easy, so, except for the brief introduction, James uses the diary form. But if the diarist is to be a man of talent and promise, how can his diary betray his weakness of projecting his fancy on, and thus falsifying, external nature? It can be done, of course, but it will be a delicate matter, and the reader will need to be alert and perceptive. Even in *The Ambassadors* (1903), which is presented from the point of view of Strether, James did not entirely dispense with narration that is independent of Strether. The narrative that introduces "A Landscape Painter" does give the reader important clues, but one feels that this is a rather clumsy patch on the tale; it would not satisfy the later James, the artist who sought neat solutions and elegant form. Within three years James was to write "A Light Man," which he thought very well of. It is a diary-story that has no other narrator, and James's solution is to make the diary's entries span the essential discovery or change in the diarist and thus tell the whole story. However, the fact that the plot and especially the dénouement of "A Light Man" have not been understood, and in fact often grossly misread, may be attributed to the difficulty of the diary form, which must necessarily make demands on the reader. James was attracted to the form in part at least because it forced the artist to avoid an aspect of George Eliot's work, which he otherwise admired intensely. In a review of *The Spanish Gypsy* published less than a year before "A Light Man" he wrote: "She puts her figures into action very successfully, but on the whole she thinks for them more than they think for themselves" (LC I, 945). James's final solution to the problem was, of course, to "invent" a method that developed a centre of consciousness, a complex and supple form that can be seen in, for example, "Daisy Miller" (1878) and, consummately, in "The Beast in the Jungle" (1903).

"A DAY OF DAYS" (*Galaxy*, June 1866, 1885)

This tale pairs with its predecessor, "A Landscape Painter," both being set in remote districts, but it is the differences rather than the similarities that strike one. Locksley and Esther have weaknesses and faults, but, in Adela Moore and Thomas Ludlow, James shows us admirable strengths: in "A Landscape Painter" the two characters guilty of deceit or folly get married, with unhappy results, and in this succeeding tale the two good characters, though strongly attracted to each other, go separate ways with an effect that is poignant, powerful, and ennobling. We think of "A Day of Days" as James's first little masterpiece. Perhaps the deliberate choice of celibacy was a theme that James already found important. There is maybe a hint of the "might have been" of Whittier's well-known poem "Maud Muller," which is mentioned a year later in "Poor Richard" (I, 140), and there is a reference to Longfellow (I, 100), but "A Day of Days" seems to be the first tale by James that is not the product of an obvious borrowing.

Thomas Ludlow, a young New York scientist, on the eve of departing for Germany to advance his studies (as William James was soon to do), comes, like Locksley in "A Landscape Painter," to a country district, not to recuperate but to consult an older scientist. The scientist is away, but his young sister is at home; she entertains Ludlow while he waits. The two young people go for a walk, their minds and feelings meet, and within these few hours they come very close to making a commitment to each other; however, in response to what is by implication a proposal of marriage from Adela, Ludlow decides that he must follow his scientific calling, catch his train, and board the ship for Europe, and so they part.

Technically the tale does not break obviously new ground, but it shows great skill in the presentation of the two central characters that is especially to be admired because, as has often been said, it is difficult to make "good" characters interesting. Villainy is more easily absorbing; usually, as Hawthorne puts it in "A Select Party," "specimens of perfection [prove] to be not half so entertaining companions as people with their ordinary allowance of faults." Adela, whose name (from the German *adel*) suggests her nobility of spirit, and Ludlow, whose origins it is suggested are lowly, are clear-headed, sincere, and high-principled, but we do not feel oppressed by their virtues, partly because, in the case of Adela, she has put imprudence behind her--"she had become rather hastily and unprudently engaged [significantly, perhaps, a common case in these early tales], but she had eventually succeeded in disengaging herself" (I, 88)--but also because she is so well-balanced: she has travelled, is experienced, and is now deliberately choosing the sincerities and simplicities of country life and sororal affection to

offset the sophistication she had learned in the city; a contrast to
Esther in "A Landscape Painter," she is intelligently self-critical,
"becoming--so she argued--too impersonal, too critical, too
intelligent, too contemplative, too just" (I, 89); she leads the
examined life, which does not exclude, as the quotation shows, a
playful mockery of herself. Thus James avoids sentimentality and
melodrama in presenting a complex amalgam of intelligence, moral
insight, and "a delightful sense of youth and *naiveté*" (I, 89), a sort
of Blakean "organized innocence" in Adela's ironic insights that
goes together with a capacity for love. She can playfully mock
Ludlow even while she is feeling strongly drawn to him: "Do you
call yourself a very common fellow because you really believe
yourself to be one, or because you are weakly tempted to disfigure
your rather flattering catalogue with a great final blot?" (I, 103).
James does not merely assign virtues to her; he makes us feel and
see them in her. Similarly, Ludlow has deep but unembittered
knowledge--he says, "Ugly sights can't make you unhappy,
necessarily" (I, 94)--is both virile and assertive, and is also a
gentleman, capable of "an emotion of manly tenderness" (I, 101).

We suggest that there is a thread that can be traced from
here to the end of James's work, a connection between the
amalgam in Adela and Ludlow and a similar compound in "The
Papers" (1903), where "the ironic passion . . . might assert itself as
half the dignity, the decency, of life"; the other half is "love" (ECT
XII, 103, 122) and the humanity and compassion that the two
newspaper reporters in that tale must learn. In a review that
appeared about a year after "A Day of Days" James writes of "that
small but essential measure of irony which accompanies real
discrimination" (LC I, 200). This is not an original or even
uncommon doctrine, but it is what James believed and practised. It
is part of his vision of virtue, and is expressed in his moving tribute to his beloved cousin, Minny Temple, who, after her early
death in March 1870, became for him a sort of lodestar: she "was
to count . . . as a young and shining apparition, a creature who
owed to the charm of her every aspect (her aspects were so many!)
and the originality, vivacity, audacity, generosity, of her spirit, an
indescribable grace and weight"; and yet, "to express her in the
mere terms of her restless young mind, one felt from the first, was
to place her, by a perversion of the truth, under the shadow of
female 'earnestness'--for which she was much too unliteral and too
ironic" (A 282-83). Some of this happy medley of qualities in
Adela will appear again soon in early tales, in Gertrude Whittaker

("Poor Richard," 1867) and Miss Congreve ("Osborne's Revenge," 1868).[17]

Having tried one approach toward narration from the point of view of one character in the diary in "A Landscape Painter," James here withdraws to conventional omniscient third-person narration. He was clearly experimenting with various methods of narration,[18] and, although a year later "Poor Richard," his most ambitious tale to that point, was also to be written in the conventional mode, it was perhaps because James felt that "A Day of Days" was unenterprising in its technique that he submitted it not to the *Atlantic Monthly* but to the *Galaxy*, which he thought less well of. When pressed by the editors of the *Galaxy* to add "5 m.s. pages" to the story, James made a virtue of necessity if, as we have suggested elsewhere, he used the expansion to show Victorian readers that Adela was by no means "forward" or brazen in virtually proposing marriage. We have argued that the effect of the addition is to make it clear "that this is a virtuous girl who is being carried by genuine emotion past the boundaries that have always contained her."[19]

"MY FRIEND BINGHAM" (*Atlantic Monthly*, March 1867)

If we exclude "A Landscape Painter," where James presents a diary framed by a narrator, "My Friend Bingham" is the first tale in which he uses a first-person narrator. The tale is told by Bingham's friend, who is nameless. What he tells us is almost, but not completely, reliable; it must be interpreted in the light of his own partiality and fallibility. He warns the reader of this in the opening paragraph by apologizing for "the superficial manner in which I have handled my facts," and by making a pother about being "unwilling to pronounce," hesitating "to assume the responsibility of a decided negative," and leaving "the solution to the reader" (I, 108). Nevertheless, left to his own judgement and making allowances for the narrator, the reader will probably accept without much cavil the narrator's assessment of Bingham as "a man of opinions numerous, delicate, and profound" (I, 109), and even agree that in the end he becomes "a truly incorruptible soul" (I, 127). The reader will have even less trouble in accepting--partly because it comes indirectly from Bingham himself--that, at the age of twenty-three, "so superficial was [Bingham's] knowledge of the real world . . . that he found himself quite incapable of intelligent action," and also that he was inclined as a young man grossly to magnify trivial irritations such as "domestic embarrassments," and even to harbour "profound resentment" (I, 109) against people among whom he had been "born and bred" (I, 108). Even so, Bingham is almost of the company of Locksley ("A Landscape Painter"), almost to be numbered among James's innocents, being sensitive, cultivated, and, incidentally, also, like Locksley, wealthy and recently jilted.

Like "A Landscape Painter," this tale has a relation, though more overt, to a well-known poem or poet. Bingham, shooting idly at a seagull while on holiday with his friend, accidentally kills a young boy who is with his mother on the beach. The parallels to Coleridge's "Rime of the Ancient Mariner" in this act and in its consequences are clear, and in fact the narrator quotes a complete stanza of the poem (I, 113). We feel, however, that in this tale the borrowing is less successful than in some others because it has neither the ingenuity of "A Tragedy of Error" nor the subtle application in "A Landscape Painter" or even "The Story of a Year"; James's plot is not notably different from Coleridge's,[20] and the moral is less dramatically and subtly achieved. James has not put his borrowing to sufficiently significant use.

Bingham eventually marries Lucy Hicks, the mother of the boy he has accidentally killed. The lesson she teaches Bingham, by example, not precept, is how to respond to suffering--suffering of an order very different from the minor "domestic embarrassments" that had so disturbed him earlier. In her loving-kindness and forgivingness, she is in contrast to Bingham, but also to her kinswoman, Miss Horner, who, not surprisingly, gives "an angry stare" after the accident (I, 114), and to the narrator, who expects a "vulgar movement of antipathy" from her and prepares to reply in the same coin (I, 116). In Coleridge's "Ancient Mariner" the protagonist, though forgiven for his wanton act of violence in shooting the albatross, is constrained to repeat his tale at intervals. Similarly, Bingham, though forgiven for his act of casual, if accidental, manslaughter, embarks on a marriage which, the narrator is careful to tell us, though happy, is fated to be childless. Thus Coleridge's and James's common theme is that we can never wholly escape the consequences of our acts.

"My Friend Bingham" is a moral fable, not a fairy-tale, and Lucy--her name comes perhaps from Coleridge's collaborator, Wordsworth--is too good to be true. We are to believe that she feels deep grief but no rancour; she indulges in no recrimination: for example, on the day of her son's death she says, "I pity [Mr.

Bingham] from my heart," and then even, "I had rather have my sorrow than his" (I, 119). The model of forgiving presented in her is a little oppressive and factitious; we might be reminded of Parson Adams's precept about submission to "the will of Providence" and how he and the precept are completely overturned by the news that his youngest son has been drowned.[21]   James never revived "My Friend Bingham."

"POOR RICHARD"   (*Atlantic Monthly*, June-July-August 1867; 1885)

    In a letter to C.E. Norton of 10 August 1867, W.D. Howells said that "Poor Richard," the first tale by James to reach his desk after his assumption of the sub-editorship of the *Atlantic*, which had already published two of James's tales, was "admirable"; he advised the editor, J.T. Fields, to publish all the stories he could get from the writer (I, xxxix, xxxvii-xxxviii; EL 89).   It was probably Howells's praise of this tale, as well as his general encouragement, that James later referred to in the title of a Note, "The Turning Point of My Life" (1900-1901) (N 437-38).
    "Poor Richard" was written in the summer of 1866 at Swampscott (on the coast just north of Boston) (I, xxxviii), "that scene of fermentation" and "unspeakable memories" (A 494). The story is of the courtship of Gertrude Whittaker by three suitors; it seems to have some relation to the situation during a holiday in the White Mountains of New Hampshire in August 1865, when two war veterans, the younger Oliver Wendell Holmes and John Chipman Gray, together with the civilian James, were all in attendance on Minny Temple.[22] In James's tale, Richard Clare is the civilian, and the other two suitors are Captain Severn, who was wounded and is later killed in the Civil War, and Major Luttrel; at the end of the tale Gertrude is still unmarried.
    It is James's longest fiction until "Gabrielle de Bergerac" (1869), and he maintains the reader's interest throughout all the convolutions in the plot and the characters' consciences. What are particularly remarkable are the detailed yet clear analyses of complex states of mind and feeling and of moral dilemmas, which were to become a feature of James's greatest work. As James was to say in a review of October 1873: "The subtlety of the conscience makes half its virtue" (LC II, 192). In "Poor Richard" we see James entering into an inheritance, a tradition proximately mediated especially by Hawthorne and George Eliot. This non-

Conformist or Puritan strain seems to have been understood by James with special clarity after he became a resident of New England, which is specifically evoked as the setting of "Poor Richard." [23] In this respect, Captain Severn makes an interesting contrast to John Ford in "The Story of a Year," the location of which is more vaguely designated as "Northern" or "Yankee." "While subject to the chances of war, [Severn] doubted his right to engage a woman's affections: he shrank in horror from the thought of making a widow" (I, 139-40). Although in his case it is a matter of betrothal rather than marriage, Ford does not have the glimmer of such a scruple in his conscience.[24] It might be objected that the comparison of Ford with Severn is invalid because James's purposes are quite different in the two tales, but James does seem to see Severn's scruple as belonging to the New England milieu and ethos.

There seems to be no conspicuous borrowing in "Poor Richard," though the title might suggest a connection with Benjamin Franklin; James's Richard, passionate in the beginning and somewhat more deliberate at the end, could be seen as a compatriot of Franklin's prudential hero. In the revision of 1885, Richard's surname is changed from Clare to Maule, which must remind one of the young daguerrotypist Holgrave of Hawthorne's *The House of the Seven Gables*, who finally reveals that his real name is Maule. Certainly James's description of Holgate-Maule in his *Hawthorne* applies equally well to his own Richard Maule: this "modern young man," says James, is Hawthorne's "attempt to render a kind of national type--that of the young citizen of the United States . . . who stands naked, . . . unbiased and unencumbered alike, in the centre of the far-stretching level of American life" (LC I, 416). Certainly James's own "Bon Homme Richard" is also in some archetypical way American, "a plain New England farmer," and, at the end, "eager to try his fortunes in the West," perhaps following his sister and her husband, who had moved to California (I, 137, 179, 134). Gertrude, on the other hand, is a New Englander who resolves "to spend some time in Europe" and "at . . . last accounts . . . was living in the ancient city of Florence" (I, 179); she is more like the kind of American that James already was or would soon become, the sort of American girl that he would often write about. Here is perhaps the first faint adumbration of the "international theme."

An allegorical element is seen in the contrast of types in "Poor Richard."   Richard and Gertrude are opposites: she is wealthy, "robust and active," "with a warm heart, a cool head, and a very pretty talent for affairs" and "feelings . . . strong, rather than delicate"; her conduct is marked by "a moderation, a temperance, a benevolence, an orderly freedom, which bespoke universal respect"; "impulsive, and yet discreet; economical, and yet generous," and "with a prodigious fund of common sense beneath all" (I, 133). Richard, on the other hand, is not wealthy, and this difference is more marked in the 1885 revision; he is "a rebellious and troublesome boy, with a disposition combining stolid apathy and hot-headed impatience," "dull, disobliging, brooding, lowering," and apparently "often the worse for liquor" (I, 134). There are not only two kinds of Americanism in the contrast, but also the Romantic and neo-classical temperaments: Gertrude is controlled feeling, and Richard is passion. "'I know my own feelings,' and [Richard] raised his voice. 'Haven't I lived with them night and day for weeks and weeks?'" All this while "gloomily folding his arms" (I, 129). Besides this Byronic touch, there is a passage describing Richard that might remind one of Beowulf-- "brute volition," "barbarous ignorance," "high opposing forces," "struggle," "Pagan hero," "slaying his dragon" (I, 137)--and one wonders whether Professor Child, the Harvard philologist, introduced James to Anglo-Saxon epic. But in "Poor Richard" James is probably neither borrowing to any great extent from the classics nor tracing the outlines of a new vision; in all likelihood he is, as we have seen, drawing mainly on an intense personal experience in the White Mountains.

Richard's early obtuseness and uncouthness, like Beowulf's, are transcended; he is educated and disciplined by Gertrude. Halfway through, after some tumultuous scenes, we find Richard has been "very busy" on his farm, can describe himself in the past as a "stupid, impudent fool," and can generously refuse to allow Gertrude to say that she has been "unjust" to him (I, 152). The second half of the tale symmetrically reverses the action: it is now Richard who with his sincerity and directness rescues Gertrude from entrapment by the insidious Luttrel. All this shows that wisdom and morality require the harmonious blending of opposite qualities, something like the blend we saw in Adela in "A Day of Days." Like that tale too, "Poor Richard" ends not with marriage but with the separation of two admirable and sympathetic young people. Gertrude, like Maud Muller (I, 140), has to watch the man she wants to marry ride away, and he, matured and now with a Franklinesque self-possession that she has helped him to achieve, forgoes any notion of marriage, like Ludlow in "A Day of Days," and plans to start a new life, not in Europe but in the West. Perhaps James himself was giving up the idea of marriage, but in order to go East.

There is in "Poor Richard" a significant technical innovation: James begins the tale with a dramatic scene--*in medias res*--between Richard and Gertrude (I, 128-33), and only after this come the circumstances and the context, beginning "To appreciate the importance of this conversation, the reader must know . . . " (I, 133). This seems to be looking forward to the exhortation, so frequent in the Prefaces, to "dramatise!"

There is another foretaste of the later James in the long, relaxed, even loquacious, passages that introduce Richard (I, 133-37) and Severn (I, 138-41) and their temperamental, moral, and social problems. Coating the psychological penetration, there is a suave, genial, and witty irony. On Severn, for instance, this produces figures that are at once complimentary and courtly, picturesque and gently facetious: "But although, in the broad sunshine of her listening, his talk bloomed thick with field-flowers, he never invited her to pluck the least little daisy" (I, 141); "field-flowers" conveys the freshness and sincerity of Severn's affection, and "he never invited her" his conscientious scruples; these delicate connotations are deftly stirred with an already masterly light touch. James's style is his own, but it may be that he consciously emulated Turgenev, of whom he wrote in 1877: "It is characteristic of his genius to throw a sort of ironical light over all things--even to some extent over the things that have his deepest sympathy" (LC II, 1001).

We think more highly of "Poor Richard" than Cornelia Pulsifer Kelley does, but we believe she is right in seeing in it the new influence of George Eliot.[25] James had recently--in August 1866, after reading *Felix Holt*--praised George Eliot's "firm and elaborate delineation of individual character," her "humanity," and her "extensive human sympathy" (LC I, 907-08), and, in a longer essay later the same year, he had especially admired "that lingering, affectionate, comprehensive quality" that was the "chief distinction" of "her style" (LC I, 926); it was to become a marked feature of his own style, his own charm.

Howells was truly perceptive when he so confidently hailed the advent of greatness in the writer, aged only twenty-three and six years his junior, who submitted "Poor Richard" to *The Atlantic*.

Chapter II

THE CROP OF 1868

In 1868 appeared James's first abundant crop of fiction, three tales in each of the *Atlantic Monthly* and the *Galaxy*, totalling six; in criticism as well as in fiction he equalled his production of the previous four years by publishing sixteen reviews during the year (LC I, 1432-33; LC II, 1362).

There are some fairly clear reasons for this spate. Besides growing confidence and skill, he was encouraged by editors who became his friends--Howells of the *Atlantic*, C.E. Norton of the *North American Review*, and E.L. Godkin of the *Nation*--and there was the need to earn money and reputation before his first visit on his own to Europe, which began in the spring of 1869. Meanwhile he was still living under the parental roof, in Cambridge, Massachusetts, which he would not finally leave until 1875. Secure access to several journals and a pressure to become more independent financially would help to explain why most of the tales of 1868 are, we must confess, after the success and promise of "Poor Richard" in 1867, somewhat disappointing.

When he told T.S. Perry in March 1868 that "I shall continue to manufacture ["little" tales] in a hackish manner, for that which is bread. They *cannot* of necessity be very good; but they *shall not* be very bad" (L I, 84), one wonders whether he was himself aware of some falling-off, of a catchpenny element in the mystery tales resorted to in order to please a readership that did not appreciate "Poor Richard," which had been roasted even in the *Nation* (EL 89). They are certainly a far cry from his later attempts at the wondrous strange; "A Problem" and "De Grey: A Romance" will not bear comparison with, for example, "The Turn of the Screw" (1898) and "The Jolly Corner" (1908).

"THE STORY OF A MASTERPIECE"   (*Galaxy*, January-February 1868)

In this tale some prominence is given to Browning's "My Last Duchess," but there is little connection between the tale and the poem unless it is that the difference between the two women who sit for their portraits is almost complete. Gilbert Baxter, the artist, may derive from James's friend and mentor at Newport, John La Farge. There is one curious puzzle: why would James give Miss Everett the name of the then well-known but now forgotten orator whose florid two-hour address preceded Lincoln's famous four minutes at Gettysburg?

If we set aside "A Landscape Painter," this is James's first fiction about an artist and art, a field that was to be fertile for his imagination; the elaborate plot demonstrates that the fullest and deepest truths about life are told by art, in this case by a portrait, even though this truth may not be recognized, and may even be resisted, by those who are closely concerned. James is presenting in a naturalistic mode a sort of parable with a concept similar to those in allegories by Hawthorne, such as "Drowne's Wooden Image" and "The Artist of the Beautiful." A Shelleyan (and indeed later a Nietzschean) view of the importance of art sustained James throughout his life, especially in difficult periods such as those after the failure of *Guy Domville* in 1895 and of the New York Edition a decade later, when James felt himself one of the types of the Innocent to whom the world was indifferent or worse.

There are interesting technical shortcomings in the tale. James's maladroitness in handling the narration tends to blur the tale's main point--that art is great and should prevail. The main fault is that we get an aggregation of fragments and views. The narrative begins and ends with Lennox at its centre; he is engaged to Marian and commissions Baxter to paint her portrait. The view from his vantage point is, however, soon interrupted by a clumsy, apologetic, but massive intervention by a disembodied narrator: "I may as well take advantage of the moment, rapidly to make plain to the reader" a previous affair between the painter Baxter and Marian, until (five pages later) "the reader has now an adequate conception" of the triangle of forces (I, 191-96); then there is a current scene between Baxter and Marian that Lennox has no knowledge of. Close reading shows a less obvious but more significant failure to deal with the protagonist's experience. Lennox has various virtues and strengths: though he is not an artist or a critic with trained insight he is "fond of reading, fond of music," and has an unusual share of sound information (I, 183); he is responsive to art. This might have allowed James to show how the full power of art could come to this intelligent and sensitive man--bringing home to him the unpleasant truth about the woman he is committed to marrying--with the force of a revelation. But James's tactics do not match this strategy. Lennox is in a "muddle" (I, 201), sensing and at the same time resisting the truth that Baxter's portrait reveals about the beautiful Marian; he constantly tries to comfort himself with the thought that what unsettles him in the portrait is not a deficiency in Marian herself--although he himself has come close to reproaching her with her heartlessness (I, 200)--but the effect of the interference in the painting of Baxter's personal feelings after his unhappy affair with Marian, and he thus never finally acknowledges the sovereign power of art. In the end he destroys the portrait he has commissioned: "with half a dozen strokes, he wantonly hacked it across. The act afforded him immense relief" (I, 209). In another tale, "The Liar" (1888), James has a portrait slashed, this time by the subject, and for a subtly different reason--that the painting had conveyed a cruel truth (ECT VI, 431), inspired apparently by the personal jealousy of the artist, who is also the narrator, which makes the picture more cruel than true. It seems possible that in *The Picture of Dorian Gray* Oscar Wilde, in attempting to dramatize the sovereignty of art, which (according to Wilde) life imitates, might be remembering James's tale when he has his protagonist finally stab the detested portrait.[1]

In a manner that the mature James would consider inartistic, the disembodied narrator, whose authority must be taken on trust, again interposes, this time to point to the proposition about art that is at the centre of the tale: "It is very certain that [Baxter] had actually infused into his picture that force of characterization and that depth of reality which had arrested his friend's attention; but he had done so wholly without effort and without malice. . . . This . . . is simply saying that the young man was a true artist. Deep . . . in the unfathomed recesses of his strong and sensitive nature, his genius had held communion with his heart and had transferred to canvas the burden of its disenchantment" with the shallow Marian (I, 202). James balks at the difficult task of leading us through an epiphany experienced by Lennox and again takes the easy but clumsy way out by letting his disembodied narrator explain the situation.[2] We are still a long way from "The Beast in the Jungle." When James made his significant technical advances, giving up the fictionist's apparent boon of an omniscient or infallible narrator for the seeming limitation of keeping close to the point of view of a protagonist, he laid the foundation for his greatest achievements. Within a year of "The Story of a Masterpiece" would appear James's first tale ("A Light Man," 1869) to rely completely on a diary--Locksley's diary in "A Landscape Painter" was introduced by a narrator's commentary--and a few years later James would attempt to represent his first thoroughgoing, if rather simple and conventional, epiphany in "Guest's Confession" (1872).

In using his narrator as an easy means of establishing the moral structure of "The Story of a Masterpiece," James sacrifices the subtle tension and the more dramatic and poignant movement towards a climax that the opening pages seem to be preparing us for when they give us only oblique hints of Marian's shortcomings, telling us, for example, that she was "quite guiltless of any aberration from the strict line of maidenly dignity" and that she "professed an almost religious devotion to good taste," being not only entertaining but thus also "irreproachable" (I, 180); this is truly Jamesian, giving the reader an inch, whereas the narrator's interventions too easily concede a mile.

The *Galaxy* editors, who had asked for an addition to "A Day of Days," which James retained when he revised the tale, asked this time for an addition that explicitly stated that Lennox did marry Marian after all (see I, xl). James complied under protest with an extra dozen lines which indicate, however, that he felt they were unnecessary and therefore a blemish: "I need hardly add . . ." and "It is not necessary to relate . . ." (I, 209). In view of this and the other difficulties we have discussed it is not surprising that James did not republish the tale.

"THE ROMANCE OF CERTAIN OLD CLOTHES"
(*Atlantic Monthly*, February 1868; 1875; 1885)

It is a little surprising that this tale should have been revised and republished twice, and that, of the six that were revised for James's first collection, *A Passionate Pilgrim* (1875), which had a planned coherence--"American adventurers in Europe" (L I, 357)--this was the only tale that was not "international," except in the incidental and insignificant contrast between Arthur Lloyd and the young men of the Colony (I, 212). In March 1873 James told his mother that he would "rather object to reissue" any of the tales he had written to that point except "A Light Man" (L I, 357), and yet, in the 1875 volume, "The Romance of Certain Old Clothes" was republished. In 1885 it appeared for a third time in *Stories Revived*, together with several other early tales. Perhaps part of the explanation is that it was written in the vein of Hawthorne and possibly at the suggestion of Howells.[3] We have already mentioned the possibility of James's conscious recall of Hawthorne's themes, if not his manner, in the previous tale, "The Story of a Masterpiece." In this tale we find Hawthorne's manner as well.

Romance always had an appeal for James. He was himself fond of Hawthorne, on whom he was to write a book (1879), and of other writers of romantic tales, such as R.L. Stevenson and H.G. Wells. He had developed a rationale for his predilection. As early as August 1870 he writes in a review of Disraeli's *Lothair*: "We are forever complaining, most of us, of the dreary realism, the hard, sordid, pretentious accuracy, of the typical novel of the period, of the manner of Trollope, of that of Wilkie Collins. . . . We cry out for a little romance, a particle of poetry, a ray of the ideal" (LC I, 862). On the other hand, five years earlier he had written that "a good ghost-story . . . must be connected at a hundred points with the common objects of life" (LC I, 742), and five years later he was to make the point that the "escape from bread-and-butter and commonplace" should not be "into golden hair and promiscuous felony" (LC I, 495).

James has not altogether avoided this last error in "The Romance of Certain Old Clothes." One of the two sisters--the central character--has, not golden hair, but "auburn tresses," and she is "tall and fair" to boot; and, although there is nothing promiscuous about the felony, the death of this young wife, brought about by the fierce unwillingness of her sister--herself already dead--to suffer her successor's appropriation of her clothes, symbolic of her wedded love, is certainly strange and horrible enough: "on her bloodless brow and cheeks there glowed the marks of ten hideous wounds from the vengeful ghostly hands" (I, 226). There being no question of parody or burlesque in the tale, we feel impelled to say that James could hardly have strained any further what he himself called "that compromise with reality which is the basis of all imaginative writing" (LC I, 948).

By placing his tale well back in the past, James employs the conventional means to give himself the licence of the traditional gothic romance. It opens: "Toward the middle of the eighteenth century there lived. . . ." The father of the two sisters, "a great reader of Shakespeare," has named them Viola and Perdita (I, 210); it is difficult to see the significance of this, unless links with *Twelfth Night* and *The Winter's Tale* suggest doors opening on to a romantic landscape.

In "The Romance" there is little of the consolatory, heartwarming human feeling that can go together with the traditional harshness of the legend or fairy-tale; we are left only with the sordid and sensational form of the eerie. James's tale has an obvious affinity with "*La Vénus d'Ille*" in its grotesque and savage ending, but it dramatizes none of the higher poetic and deeper moral truths of the Mérimée story; its dynamic derives from nothing more surprising or elevated than rather banal sororal jealousy. (Similar jealousies are the mainsprings of the two other romances of this period, "A Problem" and "De Grey: A Romance.") However, there are very obvious moral lessons in "The Romance": it demonstrates the destructiveness of jealousy and the nemesis that overtakes Viola on account of her "insatiable love of millinery" (I, 217). The final impression is of the sordid meanness of the sisters' behaviour, which contrasts starkly with the idealities associated with Shakespeare's romantic heroines.

The irony in "*La Vénus d'Ille*," and in several tales by Hawthorne that James's might remind us of, is in the construction, the plot itself. Besides this "The Romance" has an irony in the tone of the narration that is sharpened by sarcasm, a tarter element than the genial irony in "Poor Richard." Whereas in Hawthorne's "Young Goodman Brown" and "Roger Malvin's Burial," for instance, there is a whimsically detached tone that can also be sober and reach out in compassion, in "The Romance" there is a strong undercurrent of sardonic satire designed to underscore, rather heavily, the moral bearing of the tale, as in Arthur Lloyd's "little capital of uninvested affections" (I, 212) and in Viola's beginning "to feel sure that her return [in winning the affections of Arthur, her deceased sister's widower] would cover her outlay [in insidious arts]" (I, 223). The "romance" in the title is almost oppressively ironic.

It is interesting that in the 1885 revision of "The Romance" James changed the girls' family name from "Willoughby" to "Wingrave" (a surname that gives a title to a later tale) and, though retaining the name "Perdita" for the younger, more sympathetic sister, changed the older sister's name from "Viola" to "Rosalind," perhaps because, though both these Shakespearean heroines disguise themselves while they are conducting their courtships, Rosalind is the more direct and determined in securing her husband. Edel suggests that this tale of deadly sibling rivalry has its roots, like the later "Guest's Confession" (1872) and "Owen Wingrave" (1892), in James's family situation, especially his rivalry with his older brother, William.[4]

The *Nation* of 30 January 1868 praised "The Story of a Masterpiece" as "very well thought out"--referring one supposes to the intricate plot--but found "The Romance" to be "trivial altogether." William James thought "'Poor Richard' the best of your stories because there is warmth in the material," and he said that "the story of 'Old Clothes' is . . . very pleasantly done, but is, as the *Nation* said, 'trifling' for you" (I, 513, 515). We think William and the *Nation* are right about "The Romance."

"A MOST EXTRAORDINARY CASE" (*Atlantic Monthly*, April 1868; 1885)

Adeline Tintner believes this tale is James's "partially successful tribute" to Stendhal's *La Chartreuse de Parme* (TBW 246), but it is a somewhat puzzling tale, more ambitious and certainly more interesting than its predecessor. Again we quote William, who read it "with much satisfaction. It makes me think I may have partly misunderstood your aim heretofore"; but the aim William detects leaves us still at a loss. He thinks one of Henry's objects is to show that, as in life, people in his stories "come out of space and lay [their orbits] for a short time along ours, and then off they whirl again into the unknown, leaving us with little more than an impression of their reality and a feeling of baffled curiosity as to the mystery of the beginning and end of their being" (I, 515). If William is right, it makes further explanation not only unnecessary but impossible.

Colonel Ferdinand Mason, suffering still from Civil War wounds, is an invalid, lying "in bed in one of the uppermost chambers" of a great New York hotel (I, 227) when he is visited by his aunt, Mrs. Mason, who tells him that "from this moment you're in my hands"; "finally, after the lapse of years," this "war-wasted young officer" is "being cared for. He let his head sink into the pillow, and silently inhaled the perfume of her sober elegance and her cordial good-nature" and "listened to the rustle of her dress across the carpet" (I, 230).[5]

Mrs. Mason, who, like "La Sanseverina" in Stendhal's

novel, seems to feel more than an auntly love for her nephew, arranges for her English manservant to accompany Ferdinand the next day to a station of the Hudson River Railroad, where she is waiting for him in "a low basket-phaeton, with a magazine of cushions and wrappings"; she takes him to her house, "a cottage of liberal make, with a circular lawn, a sinuous avenue, and a well-grown plantation of shrubbery." He thus feels fully enveloped by "the exquisite side of life" (I, 230-31), especially when Mrs. Mason's niece from Germany, Caroline Hofmann, attractive and very polite (as her name suggests), becomes the centre of a "mild radiance" (I, 235); he is encouraged by the milieu, and is soon enamoured, despite Mrs. Mason's adjuration and warning that Caroline will "not fall in love" with him (I, 237). He experiences a "quickening" of his faculties (I, 235), and this encourages our hopes that he will recover from the unspecified and somewhat mysterious "disorder," "deeply seated and virulent" (I, 233), that stems from his wound.

But after each exertion in the course of his courtship, his recovery suffers a setback (I, 244, 250, 259). Then there is the announcement of Caroline's engagement to Knight, a young and personable doctor who has been ministering in a very friendly fashion to Ferdinand. Apparently as a result of this unwelcome news, Mason resumes what in the 1885 revision he calls "the dance of death" (I, 489), and "at last he let disease have its way" (I, 259). It seems that he loses the will to live--a notion that is given a little more emphasis in the 1885 revision.[6] But this seems a rather indeterminate or insufficiently justified cause in a young man with some achievement and endurance to his credit, who had, moreover, another "mistress, his first love . . .--work, letters, philosophy, fame" (I, 257).

Adeline Tintner suggests that "the foreshortened tragedy of James's little tale requires a supplementary gloss by the reader who, like James, has . . . fallen under the spell" of Stendhal's novel; those not under the spell will not, says Tintner, recognize the various transformations James has effected, because James had not yet come "to realize that the 'secret' of getting the reader to do 'his share of the task' [Tintner is quoting from James's 1866 essay on George Eliot (see LC I, 922)] in understanding the tale was not a simple matter of imitating the structure of relationships drawn from the model" (TBW 247). There is no specific mention of Stendhal or his novel in James's tale, and, unlike even "A Tragedy of Error," it does not stand firmly enough on its own feet. Despite some glowing passages, it is certainly not a successful case of borrowing; we cannot even be quite sure that it is in fact a product of borrowing.[7] Edel asserts that James was "reading Stendhal for the first time" in northern Italy as late as the summer of 1869 (EL 99).

In "A Most Extraordinary Case" there are hints, clearer than in "The Romance," of the international theme that is to come. Col. Mason is very American, having fought in the War; and, being "a singularly nervous, over-scrupulous person," given to "assiduous reading and study" and to "uninterrupted austerity" (I, 234), he is somewhat reminiscent of "Poor" Richard, just as Mrs. Mason, an American very much attached to Europe, is a little like Gertrude Whittaker. Besides an English manservant, Mrs. Mason has a German companion, has been "living in Europe" (I, 228), and leads a more leisured life, being fond of comforts and elegance, cultivating "those lighter and more evanescent forms of conviviality" that her nephew is "quite ignorant of" (I, 235). He is in earnest and takes life hard; she is more self-indulgent and looks for pleasure, making one think ahead, for example, to Lord Lambeth in "An International Episode" (1878-79) and to other Europeans, who tend in James's fiction to be more hedonistic than Americans.

"A PROBLEM" (*Galaxy*, June 1868)

James submitted this tale to the *Galaxy*, though he preferred the *Atlantic*--"the most respected magazine of the time" in the United States (I, xxx)--and its encouraging sub-editor Howells; this and the fact that he never revived it indicate perhaps his opinion of the tale. It is indeed a comparatively slight thing, certainly the shortest of these early tales; however, nothing that James published is entirely devoid of interest and merit, and this has several minor virtues and some marks of James's genius as well.

In its structure the tale has the strictness and simplicity of form that belong to a legend or fable, and its substance, centring on the words of an oracle, has the fascination these have had since Herodotus, especially when they are somewhat sinister or, as Aeschylus has it, "crooked and ambiguous utterances."[8] The tale has, moreover, some of the heart-stopping switchbacks to be found in dramas such as *Oedipus Rex* and *Macbeth*. The three different prophecies are unsettling, but Emma and David, just happily married, can at first persuade themselves that they are not to be taken seriously. The couple can laugh when part of the first prophecy is fulfilled in the birth of their daughter (who remains completely undeveloped as a character throughout the tale) and are mightily but deludedly relieved when the child does not die-- though her death had been foretold--of a serious illness. (In other words, the plot is, in Aristotle's sense, complex, and articulated in discoveries and reversals.) The two take comfort in the illusory belief that the second and third prophecies, that Emma and David will marry twice, are mutually exclusive, but the predictions are fulfilled in a most unlooked-for manner, like those of the witches, who "palter with us in a double sense" in *Macbeth*: after quarrelling, separation, and virtual divorce, Emma and David meet again, when the death of their daughter has fulfilled the first prophecy, and in effect marry for a second time. James borrowed from, or writes in the tradition of, classical sources, and to good effect.

Though all this could be produced by mere mechanical skill and good workmanship, there is at least one feature of the tale-- indeed its prime virtue--that is distinctive: it gives a dramatically compact reflection of the processes of the human mind and imagination, of the fears, rationalizations, velleities, and fancies of those fallible instruments, and of the human need and capacity for love. James shows the germination of suspicion, the insidious and seemingly inexorable advance of jealousy and hatred toward a tragic climax, but also the final reconciliation and miraculous restoration of love.

"DE GREY: A ROMANCE" (*Atlantic Monthly*, July 1868)

This tale is an extraordinary mixture. We are introduced to Mrs. De Grey, a quiet, retiring widow, and her comfortable New York home, where she takes her tea as, we are told, she takes life itself, "weak, with an exquisite aroma and plenty of cream and sugar" (I, 278), and into this familiar scenario is sandwiched a large slice of the flummery and fiddle-faddle of pre-Shavian melodramatic romance. "The play between two orders of determinism"--the familiar and the strange--is one of what Richard H. Brodhead calls the many "specific debts" to Hawthorne in this tale,[9] but the result is rather embarrassingly clumsy.

With Mrs. De Grey has lived, for twenty-five years, Father Herbert, a Catholic priest and a scholar, born an Englishman, and once a close friend of Mrs. De Grey's husband before her marriage.

The two young men had quarrelled bitterly, then become reconciled, and George De Grey had died two months after Herbert became a member of the household. At the age of sixty-seven, feeling lonely, and having to endure at least one more year of her son Paul's absence in Europe, Mrs. De Grey becomes interested in and hires as a companion Margaret Aldis, an attractive young woman who has lost both parents and is friendless. The great events in this household are the arrival of Paul's letters. Margaret begins to take an interest in the young man, who eventually arrives home, his fiancée having recently died in Naples (I, 288).

With this situation established, and after an opening sentence placing the story in "the year 1820" (I, 277) (and thus giving James the liberty that the past allows) and a few murky hints of "a secret in [Mrs. De Grey's] life" (I, 278), we find ourselves plunged into an abyss of the gothic grotesque: Margaret and Paul have become attached to each other, but the girl is constrained to cry out, "Father Herbert, . . . what horrible, hideous mystery do you keep locked up in your bosom?" He reads to her from the fly-leaf of "an old illuminated missal," which is the "register" of all the young girls who, through several centuries, have died mysteriously shortly after betrothal or marriage to heirs of the De Grey line, victims of "an awful, inscrutable mystery," a "curse," though this fate overtakes only those for whom it is "the first love, the first passion." This being the tenor of his disclosure, it is scarcely surprising that, as the priest sits down to impart this horrendous information, "the room grew dark with the gathering storm-clouds, and the distant thunder muttered," or that, when he has completed his task, "a vast peal of thunder resounded through the noonday stillness" (I, 296-99). We are spared few of the clichés of the genre.

Margaret is vulnerable because she has never known love before (I, 287), but, by a singular process requiring great courage and strength of character, she breaks free: "I revoke the curse. I undo it. *I curse it*" (I, 299); in other words, she will take her chance with Paul. However, "she was to find . . . after her long passion, that the curse was absolute, inevitable, eternal. It could be shifted, but not eluded" (I, 306); it shifts to Paul, who is now himself in love for the first time and therefore in danger. He dies supernaturally, Margaret loses her sanity in the trauma, and thus "an immense calamity . . . overwhelmed" the house of De Grey (I, 308). The fact that Paul is vulnerable to the curse suggests, of course, some conclusions about his relation with his earlier fiancée, and also about the situation in the previous generation involving Mrs. De Grey, Father Herbert, and George De Grey: there is "a little dark-eyed maiden buried in Italian soil who could tell . . . [a] story"; "she died of De Grey's kisses" (I, 298).

There is little in this fantastic melodrama that can be admired, but one aspect is interesting: toward the end we are told of Margaret and Paul that, "as she bloomed and prospered, he drooped and languished" (I, 306). This curious reciprocal relationship recurs often in James, most prominently in "Longstaff's Marriage"(1878) and *The Sacred Fount* (1901), and it might be related to the paradoxical affection and rivalry between the brothers Henry and William (see EL 79-80); James refers jocularly to the notion in a letter as early as October 1869 (L I, 157-58).

"OSBORNE'S REVENGE" (*Galaxy*, July 1868)

This tale is perhaps in part a reworking of the theme of "A Most Extraordinary Case": the White Lady referred to in Roger Graham's letter at the beginning (I, 309) does restore Sir Piercie Shafton to life in Scott's *The Monastery*, but in neither of James's tales does the lady work this marvel. In "Osborne's Revenge" Henrietta Congreve is an even more innocent cause of Graham's collapse and suicide than Caroline Hofmann is of Col. Mason's death in "A Most Extraordinary Case". Indeed, with her "peculiar union of modesty and frankness, of youthful freshness and elegant mannerism" (I, 317), she is a little like Adela Moore in "A Day of Days", the prototype of this early pattern of James's heroines.

But it is the differences between "Osborne's Revenge" and "A Most Extraordinary Case" that are most prominent, and not the least of these is that "Osborne's Revenge" is ironic in structure: Osborne determines to avenge Graham by seeking out Henrietta to punish her for supposedly jilting his friend, but instead he falls in love with her, finds his suit unsuccessful, and in the end discovers that Henrietta is altogether innocent in Graham's case. There are minor ironies; for instance, Osborne conceives "a harmless artifice for drawing [Henrietta] out" and tries to make her "jealous of a rival in his affections" (I, 335), which is conduct even more questionable than that of which he wrongly supposes Henrietta guilty: he had been told that she, after encouraging Graham's addresses and being "all seduction," "deliberately transferred her favours" from him to a Mr. Holland (I, 310).

There are some technical flaws, and these are more fundamental than the word "technical" might suggest. First, when we are told that "Osborne made all possible allowances for exaggeration" in the account he is given (I, 310), James is in a sense cheating; the authorial statement sounds authoritative and yet is misleading because Mrs. Dodd's report is not only exaggerated but altogether mistaken. It is as if Conan Doyle were to dismiss evidence that Sherlock Holmes is later to find crucial. Secondly, the conversation between Henrietta and Holland, her lover, like that between Stephen Baxter and Marian Everett that we have commented on in "The Story of a Masterpiece," is an awkward expedient because it is not overheard by Osborne, even though the tale is told from his vantage point. Finally, Major Dodd, "brother of [Mrs. Dodd's] deceased husband" (I, 341), is parachuted into the tale at the end in order to expose Osborne's misconceptions. The god who appeared from the machine in a classical play was at least known and always a potential participant, whereas we have neither met nor heard of Major Dodd before, nor have we had any reason to suspect his existence.

If we except "A Landscape Painter" and "The Tragedy of Error"--the element of parody or simple inversion makes them special cases--"Osborne's Revenge" is James's first thoroughgoing attempt at a demonstration (as in, for example, the much later "The Beast in the Jungle") of the capacity of the human mind for imaginative constructions, whether achievements of genius (like Gedge's in "The Birthplace" or Berridge's in "The Velvet Glove") or, as in "Osborne's Revenge," aberrations of fancy, prejudice, or rationalization. For James, men are fabricators of such constructions, inspired or illusory. The irony in "Osborne's Revenge" is somewhat obvious and clumsy, and the tale is only a doubtful success. The next two tales, "Gabrielle de Bergerac" and "A Light Man," are, however, both accomplished performances; indeed the latter is a brilliant achievement.

Chapter III

FIRST CULMINATION, 1869

"Gabrielle de Bergerac" and "A Light Man," the two tales that are the material of this chapter, form a sort of bridge between the earliest experimental period of James's work and the so-called international tales, which begin to appear in 1870, and which by any account mark a stage in his development. But these two tales of 1869 are more than merely a bridge, a means to an end; they are both, in their different ways, culminations of tendencies in James's first fictions, especially in his use of the conventionally romantic and in his borrowings.

It is clear, and hardly surprising, that James would rather see his fiction in the highly respected *Atlantic* than in any other American journal, but it is interesting to note that the "safe" romance, "Gabrielle de Bergerac," published in the *Atlantic*, was easily understood and soon popular; the daringly new and "difficult" shorter tale, "A Light Man," accepted by the *Galaxy*, has been consistently misread and undervalued. It is clear that prudential, financial, and other considerations, besides mere aesthetic or professional preference, came into play when James submitted his tales to journals. After Howells had seen and been "fascinated" by "A Light Man" in the *Galaxy*, he wrote perhaps a little ruefully to James: "I'm sorry we hadn't [it] for the *Atlantic*; though it is good policy for you to send something to the *Galaxy* now and then" (I, xlii). By the time James left for Europe in early 1869, he had written five tales for the *Galaxy* and eight for the *Atlantic*, and, although the latter are on the average distinctly longer, they are in our opinion not markedly superior.

Both "Gabrielle de Bergerac" and "A Light Man" are polished performances, the former a historical romance, a genre that it does not transcend or add much to, and one that James never attempted again, the latter a triumph in that it both solves problems presented by the diary form and is a borrowing that makes a brilliant adaptation of its great original, St. Augustine's *Confessions*. The two tales were written shortly before James's departure for Europe and appeared after he had left. It is not known which was written first, but it suits the dramatic structure of our study to reverse the order of both the Edel and the Aziz collections of tales and to discuss the historical romance first.

"GABRIELLE DE BERGERAC"   (*Atlantic Monthly*, July-August-September 1869)

Never before or after did James write a work like this. He wrote other romances, but with a supernatural or mysterious element, not a conventional historical romance in which the sentimental, the melodramatic, and the pathetic are so pure, though not altogether simple. Perhaps he wrote it to become better known; certainly it was his first popular success, and not only James's sister Alice and his mother, but also Howells, thought very highly of it (see L I, 132; I, xli-xlii). James himself, however, always a discerning critic of his own work, writing from Europe in June 1869 after reading the first instalment, told his mother that it struck him as "the product of a former state of being" (L I, 126), and in August he wrote that "it all strikes me as amusingly thin and watery . . . as regards its treatment of the Past. . . . The present and the immediate future seem to me the best province of fiction" (L I, 132).

Because the events take place in pre-Revolutionary France, the tale is set in a past between which and the present an almost unbridgeable gulf is fixed. Not only that, but the shadow of the guillotine looms; we learn in the second paragraph that Gabrielle, the exemplary heroine, "died under the axe of the Terrorists" (I, 374), and the last sentence of the tale, the longest fiction James had published, reads, "They both went to the scaffold among the Girondins" (I, 427). This pathos suffuses the action, not least because the story is told to the narrator by Gabrielle's nephew, an old man, who had, as a boy, been involved in the main events. The romantic colour is further enhanced by, for example, the evocation of La Fontaine's *Fables*, which James had translated as a boy (A 183), and by what Adeline Tintner has seen reflected from Doré's illustrations of Perrault's "Sleeping Beauty" (I, 398-99; TMW 15-16).

Some six years later James wrote in a review of the pre-Revolutionary scene a comment that is apt here:

The French Revolution rounds off the spectacle and renders it a picturesque service which has also something besides picturesqueness. It casts backward a sort of supernatural light, in the midst of which, at times, we seem to see a stage full of actors performing fantastic antics for our entertainment. . . . There is nothing in all history which, to borrow a term from the painters, "composes" better than the opposition, from 1600 to 1800, of the audacity of the game and the certainty of the reckoning. We all know the idiom which speaks of such reckonings as "paying the piper." The piper here is the People. We see the great body of society executing its many-figured dance on its vast polished parquet; and in a dusky corner, behind the door, we see the lean, gaunt, ragged Orpheus filling his hollow reed with tunes in which every breath is an agony.

(LC II, 653)

James's stereotyped historical romance is given weight and value, as well as a nostalgic colour, by the contrasts between the modern and the defunct social systems and attitudes; the France of the tale was a "different planet" (I, 375). True to the genre, the focus is on rivalry in courtship and on matrimony. In dramatic--not to say melodramatic--contrast, there is on the one hand the nobleman who can say of the hero, his plebeian rival, "A man doesn't address you; he sends his lackeys to flog you" (I, 424), and on the other there is the contemporary Victorian romantic mode, the heroine who is happy when she has "a chance to act as my heart bade me" (I, 423).

The romantic picturesque is most manifest in the description of the castle of Fossy, which "lifted its dark and crumbling towers with a decided air of feudal arrogance" and offered "the sullen hospitality of [the] empty skull" of a "sadly scathed and shattered" tower to "a colony of swallows" (I, 406-07). One notices, besides the picturesque and the deliberate archaisms, hints of unhappy far-off things and perhaps of Macbeth's castle. There is encrusted rhetoric in the pledging of "virgin faith to the chilly sanctity of a cloister" (I, 384); a doubtfully relevant deathbed scene (I, 400-02); a breathtaking climb (I, 411-12) in the vein that James was later to read and admire in R.L. Stevenson; a lover's idealization of his passion in "It is more than enough to watch you and pray for you and worship you in silence" (I, 414); the narrator's idealization of the heroine, who "paced, with the grace of an angel and the patience of a woman, the dreary corridors and unclipt garden walks of Bergerac" (I, 385); the swashbuckling climax when the villain, "with a sweep of his weapon . . . made a savage thrust at the young girl's breast," and Coquelin, the hero, "with equal speed, sprang before her" (I, 426-27). It is studded with clichés, both verbal-- something "set poor Coquelin's heart a-throbbing" (I, 409)--and iconographic--a nightingale "out of an enchanted tree . . . raved and carolled in delirious music" (I, 389). This is all very different from what we have come to expect in even the early James. There is none of the suavity of the knowledgeable but generous man-of-the-world; the tale is a direct appeal to our unqualified--one might almost say uncritical--sense of the Beautiful and the Noble. Even in "The Romance of Certain Old Clothes," when we read that Viola "would . . . drop her tapestry, and put out her handsome hands with the serious smile of the young girl whose virgin fancy has revealed to her all a mother's healing arts. Lloyd would give up the child, their eyes would meet, their hands would touch, and Viola would extinguish the little girl's sobs upon the snowy folds of the kerchief that crossed her bosom" (I, 223), our sympathetic response is held firmly in check by an undertow of satire and mockery of Viola, our questioning of her sincerity and high-mindedness. We come closer to simple romantic rhetoric and to being asked for uncritical sympathy in the other self-declared specimen of the genre in this period, "De Grey: A Romance," in which, "rescued from the turbid stream of common life, and placed apart in the glow of tempered sunshine, valued, esteemed, caressed, and yet feeling that she was not a mere passive object of charity, but that she was doing her simple utmost to requite her protectress, poor Miss Aldis bloomed and flowered afresh. With rest and luxury and leisure, her natural gaiety and beauty came back to her" (I, 283). But even here one is not asked to surrender so completely to admiration, nor expected to accept being overwhelmed by such pathos as one finds in "Gabrielle de Bergerac." We are not suggesting that in the two earlier romances--there is some irony in calling them "romances"--James failed to arrive at a mastery he achieves in "Gabrielle de Bergerac." All three represent different kinds of romance; nevertheless, we believe that in his pre-Revolutionary story James in a sense fell back on a simpler, more established form, probably in order to achieve the popular success he wanted; it is a culmination that is not an artistic advance. Gabrielle is saintly, or at least faultless, and the result is, if not altogether insipid, too smoothly sweet in flavour; it has none of the roughness, ordinariness, or incompleteness of real life. James's next tale, "A Light Man," was to be related to the life of a real saint, and it is a very different affair.

Before he wrote "Gabrielle de Bergerac" James was well aware of the difficulty of marrying the "distinctive elements and sympathies" of the modern historian and the popular novelist, of a Niebuhr and an Anthony Trollope, and yet he thought "there is no sufficient reason that we can see why the novelist should not subject himself, as regards the treatment of his subject, to certain of the obligations of the historian." Yet again, he knew that Balzac, "(if we except his 'Contes Drolatiques'), . . . wrote but a single tale of which the period lay beyond the memory of his own generation, or that preceding it" (LC I, 1154-55). In "Gabrielle de Bergerac," James attempted what Balzac, his model, avoided, and he has only a limited artistic success; but the limitation is that of the form itself.

There are some similarities between "Gabrielle de Bergerac" and *Guy Domville*, the James play that failed so signally a quarter of a century later in London: both are set in the period just before the French Revolution, though the play's setting is England, not France, and in both the sense of family solidarity and responsibility is felt very strongly by the protagonist, who must nevertheless in the end disregard it. Edel makes the interesting comment that in *Guy Domville* James's "confusion between the romantic play he was writing and his sense of reality was strong" (EL 403); we think this is a weakness in this tale of 1869 too.

The method of narration in "Gabrielle de Bergerac" deserves comment. The tactic of giving the narrative to Gabrielle's nephew ensures some immediacy in the presentation, but the narrator, an unformed boy at the time of the events, is not clearly individualized, and is thus not himself a source of interest. James solves this problem in "A Light Man": Max Austin, the diarist, has an altogether fascinating character and is in fact the centre of the interest. Moreover, in "Gabrielle de Bergerac" there is the same sort of difficulty that we noticed in "Osborne's Revenge": there are scenes in which it is unlikely that a young boy would take part, and James has to invent unlikely reasons for his presence, as, for example, when the lovers are exchanging their most intimate thoughts.   It comes as a weak apology from James when the narrator says, "It must be confessed, [I] was sadly out of place in that . . . scene" (I, 424).

The qualities and forces represented by the characters do, however, make for considerable dramatic interest. The hero, Coquelin--bearing the name of a boy who had been at school with James at Boulogne in 1857, who was already a famous Parisian actor, and who by an extraordinary coincidence was to etch the name Bergerac indelibly on the Western consciousness when he created Rostand's Cyrano de Bergerac on the stage--represents the ethos that is waiting to be born. He is "no *sans-culotte*" (I, 427), has a liberated and cultivated intellect--he sketches "indifferently from high and low life" (I, 395)--and, "among Rochambeau's troops, [has] taken part in several battles" (I, 378) in the American Revolutionary War.

There is life in the villain too; the Vicomte de Treuil is not painted in the very blackest colours. Moreover, Gabrielle's elder brother and somewhat rigidly class-conscious guardian is not unsympathetically drawn. Gabrielle, herself, as we have said, is given a real dilemma: she realizes that "if I marry in my brother's despite, and in opposition to all the traditions that have been kept sacred in my family, I shall neither find happiness nor give it" (I, 418). (This was to become a theme in *The Tragic Muse*, "Owen Wingrave," and "Covering End," as well as in *Guy Domville*.) There is thus some depth and complexity in the otherwise stereotyped plot. But when Aziz suggests that "Gabrielle de Bergerac" "may be said to close the first phase of James's apprenticeship" (II, xxix), we are inclined to demur.   The distinction belongs more appropriately to "A Light Man."

"A LIGHT MAN" (*Galaxy*, July 1869; 1884; 1885)

James thought highly of this tale; as we have seen, in his letter of April 1873 he selected it from all the tales he wrote before 1870 as the only one he would "not object to reissue," saying it "showed most distinct ability" (L I, 357). He revised it heavily for Volume 5 of *Stories by American Authors* (1884) and then again for his own *Stories Revived* (1885).   It is his cleverest, subtlest, and most accomplished tale to this point, and it is achieved in a thoroughgoing and completely consistent application of the diary form, requiring no other narrator. Though written with an almost mischievous ingenuity, it is also a serious and moving record of a cultivated and apparently frivolous young man's entry into full responsibility and the realm of spiritual truth and value: Maximus Austin is a modern St. Augustine.

Although "A Light Man" is not conspicuously "international" in theme, it is a forerunner of those that are. James makes differences between his Europe and his America function nearer to the heart of the matter here than in "A Most Extraordinary Case." Max Austin has just returned home to America after ten years in Europe, during which his "cheerful mind" and "good digestion," his devotion to "pleasure pure and simple," but obviously also to intellectual cultivation--like St. Augustine he is familiar enough with the Latin poets to quote Horace in the opening sentence--have "quite transformed [his] physiognomy" (I, 346, 348). But he is not ready for a radical change or reformation: in his first diary entry we learn that pleasure has "lost all its prettiness" and that he is "dejected . . . bored . . . [and] blue" (I, 346); he is critical of himself and somewhat contrite, knowing that he "was never an enthusiastic votary [of pleasure]. . . . More would be forgiven me if I had loved a little more, if into all my folly and egotism I had put a little more *naïveté* and sincerity"; he is aware of seeing only "through a glass, darkly" (I, 347). Moreover, he puts searching questions to himself: "What am I? What do I wish? Whither do I tend? What do I believe? I am constantly beset by these impertinent whisperings" (I, 346), and his heart "throbs with a sort of ecstatic longing to expiate my stupid peccadilloes" (I, 347), which is changed in 1884 to "little sins" (I, 495).

That America will be the scene and in some degree the cause of his regeneration is suggested by his patriotism: "I'm the citizen of a great country"--he quotes from St. Paul more often than from the pagan poets! --"and on the whole I don't blush for my native land" (I, 346); he has returned to North America, just as St. Augustine was drawn back to his native North Africa. Max is eager to see "a delicious American town" (as opposed to New York, which corresponds to Carthage in St. Augustine's story), and he is sensitive to "rural loveliness by the lake side" (I, 348). That the diary entries are made in April and May suggests the possibilities of Easter and of a spring in the world of the spirit as in Nature.

Austin's opportunity comes in a letter from his dear and intimate friend Theodore--the name means "the gift of God"--who is private secretary, "guide, philosopher and friend" to Mr. Sloane, "old, widowed and rich" (I, 349). In brief, with the vehemence of a lonely man, Sloane takes to Austin eagerly and quickly--"be a son to me" (I, 362)--and Austin finds that he has completely displaced Theodore Lisle in Sloane's confidence and affections, even to the extent that Sloane makes determined efforts to change his will, which has been made out altogether in Theodore's favour. Although Austin twice refuses to avail himself of the opportunity to "supplant" (I, 364) Theodore, the latter becomes jealous and suspicious, and descends to "cold calculation" (I, 366), even, as he himself admits, to "hypocrisy and cunning" (I, 371). When he is confronted by Austin, he does rise to the occasion and destroys the will that is in his favour, but goes off in dudgeon, leaving the friendship between himself and Max in question. Sloane dies intestate, Austin telegraphs "Miss Meredith, a maiden lady . . . nearest of kin" to Sloane (I, 372), and she comes to enter into the inheritance.

The friendship between Austin and Theodore, who corresponds to Alypius in the life of St. Augustine, is significant. They have a great regard for each other, but are very different, seeming to have that strange Jamesian sort of reciprocal relation. The "three months together in Brittany--the best-spent three months of my whole ten years abroad" (I, 353)--are a crux. We can detect James's ever-increasing penchant for symmetry in his art: the three months were halfway through Austin's ten years away because it is "five years" since Theodore saw Austin (I, 348). It was during those three months that the two friends' interests and orientations crossed: "Theodore inoculated me, I think, with a little of his sacred fermentation, and I infused into his conscience something of my vulgar indifference" (I, 353). Theodore, once a godly youth with a "shrinking New England conscience" (I, 360), becomes more worldly and like Austin; Austin, once worldly, by "sacred fermentation" becomes more spiritual. We are reminded again of the strange see-saw relation in "De Grey: A Romance."

Sloane embodies various meanings too. He is a disciple of, and in many ways like, Voltaire, as Adeline Tintner has suggested (TBW, 208-11), especially in his rationalism and his anti-Christian posture. It is interesting that he tries to make Austin his "son"--James drops various hints that Sloane might be Austin's father (I, 347, 350, 362)--for in the scheme of the tale Sloane is his double, an Austin who has never recovered from the corruption of Europe; he too had begun "to feel certain natural, filial longings for this dear American mother of us all" and had bidden "farewell to Europe" (I, 358). Allegorically, "the groundwork of [his] house," which corresponds to his American origin, is "plain, solid and domestic," and the accretions--the "*soi-disant* Gainsborough," the "fantastic mantel-piece," and the "outlandish *chinoiseries*" (I, 349), for example--correspond to that part of him, "shallow, vain, cold, superstitious, timid, pretentious, capricious" (I, 357), that has overlaid and spoilt his American nature. Austin's vehemence in firing off this string of opprobrious epithets may be taken as a sign of his unconscious feeling that he is seeing in Sloane what he himself is in danger of becoming. We shall see this effective dramatic twist to a psychological insight again in "Four Meetings" (1877).

What is extraordinary about "A Light Man" is that it has so consistently been misread, Austin being taken as a villain who tries, as Theodore believes, to displace his friend and possess himself of Sloane's fortune. Even Howells, James's guide, friend, and admirer, misread the tale, writing to James: "I confess the idea of [Max Austin] fascinated me. He is one of your best worst ones" (I, xlii). Little wonder that James, as early as the spring of 1870, complained (though this was directed at the English, he being at the time in England) that people "have such a mortal mistrust of anything like criticism or 'keen analysis'" (L I, 209). This complaint was to become louder and more frequent, especially after the failure of *Guy Domville* on the London stage in January 1895, reaching intense exasperation in a letter to Howells of December 1902: "The *faculty of attention* has utterly vanished from the general anglo-saxon mind" (L IV, 250).

What has misled many readers of "A Light Man" is presumably James's irony, which here pervades the tone, the style, and the mode of expression that Austin affects in his diary. It is almost throughout witty, irreverent, supercilious, and apparently profane, because he is facetiously posing as a cynical pagan and even as "debauched" (I, 348), although, as we have seen, some passages indicate a very different current. One is given a clue to James's strategy in what Austin says about his dealings with Sloane: "I catch myself in the act of taking--heaven forgive me!--a half-malicious joy in confounding [Sloane's] expectations--leading his generous sympathies off the scent by various extravagant protestations of mock cynicism and malignity" (I, 360). Readers have been too readily impressed by Austin's perhaps exaggerated confessions of profligacy, for it is well known that converts often magnify their sins. It is probably significant that in October 1866 James remarked that it is "very uncommon for what is called a religious conversion merely to intensify and consecrate pre-existing inclinations. It is usually a change, a wrench; and the new life is apt to be the more sincere as the old one had less in common with it" (LC I, 925); perhaps he was already pondering a conversion as striking and a change as complete as Maximus Austin's.

"A Light Man" is very different from those tales in which James adopted Hawthorne's supernatural mode and apparatus, such as "De Grey: A Romance," but it could well be that here James was aiming at something else in Hawthorne that he specially admired and that T.S. Eliot declared distinguished Hawthorne and James from their English contemporaries--"the deeper psychology."[1] In his book on Hawthorne, James wrote: "The fine thing in Hawthorne is that he cared for the deeper psychology," which is concerned with "the whole deep mystery of man's soul and conscience" (LC I, 368).

Wilhelm Meister is different from "A Light Man" in a thousand ways, but James may have been attempting to emulate it in one respect. Of Goethe's novel James had written a few years earlier: "Few other books . . . so steadily and gradually *dawn* upon the intelligence" (LC II, 944). We do not relish meanings that come to us too readily. Writing the tale allowed James, behind Austin, to enjoy his little joke too, but when no one appreciated it, perhaps it soured. He did not include it in the New York Edition, but, of course, none of his fiction written before "A Passionate Pilgrim" (1871) was to enjoy that distinction.

There is a detailed, ingenious, and thoroughgoing correspondence between Austin and St. Augustine, whose *Confessions* provide a pattern and paradigm for Austin's "bescribbled chronicle," which is "the record of my follies, as well as of my *haut faits*" (I, 365), and which is, again, significantly like and unlike Sloane's "memoirs" (I, 349). Maximus Austin's name is itself, of course, a prime clue. The reader who is curious to follow in some detail the parallels between "A Light Man" and the saint's *Confessions* should read what we have written elsewhere.[2]

Besides Voltaire and St. Augustine, there is Browning. James gives us a stanza of Browning's "A Light Woman" as epigraph to his tale, and even a cursory reading of the poem reveals a relevance: the speaker woos and wins the light woman, to whom he had seemed to be losing his friend. Winning the woman, he loses his friend for the time being at least, but the key point that serves to confirm Austin's disinterestedness is that, having won the woman, having the plucked pear in his hand, Browning's speaker has "no mind to eat it." There are, however, ironic differences between the tale and the poem, notably that Browning's speaker seeks to supplant his friend, whereas Austin does not. A year earlier, in a review of George Eliot's *The Spanish Gypsy*, James had written: "Whenever a story really interests one, he is very fond of paying it the compliment of imagining it otherwise constructed, and of capping it with a different termination" (LC I, 950-51).

Having completed his longest tale to date, "Gabrielle de Bergerac," and his most daring instance of multiple borrowing, "A Light Man," James sailed for Europe in February 1869 to make his first visit on his own to Europe. During the next year England and Italy would give him so much excitingly new food for fiction that literary borrowings would for a time become less prominent in his work, but he was always intensely conscious of imaginative constructions by other artists of other times and nations.

Chapter IV

ADVENTURE TO EUROPE AND RETURN, 1869-72

When James in March 1873 turned aside his parents' suggestion that he bring out a collection of his earliest tales, he said: "What I desire is this: to make a volume, a short time hence, of tales on the theme of American adventurers in Europe, leading off with the *Passionate Pilgrim*" (L I, 357); *A Passionate Pilgrim and Other Tales* duly appeared in 1875, but it included only one of the three tales we consider in this chapter that would have qualified under his rubric, although "Travelling Companions" and "At Isella" are as much concerned with the great adventure involving the typical American artist or intellectual as the tale that gave the 1875 volume its title.

When James set out for Europe on his "grand tour" in 1869, and even when he was acting as cicerone for his sister and aunt in 1872, he did not feel he had reached a crossroads, as he was to feel in 1875; still, the occasions were heady enough, because he was answering "that solicitation of 'Europe' our own [family] response to which . . . kept breaking out in choral wails" (A 82); as Edel says, "The great adventure of his life" was "his embrace of Europe" (EL 506). His letters from England in the early spring of 1869 exuberantly report meetings and visits: George Eliot, Leslie Stephen, John Ruskin, William Morris and his wife--"a figure cut out of a missal" (L I, 93)--the Elgin Marbles, the Kensington Museum, St. Paul's, the countryside, the Malvern Hills, Kenilworth, Oxford, Blenheim, the National Gallery, a Tintoretto, "Rubenses and Vandykes" (L I, 112), Titian's portrait of an old doge that gave one "a new sense of the meaning of art" (L I, 103), and his "Bacchus and Ariadne--a thing to go barefoot to see; as likewise his portrait of Ariosto" (L I, 121), and so on. His raptures no doubt reassured his family that he was getting his and their money's worth, but they were nonetheless genuine.   Only Italy would be more exciting. Writing of this first visit to that country a decade later, he said, "Every glance was a sensation, and every sensation a delight" (L II, 284), but Italy was to be for him, as for so many nineteenth-century English and American artists, a perpetual infatuation (see L II, 301).   At first, however, in "A Passionate Pilgrim," it was England that provided the experience that moved James most deeply, perhaps because England was more familiar and accessible, Italy still somewhat exotic.

James was laying in large stores of observation and experience for his fiction. But, as Le Clair puts it, there was "an inner struggle . . . [involving] strong native ties and the sense of 'Europe.'"[1] Even as a child, James's "young allegiance" was split into "unequal halves" (A 22); this was the basis of his characteristic and inveterate ambivalence. Beneath his ebullient enthusiasm for Europe, he was, as he told his mother in a letter of 2 March 1869 soon after leaving home, "abjectly, fatally homesick."[2] He was subject to this affliction in 1869-70 especially; in 1872 he would be with Alice and Aunt Kate. But from far back, James had felt a more deliberate resistance to Europe: as early as July 1860 he was writing, with the pressure of personal experience and a sententiousness that may be forgiven in a young man of seventeen: "The more I see of this estrangement of American youngsters from the land of their birth, the less I believe in it" (L I, 22), and seven years later: "We are Americans born--*il faut en prendre son parti.* I look on it as a great blessing" (L I, 77); before his thirtieth birthday he was fully aware of the "complex fate" of being an American (L I, 274).

His reservation about Europe was a compound of many natural feelings, among which were pride, jealousy, resentment, and a defensiveness that was occasionally almost aggressive, although usually obscured by his habitual and apparently constitutional urbanity. Readers of the early tales of Americans in Europe will sometimes feel the slight tension in the Americans, who tend to be a little apologetic, or ready to infer a slight. Putting as high a value on art, intellect, and tradition as he did, it was difficult for James to avoid feeling sometimes, in London, Paris, or Rome, that he represented a colonial outpost of culture. This must not be overstressed, however; one is impressed again and again, and generally, with the cool penetration of his insights, and with the depth of his respectful affection for these ancient centres.

James was preternaturally observant, and this makes him a

journalist of the best kind.   In the three international tales we discuss in this chapter, and in others that are to follow, we can see that he relied to a considerable extent on his own immediate observations, especially of scenery and customs, if not yet of character, as a sentimental but also sharp tourist. There are obvious correspondences between, for example, his letter of 31 August 1869 to his sister Alice and "At Isella" (1871), and between his letters from Malvern, written from mid-February until early April 1870, and "A Passionate Pilgrim" (1871).   When he got home, he no doubt made use of the letters he had written to his family. After 1875, when he was no longer a traveller in Europe but was domesticated there, and especially after 1882, when his parents died and he no longer wrote letters of a reporting or diary kind, he began to keep and rely on his notebooks. This went together with the change from reliance on something close to transcription of personal sensory experience, as in "A Passionate Pilgrim" and "At Isella," to the development of more purely imaginative constructions.   In drawing on his European adventures, as in his borrowings, James began to attain greater freedom, which meant also more scope, subtlety, and power.

It is also interesting to watch the way in which the fairly straightforward theme of the sensitive American tourist gradually acquires a deeper significance: the American comes to embody qualities that can be thought of as typically American, and eventually we find a pattern that tends to contrast American naiveté, honesty, lack of culture, and innocence with the beautiful sophistications, or the ugly corruptions, of Europe.   The superficially American characters in "Travelling Companions" and the two untypically American men of "A Passionate Pilgrim" make way in less than a decade for Caroline Spencer ("Four Meetings") and, in particular, Daisy Miller, the prototype of the American young woman in fiction.   Beyond that again, good journalism becomes great aboriginal myth: in dealing with the material that comes closest to hand, James discovers the deepest sources of his inspiration, and his protagonist, whether American, like Isabel Archer, or English, like Fleda Vetch or Maisie, would become an Innocent in the dangerous World. In the same way, Jane Austen wrote about social visits among the gentry and then discovered the universal theme of gentlemanliness and civilized behaviour, and Conrad wrote about ships and Southeast Asia, in which he discovered his theme of human solidarity. We can watch in James what he in 1876 saw in the work of Charles de Bernard: the working of "an impulse to grasp a subject nearer its roots" (LC II, 164); "Four Meetings" and "Daisy Miller" are nearer the roots of James's archetypical myth than are "A Passionate Pilgrim" and "At Isella."

"TRAVELLING COMPANIONS" (*Atlantic Monthly*, November-December 1870)

"Travelling Companions" appeared more than a year after "A Light Man" and "Gabrielle de Bergerac." Until now, James's tales were generally either traditional romances or based on borrowings; now he draws copiously on his own firsthand experience; we find the fruit of his "gaping" and "dawdling" in Europe. In this tale there is a reference to Hawthorne's "Rappaccini's Daughter," which, like "Travelling Companions," involves Padua and a young man's interest in a girl who has a father; James's tale, however, turns Hawthorne's upside down, and the connections are rather vague. In a few years' time James wrote "Benvolio" (1875), which is much closer to Hawthorne, but by that time he was back in America, where, being without fresh European material, he tended to borrow.

"Travelling Companions" appeared in the *Atlantic* and seems as if designed for the more affluent and cultivated American reader of the eastern seaboard, eager--especially after the Civil War--to make the pilgrimage to Europe, or to recall very fondly the well-known tourist sights and shrines in Italy. There are detailed and enthusiastic descriptions of churches, views, and pictures; the tale is almost a guidebook for a grand tour. Adeline Tintner refers to it as "James's museum catalogue" (TMW 25).

Apart from this, the tale caters to American readers by portraying in a flattering light a young American woman, Charlotte Evans, aged about twenty-two, from Araminta, New Jersey, who, according to the narrator, Brooke, another American, is "American to the depths of [her] soul" (II, 8). Assertions to this effect are frequent in the tale and make clear James's intention, but the fact that he felt the assertions necessary betrays perhaps that he felt that the "American" quality was not sufficiently realized in the action. This young American is like and yet unlike Daisy Miller: she only occasionally detaches herself from her father (II, 5) and does not exercise her freedom as fully as Daisy does. Her father is a forerunner of Caspar Goodwood in *The Portrait*; both are versions of the conventional American innocent in Europe but untroubled by their complex fate. (Mark Twain's *The Innnocents Abroad* had appeared the previous year.) The tone here is very different from that in James's much later Preface to *The Reverberator* (1908), where he comments on the "negative aspects" of the American character--especially of the "business-man"--though certain of the youngest women were excepted; many Americans were "passionless pilgrims" who were "unaware of life" (LC II, 1198, 1203, 1199).[3]

The portrait of Charlotte would not disturb American self-esteem; she has "physical delicacy and . . . personal elegance" (II, 2), "decision and dignity" (II, 4), "a maturity, a conscience," as well as "frankness and freedom" (II, 6), and it is upon her discretion and wisdom that the happy course of the action depends. Mr. Evans, who "bore the national stamp as plainly as [his daughter]" (II, 3), is portrayed not unkindly, to the effect of indulgent humour rather than satire, even in his indifference to aesthetic appeals, his fondness for gondolas (II, 10, 17) and absinthe (II, 10, 20), and his "habit of being in a hurry," even though, "being out of business," he has now "nothing on earth to do" (II, 8). He too will not upset national pride, having "a shrewd, firm, generous face" (II, 3), honouring the rites of friendship (II, 22, 25), and concerned that "my poor girl has a good time" (II, 3). We have enough confidence in the narrator to accept his evaluation of Mr. Evans: "He was not the least of a bore: I relished him vastly. He was in many ways an excellent, representative American. Without taste, without culture or polish, he nevertheless produced an impression of substance in character, keenness in perception, and intensity in will, which effectually redeemed him from vulgarity" (II, 20).

But we are most of all concerned with the narrator. The tale is chiefly about him and the change in him, and he is--at least in the beginning--not altogether reliable. He too is American, but, having been away from America for some time, he is "by education" a German (II, 6), though he wished "to be a good American" (II, 8). He too--a sort of surrogate for James--is on his first visit to Italy, and his enthusiasm for Italy and all things Italian is expressed lavishly and uncritically. Here James is able cleverly to capitalize on his own store of observations and feelings, and at the same time to represent the verbal flow as superficial and excessive; it is a case of having it both ways. The concept in this tactic is good, but in the implementation there are defects. It is the same sort of problem that there was in the diary of "A Landscape Painter":

unless the narrator, Brooke, is patently and ridiculously foolish, thus alienating our sympathy, how can his fault be made clear to the reader? James employs two methods to meet this difficulty. First, he devises incidents and episodes to convey the harsher truths in Italian life such as that involving the picturesque Milanese woman, who has such "nobleness of gesture and carriage," but who prays "such bitter, bitter prayers" in the Cathedral (II, 9). More obviously, the plausible Italian family in Vicenza, who sell Brooke a pretended Correggio, might afford Brooke experience enough to correct his error, but he seems incorrigible. He knows it is not a Correggio but nevertheless buys it because its Madonna is "wonderfully like Miss Evans" (II, 14). The moral is almost too clear and trite. Secondly--and this is a more serious error in James's tactic--Brooke's lack of judgement is consistently discerned and plainly commented on by Charlotte, and to be able to do this she has to be too good to be true and interesting. She checks his advances to her, realizing that "It's not with me you're in love, but with that painted picture [the view of Venice itself]" (II, 24); and she sees through Brooke so completely that she can give him chilling advice: "spend the coming three days alone. How can you enjoy Tintoretto and Bellini, when you are racking your brains for small talk for me?" (II, 19-20). James has to be at pains to reassure us that her sagacity has not been acquired at the expense of her ability to feel: she seems to weep before Leonardo's *Last Supper* (II, 4), and she bursts into "an agony of sobs" before the Tintoretto *Crucifixion* in San Cassiano (II, 26).

We suggest that what gives the tale its greatest interest are the changes that can be followed in Brooke. Here James shows us more steps than appeared in Austin's story in "A Light Man". Apart from Brooke's saying near the beginning, "I'm open to conversion" (II, 8), and giving a hint of the process that James is developing when he remarks on treasures that he and Charlotte "may help each other to find" (II, 21), it is clear that he learns from her teaching and example. His response to works of art is profanely aesthetic, whereas hers is complete and religious. If this is not absolutely clear with regard to *The Last Supper*, it becomes so when Brooke invites Charlotte to see Veronese's *Rape of Europa* at the Ducal Palace. James himself described this picture as "the happiest . . . in the world," expressing unequalled sensuous "enjoyment."[4] Charlotte is more interested in Tintoretto's *Bacchus and Ariadne*, in which "there is no shimmer of drapery, no splendour of flowers and gems; nothing but the broad, bright glory of deep-toned sea and sky, and the shining purity and symmetry of deified human flesh. 'What do you think,' asked my companion, 'of the painter of that tragedy at San Cassiano being also the painter of this dazzling idyl; of the great painter of darkness being also the great painter of light?'" (II, 27);[5] this seems to show that she is almost ready to receive the representation of the sacred meeting the profane by Titian at the end of the tale. James's meanings fit together a little too neatly and stand out a little too plainly.

It is Charlotte who suggests the trip to Padua (II, 27) to see the famous church of St. Anthony and the Chapel of Giotto. In the church they see a couple that perform in little their own drama: "she believes; he doubts," but the man "slowly approached" the woman "and bent a single knee at her side" (II, 28), thus conforming to her example. After the Chapel, Giotto's paintings supply a text for Charlotte's sermon: "we ought to learn from all this to be *real*; real even as Giotto is real; to discriminate between genuine and factitious sentiment; . . . sentiment and sentimentality" (II, 30).[6] And Charlotte is enabled to give a demonstration of what she means: she and Brooke miss their train back to Venice and so spend the night immaculately at a hotel, but Charlotte's father, feeling his daughter has been compromised, implies that Brooke should propose marriage to her to make all well, and he duly does. She refuses him, even though, as she has previously told him, she likes him "immensely" (II, 24), which shows that she can distinguish between genuine injuries and mere lapses of form: she says, "I don't believe in such injuries" as her father thinks she has suffered (II, 35).

She does not dismiss Brooke for good, however--only for a time: "Don't fancy that I think lightly of your offer. But we have been living . . . in poetry. Marriage is stern prose. Do let me bid you farewell!" (II, 35). Again, it is for his own good, and his "uppermost feeling was a sense of freedom and relief". On his journey to Florence he is already "regarding things with less of nervous rapture than before, but more of sober insight"; he admits "the truth, the partial truth at least, of her assertion of the unreality of my love" (II, 36). He takes in Naples, Capri, and Pompeii, and, when the Signora tells him "that I was a true German," he knows that "in this she was altogether wrong"--presumably because he is now all American; in any case, when he does finally reach Rome in mid-October, he is "a wiser man" (II, 37).

In Rome, Brooke and Charlotte, whose father has died in the meantime, meet accidentally in St. Peter's: Brooke has learnt "pity," of which he feels an "immense uprising" in his heart, and Charlotte says she is "bowed in humility" (II, 39)--though she is no stranger (as Brooke apparently is) to "sorrow and trouble" (II, 38), having "lost her mother in her early years" and "her betrothed in the Civil War" (II, 30); moreover, we have seen her recognize and respond to the pathos of Leonardo's *Last Supper* and the "tragedy" and "darkness" in the Tintoretto *Crucifixion*.   They meet--again not by design--at the Borghese Gallery before the great Titian, *Sacred and Profane Love*, which with its "latent symbolism," completes James's painstaking allegory: the sacred and the profane, the religious and the merely aesthetic, are joined; the Tintoretto and Veronese meet in the Titian.   Charlotte and Brooke, having helped each other, now coincide, become companions in maturity, and Charlotte says of the figures in the Titian: "One may stand for the love I denied . . . and the other ---" (II, 40).[7] It might strike the reader, however, that she has helped him a great deal more than he her.   It is a readable tale, and very ambitious, but the plot and its meanings seem somewhat contrived.

"A PASSIONATE PILGRIM"   (*Atlantic Monthly*, March-April 1871; 1875; 1884; 1885; 1908)

In any account of James's development this tale must feature prominently for several reasons.   If, as seems likely, he wrote it soon after "Travelling Companions" and before he had completed *Watch and Ward* (see II, xxxiii), the novel he later virtually disclaimed, it was his longest work to date; it was also the earliest of his fictions to be included in the New York Edition, and James revised it no fewer than four times, twice very extensively, as the textual variants provided in Maqbool Aziz's second volume show.

The young Henry James who wrote the tale was obviously surcharged with what he had seen on his grand tour, and many passages in the text recall others in his letters, especially those written from Malvern, where he was undergoing treatment for his chronic constipation in the early spring of 1870, before returning to Boston.[8]   As James himself wrote in his Preface to *The Reverberator*, "A Passionate Pilgrim," like "The Madonna of the Future," is "in the highest degree documentary for myself" (LC II, 1206).

It is interesting to compare this, his English travel anthology, with "Travelling Companions," his Italian, which was probably written just before (see II, xxxii-xxxiii). The methods are similar yet different: in "A Passionate Pilgrim," instead of having a narrator who conveys James's impressions and at the same time must be foolishly excessive, James divides the part of Brooke in "Travelling Companions" into two. He has an unnamed narrator, who speaks from first to last and is eloquent and enthusiastic enough to be a surrogate for himself; and he has a protagonist, Clement Searle, who is excessive in his response to England, but in an interesting way, as will appear. Thus the narrator, being an American with some experience of Europe, has a basis for judgement that Searle does not have; he can be close to and almost identical with Searle, exclaiming "how thoroughly I had entered into sympathy with my companion and how effectually I had associated my sensibilities with his" (II, 72), and yet later he can be critical of him: "I may say that from this time forward, with my unhappy friend, I found it hard to distinguish between the play of fancy and the labour of thought, and to fix the balance between perception and illusion" (II, 89). This is a more satisfactory solution than the one in "Travelling Companions," but James is obviously still far short of his method in, for example, *The Ambassadors*, where Strether is the centre of consciousness but the narrator is able unobtrusively to move away from him to provide the reader with an independent and authoritative view.

The narrator reels off what could be the young James's panegyrics on London, Hampton Court, Bushey Park, a "lovely budding gentlewoman," the Malvern hills and countryside, Worcester, and Lockley Park, which throws a light forward to Lord Warburton's Lockleigh in *The Portrait of a Lady* (II, 42-43, 50-51, 52, 53-54, 58-60, 61, 62-63). Searle shares his enthusiasm, though the narrator comments on Searle's "almost hysterical emotion" at Lockley Park (II, 90). But the two differing responses to Oxford, for example, are juxtaposed: the narrator says, "Of Oxford I feel small vocation to speak in detail. It must long remain for an American one of the supreme gratifications of travel. The impression it produces, the thoughts it generates, in an American mind, are too large and various to be compassed by words. It seems to embody with an undreamed completeness and overwhelming massiveness a dim and sacred ideal of the Western intellect" (II, 88-89). This praise is weighty enough, but still measured, and associated with the human "intellect," but Searle's dithyramb attempts a higher, ethereal flight: of Oxford he says, "Mightn't one fancy this the very central point of the world's heart, where all the echoes of the world's life arrive only to falter and die? Listen! The air is thick with arrested voices. It is well there should be such places, shaped in the interest of factitious needs; framed to minister to the book-begotten longing for a medium in which one may dream unwaked, and believe unconfuted" (II, 91), and so on. Searle is even more fancifully eulogistic--admittedly seeking escape from reality--than Brooke in his most extravagant praises of Italy in "Travelling Companions."

One significant difference between the narrator's enthusiasm and Searle's self-indulgence appears in the way in which what the narrator sees and enjoys is linked with literature and pictures, and therefore derives a sort of validity from these sources: he quotes from Shakespeare--*Hamlet, Othello, The Merchant of Venice*; and Johnson, Dickens, Smollett, Boswell, Mulready (changed in 1875 to Gainsborough), Jane Austen, and Tennyson are all referred to (II, 42, 43, 60, 469, 61, 62); and he says "we greeted these things as children greet the loved pictures in a story-book" (II, 60). When, for example, he meets a "British tramp," a "genus" he had "never yet encountered," he can recognize him "from afar" by bringing "the utmost keenness of my tourist-gaze" to bear "upon the present specimen" (II, 54),[9] and when they reach Lockley Park he finds that "Miss Searle [an English cousin of his companion's] was to the *Belle au Bois Dormant* what a fact is to a fairy-tale, an interpretation to a myth" (II, 66).[10] The narrator is in fact like James himself, who wrote from Malvern to his father: "all things [are] suggestive of the opening chapters of half-remembered novels" (L I, 215). In the tale the narrator refers to this kind of experience in the second paragraph: "The latent preparedness of the American mind for even the most delectable features of English life is a fact which I never really probed to the depths. The roots of it are so deeply buried in the virgin soil of our primary culture, that . . . it would be hard to say exactly when or how it begins" (II, 42-43); this passage is in substance preserved through all the revisions of the tale.

Clement Searle, the American companion the narrator meets in London, has come to claim, or perhaps just investigate, his part of the Searle family estate, Lockley Park, though his connection with the family is unrecorded or forgotten.[11] His responses to England, and in particular Lockley Park, have a source altogether different from the narrator's, and here one must explore the strange, romantic, and ghostly dimensions--so frequent in James's fiction and derived chiefly from Hawthorne--of "A Passionate

Pilgrim."

Searle, aged about forty-three, is on his first but long-looked-forward-to visit to England and Europe. Despite the narrator's early impression--"I foresaw that I should find him a true American" (II, 51)--he reminds the narrator of "a certain type of Russian" (II, 44); the narrator, like Brooke in "Travelling Companions," claims to be sensitive to, and quick to recognize, the peculiar American quality. Searle is certainly unlike the typical American businessman that in the Preface to *The Reverberator* James complained of as virtually inescapable (LC II, 1203); in fact in the New York revision James makes Searle say, "I know nothing of business" (II, 601).[12] Searle has, he says, "drifted through life. I'm a failure." His taste was "delicate," he had written "a little volume of verses," and had married at thirty, which was "a sad mistake" (II, 55), since when he has "idled along," and the current of his life "has shrunk" to an "impalpable thread." "Was I meant to come to this? Upon my soul I wasn't." "I have always fancied that I was meant for a gentler world. . . . I came into the world an aristocrat." Then "a sharp New Yorker lawyer" reminded him of his claim and undertook to "nose round" (II, 56). Meanwhile, Searle is physically debilitated and morally morbid, his illness "in great measure a matter of mind and spirits" (II, 57). After three days in England, he can say, "This is a world I could have loved" (II, 57); he expects to die within a month. In brief it seems that, in the strange, preternatural reality that James sometimes invokes, he has been all his life in the wrong place, that Lockley Park is "metaphysically" (II, 78) his real home. When, persuaded by the narrator, he goes into the western counties to visit Lockley, his spirits revive: "His almost passionate relish for the old, the artificial, and social, wellnigh extinct from its long inanition, began now to tremble and thrill with a tardy vitality. I watched in silent wonderment this new metaphysical birth" (II, 58). When he actually reaches Lockley, he soon falls in love with his cousin, Miss Searle, and there are signs that he has arrived "home": "The very beasts have made him welcome" (II, 68), and, strangest of all, he finds a portrait of a young man "in a powdered wig," who "perished at sea, going to America," and whose name is the same as his. The narrator is "immediately struck with his resemblance to my companion" (II, 64). It is a matter of strange imaginative sympathy, metempsychosis, or reincarnation.[13]

But the tale is tragic: the absent male cousin and proprietor, Mr. Searle, returns, quashes the love that has sprung up between his sister and Clement, and in effect expels the visitors.   This virtually brings about a reenactment of the sad story involving the earlier Clement Searle--him of the powdered wig--and the young woman whose ghost now haunts Lockley (II, 74-75).

Searle, now again certain that he has but a short time to live, is taken by the narrator to Oxford, where it seems Clement was, or imagined he was, once a student, but despite this stimulus he declines rapidly and is soon in a Bath-chair (II, 93).   Before he dies, however, he ritually donates what little money and few trinkets he has left to a new acquaintance, Mr. Rawson, an "elderly man" (II, 93), whose brother, like Searle's cousin, will not share his property with his relative.   Rawson, a rather contrived intrusion, is Clement's double, as it were, being English but with a longing for America: "Something tells me that my chance is in your country" (II, 97).   In a somewhat stagey ending, Miss Searle, released from her brother's thraldom by his death in a riding accident, arrives too late: Searle is dying, but his death results in a vicarious renewal, through Rawson.

It is a strange story, but it is possible to see why James set such store by it.   It carries the "storehouse of treasures" (L I, 214) of his first ecstatic adult response to England, but also some of the ambivalence in his attitude.   Besides the panegyrics on England and the points made against the distinctly American lawyer with his "vulgar nose" (II, 44) and brashness, there is a good deal in the other scale.   English arrogance is displayed in the harsh chauvinism of the aggressive Mr. Searle, who has "implicit confidence that this exotic parasite [Clement Searle] would hardly have good manners," and talks of America "rather as if it were some fabled planet" (II, 73-74); something of this can be seen even in the mild and generally sympathetically portrayed Miss Searle when she says "that she had met an American family on the Lake of Como, whom she would have almost taken to be English" (II, 66).   Further, James arranges that the two Americans should have a signal moral victory for their sensitivity, discretion, and good manners in their dealings with Mr. Searle, much as Christopher Newman was to have in his dealings with the aristocratic French family in *The American*.   Finally, in case the tale should be taken to imply from Clement Searle's yearning for England that all the advantages are on its side, James has the Rawson story to balance the score: some people--even English people--prefer America.

Despite all this, we need to find more reasons why "A Passionate Pilgrim" was so important to James, especially since, in the Preface to the volume of the New York Edition that includes this, the earliest tale in this important edition, he seems to deprecate it by speaking of "a sufficient amount of golden dust . . . kicked up in the foreground," and saying that, together with "The Madonna of the Future," it was one of the "sops instinctively thrown to the international Cerberus," one of his attempts to "substitute the American romantic for the American real" (LC II, 1204). Although the narrator feels sure he will find Clement Searle "a true American, full of that perplexing interfusion of refinement and crudity which marks the American mind" (II, 51), one feels that neither the narrator himself nor Searle is in fact a typical American.   Moreover, in 1871 James is relying on some stereotypes to depict the Europeans in this tale[14], and he will rely largely on stereotypes for his Europeans until the end of the decade. In 1878 "Daisy Miller" is a landmark, as is suggested by its subtitle, "A Study," for with it James is breaking away from stereotypes of national character and writing more from original observation.

Too much has been made of the term "international" in discussions of James's later work. As we have seen, his Preface to *The Reverberator* sounds rather like an apology for exploiting the concept, and even as early as October 1888 James tells his brother William that he is "deadly weary of the whole 'international' state of mind" (L III, 244); with his grand myth of the Innocent he had already transcended merely national contrasts. But there is some true, if still somewhat unoriginal, observation of English types in "A Passionate Pilgrim," as in the portrayal of Miss Searle, "so fenced and protected by convention and precedent and usage; so passive and mild and docile" (II, 67), reminding one of Lord Warburton's sister in *The Portrait*, and approaching what James complained of in a letter to William from Malvern: the "plainness and stiffness and tastelessness" that he found so irritating in the English women there; they were altogether lacking the sort of "intellectual grace" and "moral spontaneity" of young American women such as Clover Hooper and Minny Temple (L I, 208).

It is ironical that on the very day this letter was written, 8 March 1870, Minny, his beloved cousin, died of consumption; James was still in Malvern when he received the news. It has been seen as one of the crucial events of his youth, like his "obscure hurt." This loss had, paradoxically, a fertilizing effect on his imagination; Minny became the archetype of the Innocent for whom "life--poor narrow life--contained no place" (L I, 222); "Her character may be almost literally said to have been without practical application to life" (L I, 223); "her image will preside in my intellect . . . as a sort of measure and standard of brightness and repose" (L I, 227). James's letters from Malvern, his fiction--probably *The Portrait* and certainly *The Wings of the Dove*--and his *Autobiography* witness to the effect Minny's death had on him. It seems to have contributed to the deep and lasting impressions left by his stay at Malvern, and the conception of Clement Searle's character may have been influenced by James's view of Minny. In particular, one is struck by a sentence in a letter to William of March 1870, three days after getting the news of her death: "One thought there is that moves me much--that I should be here delving into this alien England in which it was one of her fancies that she had a kind of property" (L I, 228). Again, a few days later, to Grace Norton: "[Minny] had a great fancy for knowing England" (L I, 232). In this, and in his sense of impending death, Searle is like Minny, and the sympathy between the narrator and the unworldly Searle could well be a projection of the closeness James felt to Minny. If this is so, it would help to explain the importance of the tale to James.

There is another way in which James's stay at Malvern was crucial in his career. In a letter of February 1870 to his mother from London, just before going to Malvern, he says, "I have been feeling for some time that I owed you a report of the situation" (L I, 195-96), and he proceeds to give a detailed and circumstantial financial statement of his expenditure "exclusive of what Father paid for my passage and of 10 sovereigns he gave me before I started. I may be considered . . . to have cost you in a year about 400£. This is certainly a good round sum and as I consider it I feel a most palpable weight of responsibility and gratitude." But he goes on to say, "I know thoroughly well at the same time that any difficulty on your own part must have melted away in your sense of the great good the money was doing" (L I, 196). James feels obliged to justify himself: "One always might have spent less. I think on the whole I may claim this:--that I have spent little more than was needful for the full and proper fruition of my enterprise. To have kept myself on a materially narrower financial basis would have been to lay up a store of bitter memories and regrets for the future--memories of a stingy timid spirit, lagging behind their great opportunities" (L I, 197). This is so close to pleading that it allows one to appreciate how great the "weight of responsibility" was that he felt at Malvern, where, after travelling for almost a year and writing virtually nothing, he was undergoing treatment and was largely idle for over two months. He must have known that the only real justification for him would be in work produced and that he must now make a great new effort.

Until now James had written partly in emulation of great writers or in well established modes. "Travelling Companions" and "A Passionate Pilgrim" were the first fruits of the new effort. Now, with all the "copy" provided by his grand tour, with what D.H. Lawrence might have called a new "passional" engagement after Minny Temple's death, with a keen sense of responsibility, and within sight of his twenty-seventh birthday, he was ready to make a new beginning. It is not surprising that, when he designed the New York Edition, he felt that it was with "A Passionate Pilgrim" that his career as an artist really started.

"AT ISELLA"   (*Galaxy*, August 1871; see II, 102, re partial revision)

As a child and boy James had spent several years at various times in Europe; however, his parents had never taken him to Italy, though for much of the time they had been in Switzerland, close by. Perhaps James's eagerness for Italy was made all the sharper by this omission. In January 1868, reviewing Howells's *Italian Journeys*, he wrote with warmth of that "deeply interesting country," with its "achievements" that "represent to the imagination the *maximum* of man's creative force" (LC I, 476-77). To a writer for whom the creative imagination was to sustain and inform his central myths, Italy was from the beginning of the first importance.

"At Isella" was the second tale to be based on James's visit to Italy in 1869-70. In "Travelling Companions," Italy was of course prominent, but mainly as a soundingboard, a means of measuring the judgement and posture of Brooke and Charlotte Evans. In "At Isella" the fascination of Italy is itself the central theme, though mediated by a narrator, again an unnamed American, who is much closer to James than Brooke was; the tale seems, like "A Passionate Pilgrim," to be "in the highest degree documentary for myself" (LC I, 1206). How close it is to his own experience can be seen by comparing the detail of the journey in the tale with that described by James in a letter of 31 August 1869 to his sister; yet the letter makes no mention of a French priest, co-traveller in the coach, though the Hospice at the summit of the

Simplon is mentioned, nor is there a fascinating signora at Isella. Interestingly enough, whereas in the tale the narrator changes his route, "debating whether or not delay would add to pleasure" in his approach to Italy (II, 105), for James "'twas partly (*excusez ce detail*) a disordered stomach and partly that I had exhausted myself by carrying my knapsack from Lucerne" (L I, 128) that determined the decision to take not the St. Gotthard Pass, as he had planned, but the Simplon. Art is idealization, concerned, not primarily with mundane bodily functions, but with the "metaphysical" soul (II, 105), a term that had appeared twice in "A Passionate Pilgrim" (II, 58, 78).

The letter does indeed specifically mention "the sense of going down into Italy--the delight of seeing the north melt slowly into the south--of seeing Italy gradually crop up in bits and vaguely latently betray itself" (L I, 128), but the artistry with which this aspect informs and animates every detail and corner of the first ten pages of the tale is perhaps its most engaging feature. It colours even the description of Switzerland, which is "little else but brute Nature surely," whereas "what we seek in Europe is Nature refined and transmuted to Art" (II, 102). When the narrator seeks for the sources of Swiss history and legend, his dissatisfaction appears: he finds a "half-hideous church," a "ludicrous plaster-cast of the *genius loci* [William Tell] and his cross-bow," a "sordid lake-side sanctuary, . . . its walls defiled by cockneys." On his journey, a river is merely "a palpable foretaste of Venice," and he begins "to look out for premonitions of Italy"; he wonders whether "deserted Italian palazzos took the lingering sunbeams" at the same angle as do "certain formal burgher mansions" at the "heart of Helvetia" (II, 102-04). Later, in Italy, there is "a fancied elegance of leaf and twig," and the peasant woman who comes to the door with her naked infant, who has been squalling with a "terrible cry," makes him think of the Madonna and Child he was "in coming weeks" to see "over many an altar and in many a p[a]lace"; the "first time the music of an Italian throat [vibrated] upon Italian air," the word "*Niente*" seemed to him "delicious" (II, 110-11). The simple French priest is, in contrast to the narrator, fearful in thinking of "the possible hazards of travel," "full of . . . [the] appealing innocence of mundane things," and "possessed . . . with a sort of school-boy relish for the profane humour of things" (II, 107). At the Hospice, the narrator feels "a solemn and pleasant fitness in my thus entering church-burdened Italy through the portal of the church," although the Prior provoked the "romantic Yankee tourist" to wonder whether he was "more evil than gentle" (II, 108-09). Whereas in "Travelling Companions" and "A Passionate Pilgrim" James provides "external" checks on the excessive fervour of the enthusiastic pilgrim, here the narrator/protagonist is both susceptible and perceptive; by making ironic comments on his own attitude, he seems to provide an ironic check on himself, and yet at the same time the romantic notions hold sway over him.

The second half of the tale presents the narrator's meeting with the signora at Isella. Artistically this is less successful. The lady is a fugitive from her husband, hoping to escape to a lover in Switzerland, and her story is replete with stereotypes, stagey melodrama, and hackneyed dialogue ("Hark! . . . If it should be he--if it should be he!" II, 119); however, she floods the narrator's mind with "the memory of the rich capacity of the historic womanhood of Italy. I thought of Lucrezia Borgia, of Bianca Capello, of the heroines of Stendhal" (II, 115), and he confesses to her: "Ever since I could use my wits, . . . I have done little else than fancy dramas and romances and love-tales, and lodge them in Italy. You seem to me as the heroine of all my stories" (II, 118). (The narrator is like James himself!) A great part of the problem is the reader's uncertainty: when the narrator, after he has heard all the sorry, sad, and sordid details of her trouble, says, "I was part and parcel of a romance!" (II, 123), are we to take it that he is naive and foolish, like Brooke in "Travelling Companions"? The signora's function seems to be like that of the striking woman in Milan Cathedral who had "nobleness of gesture and carriage" and yet prayed "bitter, bitter prayers" (II, 9). Are we to assume that, despite the revelation of the horrors of Italy, this narrator, like Brooke, is so wedded to the notion that Italy provides the substance of "our consoling dreams and our richest fancies" that he cannot accept evidence that would disturb this "Platonic 'idea'"? (II, 117)--perhaps even that he has been euchred out of 170 francs by an accomplished confidence woman (II, 123)? The impression we have of this narrator is that he is too perceptive, too critical of himself to make so egregious an error. So there seems to be an inconsistency in James's portrait of him. Perhaps it was an awareness of this that prompted James to comment adversely on the second part of the tale in a letter to Grace Norton: "I send you herewith a little story ["At Isella"]--not meant for folks as fresh from Italy as you--the fruit of a vague desire to reproduce a remembered impression and mood of mine. The lady is a gross fit. At the time, I wanted something to happen; I have improved on vulgar experience by supposing that something *did*. It is not much you'll see, and such as it is, not perhaps an improvement" (L I, 259).

"MASTER EUSTACE" (*Galaxy*, November 1871; 1885)

James returned home after a year abroad, and, after three tales of Americans adventuring, the next two--and his first novel, *Watch and Ward* (1871)--abruptly return to American settings and to conspicuous borrowing. In this tale Eustace says, "I'm like Hamlet--I don't approve of mothers consoling themselves" (II, 143); there are many other echoes of the play (see II, 131, 133, 138), and some similarity in the line of the plot.[15] As Edel says, "All of Henry James's work shows that he had been saturated with Shakespeare from his earliest days" (EL 562), and the poetry and plays work as powerful yeast in James's imagination.

Like "The Story of a Year," "Master Eustace" is *Hamlet* with some large differences, especially in characterization: Mrs. Garnyer is something like Gertrude, but Eustace/Hamlet, though gifted, is a spoiled and egotistic brat with "a particular fancy for the moon" (II, 129); Mr. Garnyer, deceased, is said to have been "coarsely and cruelly dissipated" (II, 128), and Mr. Cope, who turns out to be Eustace's real father and hopes to (and does) marry Mr. Garnyer's widow, is rather more stolid and respectable than Claudius, though apparently attractive enough to the narrator, who is a sort of companion to Mrs. Garnyer and governess to Eustace.[16]

There are other technical points of interest. The story is told, long after the events reported, by a narrator who is introduced to us as making her cup of tea "with a delicate old-maidish precision" (II, 127), which predisposes us to accept the accuracy of all she has to say. The most prominent feature of her narrative is that Mr. Cope's paternity--at first unsuspected by the reader, then successively thought possible, probable, then clearly implied--is not specifically stated and definite until the last brief sentence of the tale.   The calculated effect of her narrative corresponds to the gradual dawning of this fact on the narrator over the roughly twelve years covered by the events she relates. Mrs. Garnyer's marriage had lasted only three years, and Eustace was five (II, 128) when the narrator was hired as governess and companion, but, as in Sophocles's *Oedipus Rex*, the reader will not ask some lawyers' questions, such as why it was that, in her long intimacy with Mrs. Garnyer, she never discovered how recently Mr. Garnyer had died, or how it was that Eustace was conceived or born before the marriage, or what Mr. Garnyer had thought of the matter. But it all happened a long time ago, and foreshortening can veil many improbabilities. We will not feel we are being cheated as in "Osborne's Revenge"; we will not be inclined to ask these questions when suspicions about the paternity of Eustace accumulate, late in the tale, long after the early history has been related.

Reflecting on James's development, we can now recognize that this kind of discovery by a narrator in the course of the tale is important in his fiction: a sensitive central intelligence gradually becomes aware of a complex situation, and this entails a crucial change. We have seen attempts, more or less flawed, at this sort of structure in "A Landscape Painter" and "Osborne's Revenge"; in "A Light Man" we are given a "before" and an "after" that imply a change, but we are not specifically taken round the corner that leads from the one to the other. In "Travelling Companions" we are taken through the change, but only, in a general and summary form, perfunctorily, when Brooke is travelling through Italy between Venice and Rome (II, 36-37); again we really have only the before and the after. It is not until the next tale, "Guest's Confession," that James will attempt the more delicate matter of the protagonist's actual experience of the mental and emotional change itself.

"Master Eustace" is a romance in two senses: it is the narrator's "only romance--and it's the romance of others" (II, 127), but also, because it is set in the "days of private conveyances" (II, 146)--Mr. Garnyer's book of French poems is inscribed "1802" (II, 136)--it enjoys the liberty we give to tales of former days, and events can have a higher, even sensational, colour; it ends with the death of Mrs. Garnyer, not from poison or a bullet, however, but from shock.

Edel has suggested a parallel between Eustace's sense of displacement and jealousy when he hears of his mother's projected marriage and James's when he returned in 1870 to find William "in comfortable possession" of the parental home, 20 Quincy St., Cambridge;[17] if this is valid, it is also true that James has succeeded in detaching himself very clearly from Eustace.

The tale is also, in a very obvious way, a moral fable, showing how a promisingly gifted boy can be spoilt by an over-indulgent mother as a result of her weakness of "will" (II, 127) and her sense of guilt; she gives Eustace his way as "a kind of penance," a wish to "purchase pardon" (II, 135) for her adultery; perhaps too, in indulging Eustace, she is, like Gertrude, subject to "that monster, custom," indirectly perpetuating her adultery with Cope. The result of her mismanagement and deception, and of her keeping Eustace and herself from contact with the world and reality, is the wilful and violent refusal of Eustace to accept Mr. Cope as his mother's husband, though he is in fact his real father. When Mrs. Garnyer hears the two ineffectual shots fired by Eustace's pistol, she dies, her death the consequence of her sin and her foolishness; another consequence is the never-reconciled quarrel between her son and her lover: "the son was forgiven--the father never!" (II, 150).

It is interesting to see the tale as another about an "innocent" caught in the toils of the harsh world. Eustace is richly endowed-- the meaning of the name's Greek original (heavily ironic here) is "blooming" or "fruitful"--but is finally foiled, because his egotism demands degrees of fulfilment, sympathy, and possession that life cannot give, and so the story becomes tragic; one sees some similarity in this respect between "Master Eustace" and "A Passionate Pilgrim." Soon James will, in Euphemia de Mauves, make his innocent protagonist no less sensitive than Clement Searle and no less vulnerable--though less eccentric, less demanding--than Eustace, and the tragedy will thus become more poignant.

"GUEST'S CONFESSION"   (*Atlantic Monthly*, October-November 1872)

This long tale was published nearly a year after "Master Eustace," but it may have been written at about the same time, perhaps "in the first half of 1871" (II, xxxiv). According to Howells it was "received with more favour than anything else you've printed in the *Atlantic*," but he himself seemed a little cool about it and had some reservations, the ending not coming off "with a click," which might explain why the *Atlantic* delayed publishing it for so long. James's brother William was also rather lukewarm, admiring, "though not loving it exactly," and making it the occasion for a well-known criticism of James's work: "something cold, thin blooded and priggish [is] suddenly popping in and freezing the genial current" (II, xxxv-xxxvi).

The tale might be described, somewhat unkindly, as a not altogether satisfactory mélange: borrowings, tangled relations between father and daughter and between brothers--perhaps like those between Henry and William dwelt on by Edel in his biography--as well as moral allegory. In outline, the gentlemanly Guest, to provide pleasure for his beloved daughter Laura, improperly "borrows" $20,000 by selling bonds belonging to Edgar Musgrave, an almost psychopathic stickler for "literal integrity," who does not allow Guest any time or latitude to repay the money and humiliates him, before David, Edgar's half-brother, as witness, by exacting from Guest a written confession--handed over while Guest is forced to kneel in front of Edgar--declaring himself "a swindler" (II, 167). The tale is narrated by David, who is younger than Edgar and admits to being "frivolous" (II, 178) and given to "florid and hyperbolical gallantry" (II, 177), but who we can see is tolerant, sympathetic, generous, capable of self-criticism, and is on the whole a reliable witness; he feels Guest is "a good-natured sinner. Just as he lacked rectitude of purpose, . . . he found in the mysteries of his own heart no clue to my step-brother's monstrous implacability" (II, 166).

The situation becomes very complex for David when he discovers that Guest's daughter is in fact the young girl under whose spell he had fallen when he heard her playing the organ in an empty church in the village resort where the action takes place. Guest soon utterly forbids David's suit for Laura, who knows nothing of her father's misconduct.   Meanwhile Edgar, a hypochondriac (like William James in these years), dies, leaving nothing to David, who, however, possesses himself of Guest's written confession, which would enable him to insist that, if Guest will not consent to his marriage to Laura, he will expose him to his daughter. Guest, in what David calls his "preposterous arrogance" and "stupid implacability" (II, 194), has dug a hole for himself: after crippling his estate to repay Edgar, he is abandoned by a Mrs. Beck, who finds metal more attractive in the amiable and affluent Crawford; moreover, his blind, misdirected revenge on Edgar's step-brother will alienate his beloved daughter, Laura, who loves David. In resolving that "Justice must show her sword as well as her scales" (II, 194)--in other words, by blackmailing Guest--David rationalizes that he would really be protecting Guest from himself and his crassness, which is analogous to Edgar's. Giving Guest two hours' grace, however, David repairs to "a certain shady streamside nook," and, listening to "the light gurgle of the tarrying stream and to the softer rustle of the cool grey leafage around me," he suddenly feels "exhausted and sickened"; his anger melts, leaving him "horribly ashamed," while "an ineffable change stole over my spirit. There are fathomless depths in spiritual mood and motive." He sees a man herding cows, and "there seemed to me something in this vision ineffably pastoral, peaceful, and innocent; it smote me to my heart of hearts" (II, 199-200). He goes back, and, instead of exacting the requisite handshake, which would have betokened Guest's submission to his threat, he sits beside him and lays his hand on the hand of the still stunned Guest, with "a grasp of which [Guest] felt, first the force, then, I think, the kindness"; David then gratuitously burns the confessional note, thus abjuring the sword. Asked if he is going to dress, Guest replies, "From head to foot!" (II, 201). The moral allegory is complete: generosity is the better way. In facing and solving his difficult problem, David is no longer "boyish" (II, 178, 180, 192, 195), but manly, mature, and presumably ready for matrimony.

The fundamental borrowing in "Guest's Confession" is from *The Merchant of Venice*. Some of the more obvious links are "temper justice with mercy" (II, 164); "Is it set down in the bond?" (II, 186), and two specific references to Shylock (II, 169, 186). Moreover, there is great play, as we have seen, with concepts like implacability, "Justice" (II, 194, 195), "bowels of compassion" (II, 190), "clemency" (II, 198), and mutual "forgiving" (II, 199). The moral structure and the allegory are more pointed than in Shakespeare, and the borrowings are very clear, but there are important differences between the tale and the play. The most interesting of these is that the tale has two Shylocks--Edgar obviously, but also, ironically, his victim, Guest, whose life-denying rigidity is pointedly linked with Shylock's: "His daughter and his ducats!" (II, 195). Indeed, if David had not undergone his transformation, he would have been a third Shylock in an attempt to use Guest's confessional note to extort his consent to David's marriage to Laura.[18] It is highly ironical that David should say of Guest's note, as Constantine did of the sign of the Cross, "By that sign I should conquer," and describe his as a "holy cause" (II, 197). Although James makes the connections with Shakespeare's play conspicuous, the borrowings, as in "Master Eustace," are far from straightforward.

The narration by David is noteworthy; it is both lively and reliable. James succeeds in presenting a "boyish" character who has strong feelings, and even prejudices, but whose narrative is, we feel, dependable; moreover, we can get our bearings without extraneous help. In this way the tale is more satisfactory than, say,

"A Landscape Painter." David's shortcomings are clear and confessed, but he is fundamentally generous and has a moral sensibility. This prepares us for his crucial spiritual change. For the first time James attempts to give us not merely a "before" and an "after," but the very process of change itself as experienced by the protagonist, which occurs in the scene at the "streamside."

The purpose of this scene is plain and its nature remarkable, but, compared with later scenes of the same kind in James's work, its weaknesses become apparent. The change is stated, but in rather vague generalities and with only would-be strong emphasis, such as "I felt a nameless wave of impulse start somewhere in the innermost vitals of conscience" (II, 200); "nameless" and "somewhere" echo "fathomless depths," "ineffable" change, and "ineffably pastoral" vision. James is relying on the familiar properties of a "peaceful" and "innocent" country setting to help convey the alteration in David's spirit: the "streamside nook," the "idle skiff," as well as the cows drinking at the stream and tended by a young cowherd lighting his pipe (II, 199-200), are facile counters conveying beatitude. We feel none of the conflict or urgency in David's conscience; there is nothing subtler than mere clever stage-management. It is significant, however, that James is now addressing this central dramatic process in his fiction. Mastery of it is still to come, and we see this in a fairly simple form in that penetrating tale, "The Real Thing" (1892); it reaches perhaps its Jamesian apogee in some tales of 1903 ("The Beast in the Jungle," "The Birthplace," and "The Papers"). Within a decade of "Guest's Confession," James achieves a fine instance of this kind of scene in Isabel's long reflective vigil in Chapter 42 of his early masterpiece, *The Portrait of a Lady.*

Mrs. Beck and Crawford, owner of a silver-mine in Arizona (II, 174), are amusing characters,[19] parodies of Shakespeare's Portia and Prince of Aragon (see TBW, 20), described with James's high-spirited, sardonic, and urbanely patronizing irony,[20] a vein that has scarcely appeared since "Poor Richard." But, although their courtship does serve as a contrast to the passion and sincerity of David and Laura, it is difficult to see sufficient reasons for the prominence of these two characters. Laura (who is not a central character) seems, when compared with, say, Adela in "A Day of Days" (1866), rather conventionally immaculate and idealized: "I have called her fair, but the word needs explanation. Singularly pleasing as she was, it was with a charm that was all her own. Not the charm of beauty, but of a certain intense expressiveness, which seems to have given beauty the go-by in the very interest of grace" (II, 154). The insipidity of such passages results in part from James's efforts to convey the boyish quality of young David's love; he certainly discusses Edgar, Mrs. Beck, and Crawford in a very different, spirited style.

It is not surprising that James did not reissue "Guest's Confession" in his lifetime. When he wrote it he was probably ready and eager for another visit to Europe to renew his inspiration at that heady source. This time he would be guide and companion to his sister Alice and their Aunt Kate. They set sail in the spring of 1872; his charges returned in the Fall, but James stayed on for another two years, returning home in September 1874.

Chapter V

RENEWAL IN EUROPE, 1872-74

"THE MADONNA OF THE FUTURE" (*Atlantic Monthly*, March 1873; 1875; 1879; [1883]; 1908)

"The Madonna of the Future" makes an appropriate starting point for a chapter in which we see James returning to the adventures of Americans in Europe, and renewing that theme at deeper levels.

The list of revisions of this tale and its appearance in the New York Edition make it clear that James thought it significant, and yet the extraordinary fact is that, submitted by James either before or while he escorted his sister and aunt about in Europe (II, xxxvii-xxxviii), it was "drastically altered" and reduced by Howells in consultation with the James family, especially his father, before its publication. In a letter to his son, Henry Senior attributes the changes to Howells's "timidity" apropos "episodes . . . fashioned upon French literature," which both piques curiosity and rouses some incredulity[1]; the family justified their acquiescence by saying that the scenes did not help "the understanding of the story," and in any event the tale was in its original form too long for "one number of the magazine" (II, xxxviii-xxxix). James remonstrated mildly and privately in a letter from Rome to his father, but said he was "much obliged to you for your trouble"[2] and also to Howells "for performing the excision personally" (L I, 333-34). One supposes that James was constrained to accept the changes because he was too far away to negotiate and because he was still dependent on his father's support; his letter to his parents three months later rather anxiously draws up an account of his financial standing, estimates his debt to his father as "$65, about," and refers somewhat apologetically to his "heavy anticipatory drafts" (L I, 378). But in fact, through all his revisions of the tale, James did not reintroduce the excised scenes; the tale was never revised as thoroughly as was "A Passionate Pilgrim."

Among other reasons for the tale's significance is the fact that for the first time in James there is virtually no plot; it is a "picture" rather than an "anecdote," and in his Preface to *The Spoils of Poynton* James wrote: "I rejoice in the anecdote, but I revel in the picture" (LC II, 1155). The picture is of the situation and the attitude of the American would-be painter, Theobald (Old German: "boldest of the people"), in Florence. He seems at first indeed bold, imposing on the narrator, as he had once on all Florence, which he had taken "by storm" (II, 213), and the story is really only that of the narrator discovering the ironic truth--as Mrs. Coventry, who speaks for all Florence, had done--the vanity, timidity, and pathos of Theobald's pretension, and then, tragically, of Theobald himself discovering this when the narrator perhaps unfeelingly--certainly bluntly--confronts him with the facts: in his intention to accomplish a masterpiece Theobald has "*dawdled*," and the model for his Madonna, whom he has revered for twenty years, is "an old, old woman" (II, 221), "coarse" and marked by a "vulgar stagnation of mind" (II, 218).

For Theobald this realization is a mental and moral trauma, and he soon dies. As for the narrator's attitude to Theobald, after being impressed, he becomes somewhat scornful, but in the end he has a "compassionate interest" (II, 227) born of remorse: "I began to fear that . . . instead of giving a wholesome impetus to his talent, I had brutally paralysed it" (II, 222). What we are seeing here is a further shift in James's focus: there is less emphasis on the "external" event and more on "internal" moral and psychological processes, on the discoveries and changes within the protagonists. Here it is rather stagily and abruptly managed in Theobald, but gradually and effectively in the narrator, and the reader participates with the narrator, moving through an analogous process. We have seen James's attempt at something like this in the previous tale, "Guest's Confession," but the advance here is marked.

"The Madonna" lends itself also to an examination of the development in James's methods in his borrowings. Whereas, for instance, "A Light Man" and "Guest's Confession" follow--even if at some distance and with important differences--the models of St. Augustine's *Confessions* and *The Merchant of Venice*, now James does not follow any outlines of a model but incorporates hints and notions from many sources. In "The Madonna" there are kept before us, for parallel and ironic contrast, the lives and works of the great Italian Renaissance artists--Andrea del Sarto, Michelangelo, Correggio, and Raphael, among others--and also, as Adeline Tintner has indicated, there are the examples of Washington Allston, and of Balzac's "*Le Chef-d'Oeuvre Inconnu*," this last being referred to in the text (II, 215; TBW 70, 202, 246). But there is also a specific and lengthy recall of Alfred de Musset's *Lorenzaccio* (II, 216), as well as quotations from Browning's "Pictor Ignotus" (II, 206) and Tennyson's "Love Thou Thy Land, with Love Far-Brought" (II, 207); both these poems have a bearing on Theobald's case.[3]

But more significant as a source than either Tennyson's "Love Thou Thy Land" or Browning's "Pictor Ignotus" is the latter poet's "Andrea del Sarto," for in a very real sense James's tale presents an ironic--even sardonic--reversal of Browning's monologue, in which the uxorious Andrea attributes his failure to match the genius of Raphael and Michelangelo to his too great facility, and to his fatal infatuation with his unfaithful wife Lucrezia, who was the Madonna of his paintings, but claims that he is at least half a genius. Andrea muses to Lucrezia:

. . . a man's reach should exceed his grasp,
Or what's a heaven for? . . .
I know both what I want and what might gain,
And yet how profitless to know, to sigh
"Had I been two, another and myself,
Our head would have o'erlooked the world!" No doubt.
. . . .
In this world, who can do a thing, will not;
And who would do it cannot, I perceive: . . .
And thus we half-men struggle.
(lines 97-98, 100-03, 137-38, 140, 179)[4]

One important point made in James's tale is that an artist may well become paralyzed by the feeling that his reach exceeds his grasp. He must do what he can. After all, the historical Andrea del Sarto himself, despite his mere facility and fluency, has a place in the pantheon, less exalted than Raphael's, it is true, but a secure place nevertheless. The tale indicates that fluency and facility do not prevent achievement, but dawdling, procrastination, and (in Wordsworth's phrase) infinite delay before the ineffable make it impossible. A corollary to this is that the artist must make the best of whatever opportunities are available. Thus, writing to C.E. Norton in 1871, James concludes that "the face of nature and

civilization" in America "is . . . a very sufficient literary field. But it
will yield its secrets only to a really *grasping* imagination" (L I,
252).

Although Tintner is sometimes over-zealous in her eagerness
to find borrowed patterns in James's works, she is right to
emphasize the importance in "The Madonna" of Cellini's *Perseus*,
which provides "the theme of the story" and makes Theobald's
failure "emblematic" (TBW 55). It is poetically just that both
Michelangelo's *David* and Cellini's *Perseus*, holding out "the snaky
head of the slaughtered Gorgon" (II, 203), should dominate the
first paragraph of the tale, because both depict heroes who have
overcome great odds, and both are statues, which require literal
muscular effort from the sculptor, reminding one, for example, of
Yeats's "men / That with a mallet or a chisel modelled these /
Calculations" ("The Statues"). It is precisely in these heroic deeds,
these efforts, that Theobald is deficient and belies his name. Thus
in "The Madonna" James brings and weaves together multifarious
threads from art and literature to create a rich complex. The
apparently heterogeneous material is shaped into the tale--as the
daws "drop twigs layer by layer" to make their nests in Yeats's
"The Tower"--by James's imagination, which, as we have seen,
frequently functioned through other works of art and artists. The
multiplicity of his cullings goes together with the intensity of his
art.

The earlier European stories--"Travelling Companions," "A
Passionate Pilgrim," and "At Isella"--had been overflowings from a
cornucopia of impressions of England and Italy, many of them
almost direct set-piece descriptions written soon after the
experiences themselves. But after Malvern, Minny Temple's death,
his own earnest self-examination, and another two years (May
1870-May 1872) in Boston--where he endured "chronic eastward
hankerings and hungerings" (L I, 256), the "brooding exile" of
"another quite languishing American interval" (LC II, 1205)--
James was ready for a new and more ambitious assault on the
citadel of art. He writes "The Madonna" in Europe, and in it he
addresses himself again, but with a difference, to European
material. We have seen that the earlier European stories are
something like guidebooks. Now, however, after having used
Venice, Rome, London, Malvern, and the Alps, he uses Florence--
the Palazzo Vecchio, the Uffizi, the Pitti, San Lorenzo, and the
rest--but he subordinates it more clearly to a larger purpose, to
making a statement about art, the calling to which he was now so

deeply committed. If Aziz's deduction that James wrote "The Madonna" in June or July 1872 is correct--that is, *before* his "Italian jaunt" with his sister and his aunt (II, xxxvii-xxxviii)--it means he was not writing from immediate or very recent experience of Florence, but making use of impressions gained on his visit in 1869, two and a half years before, and in a more deliberate and artistic manner.

There is another significant advance. As we have seen, the earlier European stories all present a protagonist who responds to Europe in an excessively enthusiastic, uncritical way. It might seem that "The Madonna" is like them in this: certainly Theobald has an immense admiration for the art and artists of the Italian Renaissance, but his enthusiasm is less superficial and less obviously ridiculous than Brooke's, and it is less fantastic and eccentric than Searle's is for English civilization. Theobald's is unbalanced--as Tintner shows, he even imitates the way Raphael dressed (TMW 28)--but, as far as it goes, it is sincere and perceptive, so much so that it can at first impose on intelligent people. The point is that, even though we come to see him as virtually mad, he is much closer to the narrator than even Searle is to the narrator in "A Passionate Pilgrim," and also closer to James himself. In his Preface to *The Reverberator* James wrote that both "A Passionate Pilgrim" and "The Madonna" were "in the highest degree documentary for myself" (LC II, 1206), but they are so in different ways: the earlier tale is closer to what he saw and felt at the time, to his sensational self, and "The Madonna" is closer to the thought and agitations of James's artistic conscience.

There is certainly high-flying eloquence in Theobald's midnight disquisition near the beginning in the great piazza beneath the Palazzo Vecchio (II, 203-06), but there is nothing in the substance of it to rouse the narrator to contradiction or embarrassment, nothing that James himself could not in sufficient measure presumably have assented to. The prompt enthusiasm with which Theobald echoes the narrator's insistence--"Invent, create, achieve!" (II, 205)--veils and disowns his own weakness. Even next day, in the Uffizi, there is little to separate the narrator from Theobald. It is not until they come to Raphael's *Madonna in the Chair* at the Pitti (II, 208) that the narrator begins to voice, and the reader to discern, a difference. This picture is for Theobald the pinnacle of art: it is not "of Raphael"; it "*is* Raphael himself" (II, 209). But the narrator has a good deal to say about the picture too, and even here there might seem to be agreement: "Of all the fine pictures of the world, it seemed to me this is the one with which criticism has least to do" (II, 208).[5] Only when Theobald waxes ecstatic about the "spotless image" and the contrasted "foul vapours of life," does the narrator demur: "Don't you imagine that he [Raphael] had a model"; when Theobald expatiates on "idealism," the narrator says, "Go to, you're all wrong" (II, 209), and the gulf is clear. It is perhaps significant that, soon after this, Theobald twice uses the epithet "ineffable" (II, 210, 211), which David used in describing his crucial conversion in "Guest's Confession" (II, 200). It is tempting to suppose that, between writing the two tales, James has come to see the weakness of that scene in "Guest's Confession." Here we see another distinct advance in James's presentation of a narrator's experience in discovering the central truth.

If James was accompanying his sister and aunt about Europe when writing "The Madonna" (see II, xxxvii-xxxviii), it seems likely that he was reflecting earnestly, though not bitterly, on the likeness between himself and Theobald. James too had the highest, most idealistic conceptions and a passion for art, and he too, though for different reasons, was unproductive, his creative powers pent up within him. Theobald could well be a somewhat exaggerated projection of himself. James had not produced fiction at all copiously since 1868, and the novel he had just published, *Watch and Ward*, was a work by which he set little store. "Invent, create, achieve" could well be directed to himself. Before he saw Alice and Aunt Kate off back to America in October, the year 1872 had produced little except some travel pieces that appeared in *English Hours*, and he felt that, despite the distractions of Europe, he must get down to writing fiction. Richard H. Brodhead suggests that James was concerned about "becoming stalled in the phase of apprenticeship."[6] His letter to his parents of 29 September looks forward to hard work: "I expect this coming year or two, over here, to do a great deal for me. . . . Once I get started I have little fear of not keeping afloat. If I had had a more disengaged summer I should have a larger capital to begin upon" (L I, 303). Two weeks later he writes: "On my return to Paris, I expect to get in some sort regularly at work" (L I, 306). A little over a year later, still in Europe, he was able to tell Howells: "The *Atlantic* can't publish as many stories as I ought and expect to be writing" (L I, 424). He was, moreover, ready to write *Roderick Hudson*, his first important novel; as Aziz says, by the end of 1873 James had become "so prolific that the four magazines to which he had been contributing [fiction and reviews] . . . simply could not keep pace with him" (II, xliv).

"The Madonna" emphasizes the necessary relation between art and life and the labour and perhaps agony that the artist must endure in the fulfilment of his ideal conceptions. This was to be fundamental in both James's theory and practice. So much--indeed all--was in the *doing*; as late as 1914 he was to write of "the way to do a thing that shall make it undergo most doing" (LC I, 147). In 1908 he would tell Howells that it was "really, at bottom, only difficulty that interests me" (LL II, 119). R.P. Blackmur explains this in his Introduction to James's Prefaces: James "would push his rendering [of his theme] to the most difficult terms possible. So alone would he be able to represent the maximum value of his theme."[7] In "The Middle Years" (1893), Dencombe dwells on an aspect of this: "A second chance--*that's* the delusion. There never was to be but one. We work in the dark--we do what we can--we give what we have. Our doubt is our passion and our passion is our task. The rest is the madness of art" (ECT IX, 75). Of this passion Theobald knows nothing.

Because in "The Madonna" James is dealing with what one might call the philosophy of art, he gives prominence to scenes that Howells deprecated but did not excise; he told James: "The sole blemish on it to my mind is the insistence on the cats and monkeys philosophy. I don't think you ought to have let that *artista* appear a second time" (II, xl). James does labour that aspect, but for a very good reason. The return of the "ingenious artist," who is in contrast to Theobald and in fact his rival for the attentions of his "Madonna," leads to the final words: "I seemed to hear a fantastic, impertinent murmur, 'Cats and monkeys, monkeys and cats; all human life is there!'" (II, 232). But this points a moral about art that was as important for James as the other truths. Art meant loneliness and hard work, but it had a noble, even a priestly task-- that of dignifying life, transcending "all the ugliness, the grossness, the stupidity, the cruelty, the . . . brutality and vulgarity" (JF 605). The "ingenious artist" who displaces Theobald in the orbit of the woman who was his model specializes in sculpting miniature figures of cats and a "menagerie of monkeys." The creator of this menagerie, "a small, wiry man, with . . . a sharp little black eye" (II, 223), proudly declares, "To combine sculpture and satire . . . has been my unprecedented ambition" (II, 226), but to the disgusted narrator the little figures, in their suggestive poses, "seemed . . . peculiarly cynical and vulgar" (II, 227). When Theobald admits the

accuracy of the exasperated narrator's accusation that he has
"*dawdled*" (II, 221)--a term James often uses, together with
"gaped", for a propensity in himself (A 17, 20, 493)--he, like
Andrea del Sarto, says, "I'm the half of a genius! Where in the wide
world is my other half? Lodged perhaps in the vulgar soul, the
cunning, ready fingers of some dull copyist or some trivial artisan
who turns out by the dozen his easy prodigies of touch!" (II, 229).
It seems clear that James views the little sculptor of the animal
figures, with their slightly obscene poses, as Theobald's other half.
Without a feel for, and some contact with life, Theobald is
condemned to a sterile and barren existence. But it is just as true
that without an awareness of the ideal--the "ineffable"--the little
sculptor will emulate Bernini in vain, for he will never rise above
the vulgarity, brutality, and cruelty of his limited view. His kind of
art, without Theobald's vision, degrades man and his life, and is
therefore anathema to James.[8]   Art should be uplifting.   In his
Preface to *The Lesson of the Master* James was to defend with
"passion" his characters and cases which were said to be
unrealistic, or, as he put it, "rich and edifying where the actuality is
pretentious and vain," saying defiantly, "If the life about us for the
last thirty years refuses warrant for these examples, then so much
the worse for that life" (LC II, 1229).

Many commentators, misled by the young James himself,
count "The Madonna" as an "international" tale. It is true that
Theobald's artistic paralysis might in part be attributed to his notion
that Americans "are the disinherited of Art! . . . The soil of
American perception is a poor little barren, artificial deposit" (II,
205). It may be true that James himself, in some of his moods,
shared this view, but James's narrator in "The Madonna" scouts it;
to agree with Theobald and to see a causal connection between
Americanness and failure in art is surely to make a diminished thing
of the tale. Americanness cannot be identified with a naive or
callow idealism. James was writing not so much about a typical
American as about a type of would-be artist, who has some
aesthetic insight, and even some talent--as Theobald's drawing,
which the narrator "vastly" admires (II, 219), clearly demonstrates--
but, being without will, the "madness" of art, or some other
necessary quality, he will always attribute his failure to some
circumstance beyond his control. It is a universal rather than an
"international" tale. Indeed, it is possible to say that in "The
Madonna" James comes closer to the vein that will be most
important of all to him. Theobald is the prototype of the Innocent

who, though intelligent and sympathetic, is vulnerable because unwilling, or unable, to deal with the actual world, with--as the Innocent sees it--the world's vulgarity and cruelty.[9] Philip Grover has seen that, in Theobald, James has presented the tragedy of the artist who tries, as James was always trying, to make his art an expression of "moral idealism."[10] James was able, however, as Theobald was not, to face up to and come to grips with unpalatable truths. Significant art depends on this ability, and Theobald's inability to put pencil and brush to canvas is the result of this metaphysical failure. James himself knew the dilemma of this kind of idealist, and for this reason "The Madonna" evokes a compassion and a keenly felt sense of tragedy. We are told before the narrator begins his story that it brought "a tender tear in each of" his charming hostess's "beautiful eyes" (II, 202). This is close to the effect achieved--one might rashly say--in all James's greatest works, and explains why James constantly revived "The Madonna" and finally included it in the New York Edition, in which it is, after "A Passionate Pilgrim," his earliest work.

"THE SWEETHEART OF M. BRISEUX" (*Galaxy*, June 1873)

As soon as he had seen Alice and Aunt Kate off from Liverpool in mid-October 1872, James returned to Paris and wrote this tale, which has a French setting. William read it "without . . . the delight I have so often got from your things" (II, xlii), and James may have acquiesced in this disparagement; the tale was never revised.

James was soon to have a painter as narrator in "The Last of the Valerii," as he had in "A Landscape Painter," and here in "The Sweetheart" he deals with painters and painting itself, as he had done in "The Story of a Masterpiece" and "The Madonna of the Future"[11] and was to do again in *Roderick Hudson* (1875), *The Tragic Muse* (1890), and throughout his life in tales such as "The Real Thing" (1892), "Glasses" (1896), "The Special Type" (1900), "The Tone of Time" (1900), the unfinished "Hugh Merrow" (c. 1900; N 589-96), "The Beldonald Holbein" (1901), and "Flickerbridge" (1902). In his criticism, as in his fiction, painting was as often the vehicle for his writing on art as was writing itself.

The weakness of the tale is that the portraits of the two contrasted painters are too stereotyped: Harold Staines, the non-starter as an artist, is unimaginative, earnest, conventional, well-heeled, proper, diligent (II, 246), "comely, elegant, imposing," with a "narrow . . . ineffectual self"; and Briseux, the true artist, is poor, "ugly, shabby, disreputable" (II, 256), "without any visible linen" (II, 249), vehement (II, 250), underfed (II, 251), and sarcastic (II, 252)--but a genius. It is all too pat and predictable. Adeline Tintner suggests that the tale "incorporates the Ingres-Delacroix, Neoclassical-Romantic controversy" (TMW 9), but the tale must not be regarded as a contribution to that discussion. James was not attempting to deliver any kind of justice to Ingres, though it is true that all James's comments on the art of Ingres--these are between 1868 and 1875--are less than enthusiastically appreciative (see LC I, 1034-35, 1037, 1139).

There is one aspect of the tale that is brilliantly executed and of great interest: the character of the narrator and the method of her narration. She tells her story from her twenty-first year until she breaks off her engagement to Staines. She is one of James's innocents: she is young, prefers "imagination" to "cultivation," is a lover of Shelley's "Stanzas Written in Dejection" (II, 245), and is far from "worldly-wise" (II, 246), but obviously intelligent. An orphan, naive and vulnerable, she is imposed on by Staines, the son of her guardian, but her integrity and increasing insight bring her to the point of perceiving his emptiness, and the advent of M. Briseux, who brashly takes over the painting of Harold's portrait of her, seals this discovery, and she liberates herself. This is James's central myth, but here it is without the pathetic element so prominent in "The Madonna of the Future," "Daisy Miller," *The Portrait of a Lady*, "The Pupil," and *The Wings of the Dove*.

What gives point and value to her story is the skilful way in which James brings her from her early naïveté, through a gradual acquisition of insight, to the full discovery. The nature of her discovery, involving nothing less than the narrator's whole intellectual and moral being, is far more momentous and convincing than the change in the narrator in "Guest's Confession."

How it was that the narrator had so much to do to liberate herself, why she had to undergo such a long process of discovery-- what James in the Preface to *What Maisie Knew* would call "'subjective' adventure" (LC II, 1170)--is fully justified by the circumstances. Apart from being young, she is under obligation for being received with "substantial kindness" (II, 238) by her mother's friend, Mrs. Staines, in whose family "there had been nothing . . . but judges and bishops, and anything else was of questionable respectability." Harold's good looks were those of "a decorous young Apollo"; "never was a handsomer, graver, better-bred young man." She had "never seen so fine a gentleman, and I doubted if the world contained such another. My experience of the world was small, and I had lived among what Harold Staines would have considered very shabby people" (II, 239); the term "shabby" appears later for Briseux (II, 256). Little wonder that the girl was "vastly impressed from the first" by the young man, who had "in perfection the *air* of distinction," was "perfectly honourable and amiable" (II, 239), and above all "proper" (II, 243); in "the blessed simplicity of youth" she was unable to distinguish between a real talent for art--the vocation Staines sets his mind on, though this was "not the career" his mother would have "preferred"--and "a mania for pictures and bronzes, old snuff-boxes and candlesticks" (II, 240). Inexperience, ingenuousness, and gratitude are all forces in her that impede her perception of the truth, which nevertheless does go forward. As she says, she "observed my emotions, even before I understood them" (II, 243-44); her final realization is constantly and more and more clearly foreshadowed, and the reader follows this gradual progress closely. She does hear, but at first dismisses, other opinions: a young man is overheard referring to Harold as "*that confounded prig*" (II, 242); a critic of painting mistakes Harold's work for that of "a *jeune fille*" (II, 245). Even before this, however, she had "always thought it strange . . ." (II, 243), and now she "allowed [herself] to wonder" (II, 245), so that she would "take refuge in a silence which from day to day covered more treacherous conjectures," her "doubts" being felt as "immoral" (II, 246). Her situation has something like the poignancy of Maisie's (in *What Maisie Knew*) or Morgan's (in "The Pupil"), where youthful intelligence and goodwill are also struggling to emerge from a cocoon woven by adult stupidity or deceit. The effect is dramatic, and the fascination is in seeing her unsupported youthful spirit working against a received, respectable orthodoxy. She pleads for "another month's delay" of their marriage, though "what I wished to wait for I could hardly have told" (II, 247). She suggests that Harold use the time in painting her portrait instead of copying Leonardo's *Joconde*; this provides the occasion for Briseux to arrive and complete her enlightenment, and she has the intellectual integrity and moral courage to act on it.

The narrator's story is picturesquely and piquantly framed by her encounter in a provincial art gallery with the primary narrator, who recognizes her as she is examining the portrait of herself painted some thirty years earlier by M. Briseux. Her narration is skilfully managed by James in the manner we have indicated. But this method of using a narrator is not altogether satisfactory for what seems to be James's main purpose, which is to take us through the change or conversion of the protagonist. The difficulty with this method is that the protagonist, now older and wiser, knows the truth that she was groping toward, and thus will either delay the disclosure until the end--as in "Master Eustace"--to get the maximum effect of surprise, or--as in "The Sweetheart"--make the truth discernible from near the beginning, thus getting the maximum tension from the protagonist's being on the verge of a precipice, but sacrificing some of the shock of the final surprise. Better than either of these methods, James found, was the one he used in, for example, "The Beast in the Jungle" (1903), *The Ambassadors* (1903), and *The Golden Bowl* (1904). In "The Beast" the protagonist, John Marcher, is not the narrator, but the author uses his privilege to follow Marcher's thought and feelings closely as well as to create atmosphere and to artfully insinuate, and thus he has the best of both worlds. The dénouement can be implied without being so clearly foreshadowed; the reader has all the excitement of anticipation and in addition to this a highly dramatic emotional climax. Paradoxically, the mounting tension of the run-up seems to heighten the intensity of the reader's reaction to the impact of Marcher's full realization at the end. But, in the meantime, "The Sweetheart," though in its entirety somewhat disappointing, is a clear step forward in the techniques James was developing.

"THE LAST OF THE VALERII" (*Atlantic Monthly*, January 1874; 1875; 1885)

This was one of five tales--including "Mme. de Mauves," James's longest to date--to be published in 1874. It is one of his strange tales, reminding one of "The Romance of Certain Old Clothes," "De Grey: A Romance," and Hawthorne--the transformation of the Italian Count recalling that of Donatello in *The Marble Faun*. This tale is not gratuitously eerie, however, but, like Mérimée's "*La Vénus d'Ille*," is based on psychological and religio-social insight.

The serious aspect of this fantastic story is its presentation of the gulf between a sophisticated modern view of life, history, and religion and an earlier, more instinctual, and "heathenish" world-view of the "natural man" (II, 264); in spite of the knowledge that it encompasses, its aesthetic eclecticism, and the assurance it expresses, the modern does not comprehend the old view. The tale lifts a curtain on a forgotten life.

Once again, as in "A Landscape Painter," James has a painter as his prism, but as a narrator, not a diarist. The point of this is that the narrator, together with Martha, also an American--whom he calls "*figlioccia mia*" (II, 268) and constantly refers to as his goddaughter, thus emphasizing the similarity of their attitudes-- represents an enlightened modern aesthetic, which, for example, cultivates archaeological interests, leads to being "in love with" a Roman villa, and manifests "amusing horror" at the "*scraping*" of a mossy coat from an ancient sarcophagus (II, 260); its general feature is a sense of the "picturesque," including a relish for "precious antique rubbish . . .[and] half-historic echoes" (II, 262). Seeing his goddaughter and her new husband walking arm-in-arm "across the end of one of the long-drawn vistas" of his villa, the narrator "could easily believe that I was some loyal old chronicler of a perfectly poetical legend" (II, 265). The tale can be read as James's backward look at, and criticism and recantation of, the worship of the "picturesque," a term prominent in the vocabulary of Brooke in "Travelling Companions" (II, 9-10) and frequent in James's own travel pieces, though by 1873 he is beginning to be more critical of the term and the attitude; for instance, in "The Autumn in Florence" he writes of "our preference for what we are pleased to call the picturesque,"[12] and in a letter from Perugia he tells William, "The *keen* love and observation of the picturesque is ebbing away from me as I grow older." He associates this change with "the growth of one's mind" (L I, 385). (One thinks of Wordsworth's "Tintern Abbey.") The sophisticated aesthetes in "The Last of the Valerii" are not altogether different from Brooke before his mind expanded under the influence of Miss Evans in "Travelling Companions."

The tale is suffused with an irony, deeper than any in previous tales--with the possible exception of "A Light Man"-- which was to become common in James's work. Here there is the obvious irony in the fact that it is Martha who has to persuade her aristocratic but apparently simple husband to consent to the excavations at his villa: he had been "indifferent," and "even averse, to the scheme"; "Let them lie, the poor disinherited gods," he said (II, 266). In view of what happens, the irony is deeper when we learn that he lacks the cultivated sensibility of his wife and her godfather, who finds him "fundamentally unfurnished with 'ideas'" and having "nothing but senses, appetites, and serenely luxurious tastes" and who even wonders whether he had "anything that could properly be termed a soul"; the Italian Count does not share his wife's interest in Dante or Vasari (II, 264) and can be seen "occupied by the half-hour, playing the simple game of catch-and-toss" (II, 265).

The profounder irony--irony at the reader's expense--comes into full play when the magnificent Juno is disinterred. The narrator, Martha, and the cognoscenti are delighted and excited-- for the narrator the statue is "an embodiment of celestial supremacy and repose" (II, 267) (in other words, comfortably dead)--but the Count, apparently so lacking in cultivated sensibility, is transported by it back to the ancient world to which it belonged. He pays no attention to his new wife, whom he has loved very much, stands before the goddess in "fixed contemplation," manifesting "a still deeper emotion" (II, 268), and looks "over [his wife's] head with an air of superb abstraction" (II, 271). It is significant that the statue is a Juno, not a Venus, which would allow an easier explanation of the Count's worship! He makes a libation (II, 269) and a blood sacrifice at a "roughly extemporized altar" (II, 280).

The narrator and his goddaughter are horrified, mystified, and completely at a loss; they have another of James's "subjective" adventures. The narrator first "grew to hate the Count" (II, 272) because the case seemed to him "so fantastic, so apparently far-fetched, so absurd," but he tries to deal with the situation, saying, "Refined feeling seemed to dictate a tender respect for his delusion" (II, 276). To make sense of it he needs the Italian foreman of the excavations, who says: "There's a pagan element in all of us,--I don't speak for you, *illustrissimi forestieri*,--and the old gods have still their worshippers" (II, 278). The narrator conveys this to Martha: "Your enemy is the Juno. The Count-- how shall I say it?--the Count takes her *au sérieux*" (II, 279). He is struggling with the concept and recognizes the ridiculous inadequacy of his expression.

To win back her husband, Martha boldly has the Juno re-interred. The Count's reaction is interesting: "His eyes were brilliant, but not angry. He had missed the Juno--and rejoiced!" (II, 283). His infidelity had been not wilful, but exacted by the goddess in spite of himself. Juno's power and the Count's response are thereby made all the stranger to the narrator and Martha, and all the more real.

There are several supporting ironies. At first Martha, an

American Protestant, responds to the splendours of St. Peter's (II, 261), an edifice that always "stupefies" the Count, and--though perhaps not altogether seriously--she offers for the Count's sake to convert to his Catholicism, but he says, "I'm a poor Catholic!" (II, 262); in fact he feels much more at home in the pagan Pantheon, "the best place in Rome. . . . It's worth fifty St. Peters" (II, 275). Religion for her is a choice, almost a fashion; for him it has deep roots, within his inner being, though he is only half-conscious of them.

One cannot be altogether satisfied with the classification of even this as an international tale. It is true that, being both American and a modern artist, as well as a polymath, the narrator is perhaps at a disadvantage in comprehending the Count's response, but this is no simple contrast between Americans and Italians. The "half a dozen . . . cognoscenti"--at least one of whom is a German--who "posted out to obtain sight of [the statue]" are said to be "inquisitive" (II, 269), which puts them in a scientific category, not unlike the aesthetic, and thus very different from the Count. Even the Italian foreman, who can supply the explanation, says the Count's is a "rare" case and distances himself from the "monstrous heritage of antiquity" (II, 278); his interest in the statue is limited to its value in the market. So the tale really involves at its base the contrast between a modern and an ancient sensibility, such as that described in Lucania in the 1930s by Carlo Levi in *Christ Stopped at Eboli*.[13] All one can say is that there are no relics of the ancient Roman ethos in America, so the story could not be set in Massachusetts. But it is ironical that a similarly ancient civilization was more available to Americans--even perhaps than the Roman to Europeans--in American Indian Reserves, which were of course far beyond the purview of James the novelist. But the tale shows how deeply James was aware of and interested in the protean potentialities of the human psyche and culture, and it is possible that it was James's American background that helped him to this insight. He knew the fiction of Fenimore Cooper and Hawthorne, but more immediately relevant may be the histories of Parkman, James's reviews of which appeared in the *Nation* in 1867 and 1874. In the 1874 review of *The Old Regime in Canada* James wrote: "[Parkman's] Jesuits and trappers are excellent, but his Indians are even better, and he has plainly ventured to look at the squalid savage *de près* and for himself" (LC I, 575). It is clear that one can apply the term "international" only with qualifications.

"MME. DE MAUVES"   (*Galaxy*, February-March 1874; 1875; 1879; [1883]; 1908)

In a letter of 14 August 1873 to his parents, James wrote that this tale "is the best written thing I have done" (II, xlvi); William thought it "one of your best things" (II, xlvii); Aziz refers to it as James's "first small masterpiece" (II, xlv). None of these opinions provokes specific dissent, and yet there is a good deal in the tale that calls for criticism.

For settings James had already used Rome, Venice, Florence, an Alpine pass, London, and English country towns and countryside; now it was to be Paris, its environs, and the French countryside. The French (the French upper and fashionable classes in particular) are shown in constant contrast to America and Americans, and in a most unfavourable light. With scarcely an exception, the French are cynical, selfish, unfaithful, and narrowly snobbish. As the American Longmore tells Euphemia, Mme. de Mauves (née Clive, and American): "You are truth itself, and there is no truth about you" (II, 317); the Americans have standards of honour and morality that the French cannot "conceive" (II, 339) and do not "understand" (II, 345). Longmore is told by Mrs. Draper, Euphemia's friend, that hers is "the miserable story of an American girl, born to be neither a slave nor a toy, marrying a profligate Frenchman, who believes that a woman *must* be one or the other" (II, 288). The tale is the story of Longmore's meeting with, attraction to, affection and then love for, and eventual parting from, Euphemia. It is not surprising that his view of her situation is not flattering to her husband; in fact, even before he sets eyes on him, but informed by Mrs. Draper's report and "edified by his six months in Paris," Longmore's comment is "What else is possible . . . for a sweet American girl who marries an unclean Frenchman?" (II, 287). The reader is not expected to score these comments against Mrs. Draper and Longmore, because the author himself, who describes Euphemia's sister-in-law as "very positive, very shrewd, very ironical, very French" (II, 290), tells us that Euphemia's husband is "a thoroughly perverted creature" with a "luxurious egotism" (II, 294) that seems to be the mark of his class. For his sister it is a boast that "there has never been a De Mauves who has not given his wife the right to be jealous" (II 324). One notices that James does not allow his French characters to make as much of the argument for "the prosperity of [the] house" (II, 292) when weighed against scruples of conscience as he did in "Gabrielle de

Bergerac" and would do much later in *Guy Domville*. This is the more surprising as it comes from one who had a lifelong respect and love for France and French--if not all aspects of Parisian--culture, and who numbered, for example, Sainte-Beuve and, above all, Balzac among his intellectual and artistic paragons. Moreover, in a review published as early as January 1865, James criticized T. Adolphus Trollope's *Lindisfarne Chase* in these terms: Trollope "desires to represent a vicious and intriguing young girl; so he takes an English maiden, and supposes her to have been educated in Paris. Vice and intrigue are conjured up by a touch of the pen. Paris covers a multitude of sins" (LC I, 1356). In the same year James referred to the French as "the most brilliant nation in the world" (LC II, 472) while also, in a review of Balzac's *Correspondance*, pointing to "the Gallic lightness of soil in the moral region" (LC II, 82). It is another instance of James's characteristic ambivalence. Vivien Jones has put the case very well: "In [James's] criticism of the 1870s the coherent morality with which James eventually circumvented the French lions in his path jostles with a tendency to resort to unthinking *idées reçues* about French dirtiness and pessimism."[14]

In "Mme. de Mauves" the trouble is precisely that James's ambivalence is not at work, that in consequence he offers one-dimensional, stereotyped figures who have none of the rich complexity of feeling and motive that, at an even earlier stage, he was presenting in, for example, Richard Clare ("Poor Richard," 1868), and that is seen here in Longmore, the American who is in contrast to the De Mauves family. The cardboard French characters are of the aristocracy, a class that James had depicted with some sympathy a few years back in "Gabrielle de Bergerac." Now, involved in "international" contrasts, and writing for the American reader, perhaps James felt that he might lean on national and class prejudices. In this too he is not being true to his genius because, for reasons that are not difficult to see, he tended to write about the wealthy upper-middle class and the aristocracy: it is among these that good taste and intelligence will be most cultivated and conspicuous. He is able, in a review of 1877, to make fun of the French novelist, Octave Feuillet, who "relates exclusively the joys and sorrows of the aristocracy; the loves of marquises and countesses alone appear worthy of his attention, and heroes and heroines can hope to make no figure in his pages unless they have an extraordinary number of quarterings" (LC II, 286-87). The faults we see most clearly in others are often those we ourselves are most prone to and only more or less narrowly manage to avoid.[15]

It is perhaps not until more than a decade after "Mme. de Mauves" that James got quite clear of a tendency to rely on national stereotypes; in "Mrs. Temperly" (1887) he introduces Mme. de Brives: "an agreeable Frenchwoman is a triumph of civilisation" (ECT VI, 213), but even as late as 1889-90, a Frenchman, de Montaut ("The Solution") is somewhat stereotyped; he is "born for human intercourse" (ECT VII, 358), in which he amuses himself unfeelingly, with no "compunction" (ECT VII, 387). In the Preface (1907) to *The American* (1877), written a few years after "Mme. de Mauves," James recognizes his "affront to verisimilitude" in representing the Bellegarde family, which "would, I now feel, . . . have comported itself in a manner as different as possible from the manner to which my narrative commits it" (LC II, 1067, 1065).

"Mme. de Mauves" is, on the other hand, most flattering to the American self-image. Besides having two obviously likeable or admirable American main characters--Euphemia is described by old Mme. de Mauves as an "angel of innocence" (II, 293)--James presents even the less perfect American characters with genial tolerance: Mrs. Clive "belonged to that large class of Americans who treat America as a kind of impossible allegiance, but are startled back into a sense of moral responsibility when they find Europeans taking them at their word" (II, 298). Terms that echo throughout the tale in establishing the American aura are "innocence" (e.g., II, 293, 295, 297, 305) and "conscience" (e.g., II, 288, 292, 293, 319-320, 339), and, beyond the "excessively artificial garden" (II, 299) that represents French culture, it is the forest (e.g., II, 299, 303, 307, 316, 320, 322, 333) that provides the conditions in which American naturalness and innocence can feel at home.

It is interesting to note that at this time (1873-74) James was still not publishing in England. Aziz says James "did not think his work was good enough for English magazines" (II, xliv). One would not want to accuse James of pandering to American readers, but it is clear that the schemas that he was using in this phase of his "international" fiction would have been more acceptable in America than in Europe. He was not published in England until he presented a more balanced account of American and European qualities in "Daisy Miller" (1878). Some awareness of this might be behind James's explaining to his parents in a letter of 14 August

1873, shortly after completing "Mme. de Mauves," that he wanted to "approach English organs on some other basis than American subjects" (II, xlvi). How sensitive the matter of national image was at this time--as it still is--is indicated by the fact that, according to Aziz, both James and Howells later believed that "Daisy Miller" had been rejected by *Lippincott's Magazine* "because it was seen to be presenting an unfavourable image of American girlhood" (III, 16). And James did have his ear tuned to the market: a few years later he felt that "An International Episode" (1878-79) had offended British pride, and he told his mother in a letter of 18 January 1879 that he would "keep off dangerous ground in future" (L II, 213).

Euphemia de Mauves is a model of virtue under difficulty, bearing suffering with exemplary "stoicism" (II, 304) and achieving even a "studied gaiety" (II, 307); Longmore hears of her unhappiness only from Mrs. Draper and Mme. Clairin, before he observes it and its causes for himself. Apart from "innocence" and "conscience," a key word for her is "gentle" (II, 285, 287, 304), and James used the epithet for her in his Preface many years later (LC II, 1206). Her virtue is not always oppressive, because in the flashback to her girlhood before her marriage (II, 289-99) James makes pleasant fun of her romantic ingenuousness and naïveté. She has a "radical purity of . . . imagination" (II, 289). "Radical" is changed in the 1879 revision to "primitive," and in 1908 the phrase becomes "the prime purity of her moral vision" (II, 538). She is "utterly incorruptible" (II, 289), but her "convictions"--for instance, that "a gentleman with a long pedigree must be of necessity a very fine fellow"--"were the fruit, in part, of the perusal of various ultramontane works of fiction," and "a matter of transcendent theory" (II, 289). An easy prey for the predatory M. de Mauves, she is a more prototypical Jamesian innocent than is the protagonist in "The Sweetheart of M. Briseux," and her story is invested with infinite pathos. James does, however, make her too immaculate a heroine: the last sentence of the tale reports Longmore's final feeling for Euphemia as something like "awe" (II, 347), a term that survives all the revisions, and the reader is not invited to qualify Longmore's judgement. Putting her on so high a pedestal leads James to allow her to deliver some rather piously and pompously sententious speeches: "'If I were to find you selfish where I thought you generous, narrow where I thought you large'-- and she spoke slowly, with her voice lingering with emphasis on each of these words--'vulgar where I thought you rare--I should think worse of human nature'" (II, 336-37); this might be a speech from sentimental comedy.

The teasingly ironic note James sounds in dealing with Euphemia's naive girlhood is not unlike Jane Austen's in recounting the errors of Catherine Morland (*Northanger Abbey*) at Bath and as a guest at the Tilneys', and those of Fanny Price (*Mansfield Park*) in the chapel at Sotherton--all attributable to the uncritical reading of romances. For example, Euphemia found the castle in the Auvergne. . . "delightful as a play. It had battered towers and an empty moat, a rusty drawbridge and a court paved with crooked, grass-grown slabs" (II, 291). "Miss Austen's heroines" are mentioned in "A Passionate Pilgrim" (1871) (II, 61)[16]. There is so much fun at the young Euphemia Clive's expense, and such a degree of "awe" expected in the reader's response to the mature Euphemia de Mauves, that one might apply to her portrayal the criticism that James, two years later, allows his character Pulcheria to make in a dramatized discussion of George Eliot's *Daniel Deronda*: "The second Gwendolen doesn't belong to the first" (LC I, 989). James might have presented the mature Euphemia with some touches of the not unkind irony that was soon to play on Christopher Newman (*The American*, 1877) and Isabel Archer (*The Portrait of a Lady*, 1881).

In general, James lays on the moral meanings in "Mme. de Mauves" rather thickly. Euphemia is too good, and her husband the Baron's perfidy and cynicism are demonstrated and insisted on at unnecessary length. The Baron's speech to Longmore starting, "Being as you are her fellow-countryman . . ." (II, 310-11) sounds like one of Gilbert Osmond's (in *The Portrait*) and is effective because his irony is brazen, controlled, and sardonic, having the quality of witty sarcasm, and his corruption is there to be seen and felt; but in other passages we find statements that leave the impression of flatness: "The Baron was a pagan and his wife was a Christian, and between them, accordingly, was a gulf" (II, 305). This somewhat heavy-handed mode appears also in the extraordinary ending, in which we are suddenly to accept, according to Mrs. Draper's perhaps only slightly coloured account, that the Baron "fell madly in love" with the wife he had coldly and consistently humiliated and betrayed and "asked her forgiveness," and then that she, the model of sensitive Christian virtue, "had inexorably refused," with the result that "he had blown out his brains" (II, 347). Sentimental comedy has become the purest melodrama. Aziz sees James's "sentimentality" as the "real source" of the strength of the tale (II, lix), but we find this as difficult to accept as James Kraft's suggestion that James intends us to see Euphemia as "deliberately and hypocritically playing the role of the martyr."[17] Adeline Tintner's reading is not unlike Kraft's: she says that at the end "the reader infers that [Longmore] considers himself lucky to have escaped" (TMW 34).

Much more successful--in fact the real strength of the tale--is James's presentation of Longmore--his reflections, feelings, varying impulses, motives, scruples, and hesitations are followed throughout not by a narrator but by an author who has free access to Longmore's mind and conscience but remains discreetly invisible and unobtrusive. Longmore, sharing a good deal of Euphemia's American virtue, is the centre of consciousness; he is less impeccable, or more fallible, than she, and is the butt of authorial banter because of his comic uncertainty as he is "twisting his picturesque moustache, with a feeling of irritation which he certainly would have been at a loss to account for," and also because of his "bad French" and his outspoken--but apparently not unforgiven--opinions after six months in Paris, about "a sweet American girl who marries an unclean Frenchman" (II, 287). But from the beginning we notice his moral integrity, his reluctance to go "fishing in troubled waters" (II, 288) by approaching the unhappy wife with his admiration, and this prepares us for and gives point to a typically Jamesian crux in the story, the "painful confusion" of his dilemma near the end: "his presence now might be simply a gratuitous cause of suffering" to Euphemia, but, on the other hand, "his absence might seem to imply that it was in the power of circumstances to make them ashamed to meet each other's eyes" (II, 334).[18]

One interesting phase of Longmore's "'subjective' adventure" (LC II, 1170), reminiscent of--yet ironically different from--the "conversion" scene by the "shady streamside nook" in "Guest's Confession," is the sequence which begins when the troubled Longmore "strode away into the forest" and then found himself in an "unfamiliar region," a "characteristically French" landscape with a village inn (II, 327-28); he encounters a young artist and a young woman, apparently unmarried, whose happiness together inspires Longmore with "the urgent egotism of the passion which philosophers call the supremely selfish one" and mocks "his moral unrest like some obtrusive vision of unattainable bliss" (II, 332-33). He returns to Euphemia ready to "grasp unsparingly at happiness" (II, 334) and to dismiss all the conscientious scruples that have inhibited him, thus renouncing his Americanness and becoming hedonistically French, but she cools his ardour, appealing to his better chivalric self: "*Don't disappoint me* . . ." (II, 336), "preaching reason with a kind of passion" (II, 337); she goes "to the trouble of conceiving an ideal of conduct for him" (II, 338), and he abandons his temptation.   One more brief visit allows Longmore to part from her formally and announce his return to America.   She, though strongly drawn to him, sends him on his way as decisively as Isabel will dismiss Caspar Goodwood at the end of *The Portrait of a Lady*, and in doing so she inaugurates what Aziz calls "the repeated ritual of renunciation in James" (II, lix).

The portrait of Longmore is credible and moving; moreover, with this flexible method of narration, James enters a territory that is distinctively his own: the following of nuances and scruples in a protagonist who, being honest, impressionable, imaginative, vulnerable, and therefore in some degree the focus of pathos, is an effective instrument for reflecting the moral dilemma of the tale.

The tale is also in a new sense international in that, with whatever partiality and prejudice, it makes differences between American and French cultures a basis of the action.   James even invokes, through Longmore, though without any qualifying irony, a broad and sweeping generalization that in contemporary phraseology would be stigmatized as "racist": Longmore wishes for Euphemia a husband with "a good deal of solid virtue; jealousies and vanities very tame, and no particular iniquities and adulteries. A husband . . . of your own faith and race and spiritual substance, who would have loved you well" (II, 319).

For all the criticisms that can be directed at the sentimental idealizations of innocent American womanhood in Euphemia and the stereotypes of aristocratic French arrogance, faithlessness, and cynicism in the De Mauveses, "Mme. de Mauves" is, if not a "small masterpiece," at least an absorbing tale, perhaps the first with the full-blown charm that is distinctively Jamesian.   The charm here is a compound of many varied elements.   There are the beauty of what might be called a sophisticated pastoral setting, which is also heavy with symbolic overtones--Euphemia "lived in an old-fashioned pavilion, between a high-walled court and an excessively artificial garden. . . . After a while she came out and wandered through the narrow alleys and beside the thin-spouting fountain, and at last introduced him to a little gate in the garden wall, opening upon a lane which led into the forest" (II, 299)--the genial and suave irony, "languorous and lyrical" (II, lix), of an expansive, circumstantial, apparently unhurried narrative--"Though not in the least a cynic, [Longmore] was what one may call a disappointed observer; and he never chose the right-hand road without beginning to suspect after an hour's wayfaring that the left would have been the interesting one" (II, 284)--and the appeal of romantic chivalric attraction, gently coloured by the pathos of unhappiness and frustration. When one adds to all this the spice of treachery and intrigue, one recognizes the tale as an ancestor of *The Golden Bowl*.

"ADINA" (*Scribner's Monthly*, May-June 1874)

This, the first tale James published in a journal other than the *Atlantic* and the *Galaxy*, reminds one of "The Last of the Valerii" and Hawthorne again: there is the Roman setting and the discovery of another ancient treasure, an imperial topaz inscribed for the Emperor Tiberius, accidentally discovered by an Italian young man, Angelo Beati, for whom the treasure has a great spiritual significance. The tale is also curiously related to "Travelling Companions": Brooke's--the narrator's--weakness for the Italian picturesque has its opposite here in Sam Scrope, who is an embodiment of the recent reaction we have seen in James against the familiar tourists' glib romanticization of Italy and Italians.[19] Brooke's story ends in wedding bells, but Scrope loses his betrothed and ends as a "professional cynic" (II, 379). Brooke's philosophic "opponent" becomes his wife; Scrope's is his unnamed friend who narrates the story, who represents "the sentimental business--the raptures, the reflections, the sketching, the quoting from Byron" (II, 349), and who invokes a received and almost stereotyped "poetic" notion of the Italian character, but a good deal more flattering than that of the French upper class operative in "Mme. de Mauves." Scrope is an American and a counterweight to the series of sympathetic if naive Americans in the preceding tales. In sum, "Adina" seems to be born of ideas rather than of any deep vision or urgent experience.

Technically the tale is interesting. James starts his career, perhaps like most writers of fiction, with straightforward third-person narration, the narrator being omniscient and impartial in the sense that he has access to the minds of all the characters equally. James recurs to this method, but less and less frequently. His mature method was generally a special third-person narrative, which--as we have seen--he approaches in "Mme. de Mauves," and in which an undeclared and as it were invisible narrator, or author, slips in and out of, and does not move far from, the experience and point of view of the central intelligence, often the protagonist. But in developing this method James experimented with many intermediate modes, aiming always to enliven the common, impartial, and often flat third-person narrative, to get closer to personal experience and "'subjective' adventure" (LC II, 1170), and yet at the same time to have the satisfaction of writing within the limits of a specific form. He tries first-person narration of the semi-confessional kind ("Travelling Companions" and "Guest's Confession"); the diary form, framed ("A Landscape Painter") and unframed ("A Light Man" and, later, "The Diary of a Man of Fifty," 1879); letters ("A Bundle of Letters," 1879, and "The Point of View," 1882). Another method James used was to have a first-person narrator who was the friend of, or in some special relation to, the protagonist. This established two centres of not competing but reciprocal interest, bringing the reader into a highly charged field where he might have to work hard to get his bearings: a character or point of view is established in the narrator, and this must be taken into account by the reader as he watches the protagonist. James uses the potential of this method more fully in "A Passionate Pilgrim" than he did in "My Friend Bingham." The method can be carried a step further, however, by putting the narrator himself within a frame, by providing an occasion or setting for him to tell his story. James did this in "Gabrielle de Bergerac," "Master Eustace," and "The Madonna of the Future"; "Adina" is another in this form. But even here James does not use the frame to much purpose beyond the achievement of pathos: the events occurred long ago, or the protagonist has died. The first sentence of "Adina" reminds us of "the rule *de mortuis*" (II, 348); "The Solution" (1889-90) starts with "Oh yes, you may write it down-- every one's dead" (ECT VII, 351). It was not until "The Turn of the Screw" (1898) that James put the device of the frame to its full use, and in the following year Joseph Conrad's "Heart of Darkness" was to provide a brilliant exhibition of the possibilities of the method. "Adina," however, falls far short of that.

Scrope is chronically antipathetic to the Italian "picturesque"--the significance of the term is indicated by its frequency in the tale (II, 348, 349, 350--twice, 360, 365, 369-- twice, 370, 373, 382)--and he himself is without charm or grace. When he, by means doubtfully legitimate but certainly sharp and ungenerous, has relieved Angelo of his gem for a mere eleven *scudi*, though hoping and believing it is a treasure and worth very much more, he shows he has a bad "conscience"--a term that James associates particularly with Americans at this stage--by resorting to "ingenious" rationalizations of his conduct: "I rescued it in the interest of art," and "Money would have corrupted him" (II, 354-355). The nub of the tale is the character of Scrope, which is a "puzzling mixture" (II, 354), because, though "not an amiable man," he is "an honest one" (II, 348). Even the dogged vehemence with which he "used to swear that Italy . . . was a land of vagabonds and declaimers" (II, 349) is a facet of the sour sort of honesty in his "unsweetened wit" which did not easily allow him, even when he was in love, to "gush" (II, 359), whereas the narrator, owing it (as he confesses) to his "reputation for Byronism," finds a "careless, youthful grace" in the attitude of the sleeping Angelo, whom he refers to as "our rustic Endymion" (II, 350).

When, later, Angelo has become aware of his grievance against Scrope, the narrator believes that Scrope, whom he knows well, "might have stiffly admitted that there was a grain of reason in Angelo's claim," and in fact Scrope does make a "conscientious effort to shirk none of the disagreeables of the matter." But Scrope is so upset by strictly marginal issues--he calls Angelo a "theatrical jackanapes" and the narrator supposes that Angelo has challenged his sympathy "in too peremptory a fashion" (II, 365)-- that he is unable to do Angelo the justice that he knows he should.

In the end, when Angelo exacts his revenge and, with the charm and passion so different from Scrope's "meagre faculty of pleasing" (II, 356), he induces Adina to break her engagement to Scrope and elope with him, it is understandable that Scrope should say, "I don't know what under heaven I've done [to deserve such treatment]!" (II, 375). The gulf of incomprehension between the De Mauveses and the Americans in "Mme. de Mauves" exists here between the attitude of this type of American and the "Italian" view, to the detriment of the former in each case. We feel sorry for Scrope, despite his questionable conduct and lack of amiability. Adina, "a blonde angel of New England origin" (II, 367), finds happiness with Angelo--a case of "the intercourse of angels" in Yeats's "At the Tomb of Baile and Aillinn"--having responded to the Italian picturesqueness against which Scrope hardened himself. It is a perceptible irony that Scope's undoing is brought about by

an Italian closely associated with Lariccia (II, 352), the ancient
Aricia, a centre not merely of the picturesque but of ancient pagan
mysteries that are given central importance in J.G. Frazer's *The
Golden Bough.* The moral fable completes itself when Scrope
flings the topaz--"it had been a curse"--into the Tiber from the
parapet of the bridge bearing the name of the saint for whom
Angelo was named (II, 382).

"EUGENE PICKERING" (*Atlantic Monthly*, October-November
1874; 1875; 1879; [1883])
      In general we are following the order in which the tales were
published, but we depart from it here, our justification being that
"Eugene Pickering," though published after "Professor Fargo," was
written before it (see II, xlviii-xlix), and this suits our purposes well
because it allows us to deal with it in this chapter, which is
concerned with the series of six tales that belong to 1872-74 and
have Europe as their setting.
      James twice revised "Eugene Pickering" and reprinted it
three times. Adeline Tintner has demonstrated that in it there are
extensive analogues to *Romeo and Juliet* and *Antony and
Cleopatra* (TBW 23-28): Pickering was once nicknamed "Juliet"
(II, 417), and a letter is as important in the tale as another is in
Shakespeare's earlier tragedy, though here the business of the letter
makes for a happy and not a tragic ending.   In the tale Mme.
Blumenthal has written a "*Trauerspiel*" in five acts, entitled
'Cleopatra'" (II, 429), and, because what reaches anyone who
observes her is "simply a penetrating perfume of intelligence,
mingled with a penetrating perfume of sympathy" (II, 430), she is
fascinating to men, as was the Egyptian queen, from whose barge,
in Shakespeare's play, "A strange invisible perfume hits the sense /
Of the adjacent wharfs."   There are many such points of contact,
and James's fondness for the tale could well have sprung in part
from the fun he had in ingeniously assembling and rearranging
these pieces with some of the mischief that probably went to the
writing of "A Tragedy of Error."   This leads Tintner to say that
"Eugene Pickering" is James's "first and only burlesque, fashioned
from Shakespeare's two sets of doomed lovers, whose stories are
reshuffled," and in which there is, for example, a "miniaturization
of the great deeds in *Antony and Cleopatra*" (TBW 28). James
achieves this in part by contriving a narrator who is man of the
world enough to be described as "a sceptic, a cynic, a satirist" (II,
430), somewhat like Enobarbus. Certainly there is a great deal of

"borrowing" in this tale.

Tintner's analysis is valuable, but we believe that--perhaps because of the excitement and exhilaration of her treasure-hunt-- her account of the tale is distorted. The tale does show "the extent of [James's] confidence," but not confidence that in this "yoking of the plays" he "could improve" Shakespeare (TBW 28). His confidence is in his use of the theme of the vulnerable innocent abroad in the world. In "Professor Fargo" James develops the theme without relying on the American-European contrast and by epitomizing innocence in an old man. Now, in "Eugene Pickering," he does make something of both Eugene's Americanness and the German Mme. Blumenthal's relation to America: her talk of "the wonderful spectacle of a great people free to do everything it chooses" (II, 437) is sharply ironical in view of Eugene's own very restrictive upbringing. But the remarkable innovation in the tale is to make the innocent protagonist a somewhat comic, but not burlesque, character, and not merely in adolescence, when Euphemia was comic, but in his young manhood. James can now use his great myth for comedy as well as for pathos and tragedy, as in "A Passionate Pilgrim" and "Mme. de Mauves," and this is an indication not only of secure possession but of his feeling about the universality of the theme's validity.

To confirm that this is indeed the thrust of the tale one has only to draw attention to the emphasis, in the seven pages mainly devoted to Eugene's upbringing (II, 417-24), on his being "over-governed" (II, 424), "watched and watered and pruned" (II, 420), and subject to all that "muffling and coddling" (II, 419) until he was twenty-seven: "although I was a man grown, I lived altogether at home" (II, 420). Eugene's upbringing is reminiscent of that of Rousseau's *élève* in *Émile ou de l'éducation* (1762). Eugene, like Émile, was taken to live in the country, "to protect the lad's morals." "A tutor was provided for him," just as a tutor took charge of Émile. The mature Eugene, like Émile, was "the fruit of a system persistently and uninterruptedly applied." "His education . . . . had bequeathed him, now that he stood on the threshold of the great world, an extraordinary freshness of impression and alertness of desire," but the narrator trembles for his "unwarned innocence" (II, 418-19).[20] The word "innocence" itself recurs frequently for Eugene (II, 416--twice, 419 ["unwarned innocence"], 420, 427, 437); the concept of innocence and its opposite, disillusionment, appears in statements such as "life offered itself to me for the first time" (II, 420) and "He was pale

and haggard; his face was five years older. Now . . . he had tasted
of the cup of life" (II, 446). It is clear what Eugene looks forward
to: terms such as "liberation" (II, 421, 449), "liberty" (II, 422),
"freedom," and "the right to be free" (II, 432, 437, 443) abound in
the text; Eugene's images are of climbing "fences" and taking a
"plunge" (II, 419, 422). One feels James is getting closer to Daisy
Miller, "a child of nature and of freedom" (LC II, 1269). It is no
wonder that Eugene, with his "radiant intelligence" (II, 420),
should have a "cloister face" and that he "blushed to his eyes" (II,
419, 437); he was emerging as from a convent into the raw world.
In a letter to Henry of 22 March 1874, William refers to "your last
story about the ingenuous youth in Baden [this should be
Homburg] and the Coquette" (II, xlvii).

   Adeline Tintner's analysis is most clearly misleading in what
she suggests about the word "world": "Since Shakespeare's play
[*Antony and Cleopatra*] is about world power and domination and
the dividing of the known civilized world among the Triumvirate, it
is not surprising that the word 'world' occurs more than forty
times, more than in any other play by Shakespeare. It also occurs
very often in James's story, for he pushes and parodies the analogy
between world curiosity and desire for conquest shared by
Shakespeare's characters and his hero. 'World' is mentioned ten
times in the first ten pages of 'Eugene Pickering' before the story
really gets under way and twenty-one times in all of its fifty pages"
(TBW 25). This passage illustrates part of Tintner's method and
shows how she supports readings by using statistics. This has on
occasion been fruitful in literary studies, but unless it is used with
discretion and with regard to the large issues, it is a pitfall. She
oversimplifies and distorts James's tale by pressing too hard on the
similarities between Eugene and Antony. There are of course
similarities, and there are elements of comedy in the discrepancies
between Eugene's naive curiosity and Antony's lust for sexual and
political conquests. Eugene's plight is funny, but it is also
touching. "Eugene Pickering" is almost as far from burlesque as
Othello is from being a bloody farce. It is a mark of James's genius
that he can bring out the comic and also, at the same time, the
serious and pathetic--even the potentially tragic--aspects of the one
situation. Here we are seeing the rites of passage of a young man
of ability and promise--"his natural faculties were excellent," and
he is frequently credited with "imagination" (II, 420, 430, 439,
446)--who has been immured and is now, inexperienced and
vulnerable, suddenly among the rich, the idle, and the predatory of

Homburg spa, in the midst of the world's "sharp intricate actual living facts" (L IV, 641). Mme. Blumenthal is not merely a parody of Cleopatra, but a valid translation of her into a demi-mondaine of contemporary fashionable society. James even transforms her, quite convincingly, into a "revolutionist" with a "passion for freedom" (II, 437), thus giving her a special appeal to Eugene. It is of course an irony that Eugene's true "liberation" (II, 449) should come from the letter he has put off opening for so long because he supposed that it would lead him straight into a marital prison that his father had designed for him; because the letter in fact releases him from the contract to marry Miss Vernor of Smyrna, he is-- paradoxically--free to marry her, as in due course he will do.

In dwelling too insistently on the correspondences, Adeline Tintner has in effect gone back on the insight she had into James's development when she said that he moved from "a one-to-one correspondence" with his source to "a freer, more subtle, and more generalized attitude" (TBW 4). James does not turn Shakespearean tragedy into easy and mechanical burlesque, but borrows subtly from the plays to create an effect that may be comic but is also complex and poignant. In art he is moving from emulation to empire. In life he was having to turn his thoughts homeward again toward America and 20 Quincy St., Cambridge, Massachusetts.

Chapter VI

AMERICAN INTERRUPTION, 1874-76

James returned home to Cambridge in September 1874 but soon moved to New York, where he was more conveniently placed for his literary trade. After little more than a year, however, he was off again to Europe, not to travel this time but to live in Paris. He abandoned his attempt to live and work in America, and the decision to go to Europe was the turning point of his life: from now on he would live in Paris, then London, then Rye. By Christmas 1875 he was installed in Paris, supporting himself by an engagement to write articles for the *New York Tribune*.

James worked hard during his 14-month stay in America. He finished *Roderick Hudson* and did a great deal of reviewing, especially for the *Nation* (see LC I, 1434-36; LC II, 1363-64). His production of tales was comparatively meagre. Of the four tales considered in this chapter, "Professor Fargo" was written and published before he left Europe in 1874, and "Crawford's Consistency" and "The Ghostly Rental" were written, or at least completed, after he had taken up residence in Paris; only "Benvolio" was written and published during his American stay, and, oddly enough, of the four it has most to do with Europe and comes closest to the international theme. Nevertheless, all four tales may be regarded as belonging to James's American stay of 1874-75.

"PROFESSOR FARGO" (*Galaxy*, August 1874)

The basis of this tale is the contrast between two performers, Professor Fargo and Colonel Gifford, the former "impudent," a "rascal," "vulgar," and a "ranting charlatan," who with his "windy verbiage," "brazen foolery," and "general humbuggery" (II, 385,

394, 398, 399, 392, 398, 397) brags of his powers of "spiritual magnetism," though "some folks call it animal magnetism" (II, 403). Gifford, on the other hand, who has by misfortune been "cruelly" "yoked" (II, 402) to Fargo, is a "melancholy old mathematician" (II, 393) with a "simple, unpretentious tone" and a "single idea, but his one idea was a religion" expounded with "mild sincerity" and "intensity of faith," though far above the heads of the sparse rural American audience--and of the sophisticated narrator's as well--so that he is "benignantly but formidably unintelligible" (II, 392); he has "always had a passion for scientific research, and I have squandered my substance in experiments which the world called fruitless" (II, 397). What James wrote of André Ampère in a review the following year might be applied to Gifford: "He was a signal example of the almost infantile simplicity, the incorruptible moral purity, that so often are associated with great attainments in science" (LC II, 22).

Gifford has a daughter born a deaf-mute as a result of an explosion during one of his experiments; she is not only dearly loved but felt to be a particular responsibility. Fargo's demonstrations of spiritual magnetism are "heavy, vulgar, [and] slipshod" (II, 405); he has more luck with animal magnetism, which he uses to detach Gifford's daughter from him, and in the end he makes a "triumphant escape" with her, taunting Gifford as he goes. This results in Gifford's becoming "mad" and having to enter an "asylum" (II, 411).

Edel dismisses the tale as "clearly one of James's recurrent potboilers" (ECT III, 10); Aziz's comment is that it is "a curious oddity in the present sequence of 'international' studies" (II, xlvii), and he "wonders why James wrote this curious piece at this juncture in his career" (II, xlix). But the tale is more significant than it might at first seem: Gifford is James's latest and, thus far, most original avatar of the Innocent--pure-minded, devoted, brilliant, but pathetically "astray in the modern world" (II, 397), and in the end cruelly trapped by it. What is unusual in this version of the myth is that James does not rely on inexperience and youth for the pathetic effect, and it is not thereby diminished: the narrator says, "I couldn't bear any longer to look at the Colonel" (II, 409). Furthermore, James does not buttress the theme by playing up American naïveté and morality as opposed to European corruption: Fargo is as American as the Duke and the King of *Huckleberry Finn*, with their Royal Nonesuch, and, although the daughter is described as having the "grace, the delicacy and fragility of the characteristic American type" (II, 392), there are no "international" implications. In this tale James has identified his deepest theme and stripped it of adventitious support or admixture. Although Aziz sees that, in the international tales, "it is not internationalism *per se* which is at issue, but its fearful concomitants--the perils of dispossession, disinheritance, alienation, the moving away from one's spiritual and cultural orbit" (II, lix), he does not apply his insight to "Professor Fargo," a tale that indicates that James is now far more aware of what he is about.

The narrator too is interesting, as James's narrators increasingly are. This one, though a commercial traveller visiting out-of-the-way places and putting up at "rural hostelries of New England" (II, 395), is clearly sophisticated: in the first dozen lines of his narrative he refers to "the elastic philosophy of a commercial traveller," and he complains that "the dullness of the landscape [is] a weariness to the spirit" and speaks of bruises "physical" and "intellectual" (II, 383). The rest of his narrative bears out that he is well-read, well-travelled, knowing France and Italy (II, 384), and sceptical, with an ironical and supercilious wit--he is disappointed in the epitaphs in the cemetery because they are "posterior to the age of theological *naïveté*" (II, 387)--but he has sympathy to go with his irony. He is indeed a surrogate for James himself, even down to his boredom with provincial America. One disadvantage in this is that we are not invited--nor are we able--to stand aside from him to see and criticize his prejudices and faults, as we shall be able to do, for example, in "Four Meetings"; the narrator has a lively and amusing style, but the lack of this extra dimension has a somewhat flattening effect on the tale.

Another significant feature of the tale is James's "borrowing" from *Don Quixote*, which has been discussed in detail by Adeline Tintner (TBW 201-08). The narrator in "Professor Fargo" becomes absorbed in a copy of Cervantes's great book that he finds in the tavern parlour (II, 387), and references to the great novel recur like a motif, culminating in the narrator's identifying Gifford with the Don: "he was Don Quixote . . . with his sallow Spanish colouring, his high-browed, gentlemanly visage, his wrinkles, his moustache, and his sadness" (II, 390), to which he might have added his "incorruptible conservatism" (II, 404), his "military precision" (II, 394), and his "stately gravity" (II, 405); the narrator even seems, himself, as Tintner observes (TBW 205), to come to emulate Sancho Panza (II, 393), thus making it something like--but short of--a conversion experience for him.

Don Quixote seems to have been important to James at this time; he refers to him in "A Passionate Pilgrim" (II, 88) and "Mme. de Mauves" (II, 293), but in carrying Don Quixote over into James's tale too completely, Tintner has somewhat confused James's purpose. She is right in saying that "in essence, the Don Quixote of Cervantes is for James an embodiment of the artist," but mistaken in arguing that "fanatical visions are necessary for the writer while he writes" (TBW 207); she is assuming that Gifford's work is not truly, but only "so-called," scientific, a "figment of the imagination," and so worthless. James's point is that Gifford's work is not only disinterested, but has the purity and the validity and exactness of "his system of transcendent multiplication" --using which his daughter was "invariably found to have hit the mark" (II, 393)--in contrast to the immediately preceding performance by Fargo. Moreover, the narrator with his intelligence and cultivation finds Gifford's show "a lesson in culture" (II, 393). Gifford does not suffer, as Quixote does, from delusions. If any more evidence is needed for this, it can be found in Gifford's reasoned disgust at Fargo's antics, his own rational conduct--"It's doubtless the height of indiscretion in me to take you into my confidence. My subsistence depends on my not quarrelling with my companion"-- and especially in the way he can satirize himself: "Like all inventors whose devices are of value, I believe that my particular contrivance would be the salvation of a misguided world" (II 396). On the other hand, Quixote had to reach the end of Cervantes's book and recover his sanity before he could see himself clearly. James's "conversion of *Don Quixote* to his own needs" is more complete than Tintner allows, but the tale does bear out what James wrote toward the end of his life: "all simple and imaginative men" have "a shade of resemblance" to the knight of La Mancha (A 286).

"BENVOLIO" (*Galaxy*, August 1875; 1879)

After his two-year absence, James returned to America in a frame of mind that was far from sanguine: "I shall not find life at home *simpatico*," he told his mother, "but . . . as regards literary work, obstructively the reverse" (L I, 449). "Benvolio" is only incidentally "international," and has little to do with the theme of the Innocent. Moreover, James's experimentation with forms of narrative is abandoned, or rather takes on an altogether new turn: an omniscient third-person narrator is telling the story in a highly ambiguous manner that brings Hawthorne immediately to mind.

He starts: "Once upon a time (as if he had lived in a fairy tale) there was a very interesting young man. This is not a fairy tale, and yet our young man was, in some respects, as pretty a fellow as any fairy prince" (III, 23). It is told in the manner of a fairy tale, and yet it is not one; the reason for this appears at the end of the tale.

Adeline Tintner says the tale is "the only allegory that James ever wrote" (TBW 51), and Edel that it is "an unashamed personal allegory" (ECT III, 10). But we must use the term "allegory" carefully. Even *The Golden Bowl* has been declared to be to some degree allegorical, and we shall endeavour to demonstrate that, if James did write a personal allegory, it is "The Ghostly Rental," published a year later. "Benvolio" is an allegory, but not particularly personal; it is an allegory of the kind that Bunyan and Hawthorne wrote. Bunyan and Hawthorne were in the tradition of Puritanism, and James, living in New England, knew the tradition at first hand, but he wore his Puritanism with a considerable difference. As "The Ghostly Rental" was soon to show, James's attitude to Puritanism and New England was ambivalent; in *Notes of a Son and Brother* he records his satisfaction in being "in New England without being of it," the latter condition being a "danger" that he had "after all escaped" (A 305). But, through Hawthorne, he was closer to New England than this suggests or than he himself perhaps realized.

We have seen that, apparently at the suggestion of Howells, James wrote the Hawthornesque "The Romance of Certain Old Clothes" (1868). But James had always loved Hawthorne: "The Wonder-Book and Twice-Told Tales had helped to enchant our childhood"; "the Seven Gables, the Blithedale Romance and the story of Donatello and Miriam (the accepted title of which [*The Marble Faun*] I dislike to use . . .)," were placed "somewhere on a shelf unvisited by harsh inquiry" (A 478). What could be more natural than that James, making his last attempt to take literary root in America, should look to Hawthorne for his model. He had not until now written an allegory like "Rappaccini's Daughter," and he would not try again; in "Benvolio" he achieved an ironic and mannered *tour de force* that was unrepeatable. Within a few years he was to say in his book on Hawthorne (1879) that this kind of allegory--presumably unfortified by the specific sardonic adaptations that James makes in "Benvolio"--was, to his sense, "one of the lighter exercises of the imagination" (LC I, 366). Before we discuss the particular use James makes of Hawthornesque allegory in his ambiguous fairy tale, we should see what he borrowed from *The Marble Faun* for his tale.

At the centre of *The Marble Faun* is the contrast between the joy of unreflecting innocence (in Hilda and the pre-lapsarian Donatello) and the gloom of sin and experience (in Miriam and Donatello after the Fall); this is reflected in "Benvolio" in the competition for Benvolio's affections between the fun-loving Countess and the pensive Scholastica, and both Hawthorne's and James's fictions borrow from the formal contrast between Mirth and Melancholy in Milton's "L'Allegro" and "Il Penseroso." Beyond this, Hawthorne, unlike James, treats of the attainment by Donatello of "a higher innocence than that from which he fell,"[1] which obviously relates the novel to *Paradise Lost* and *Paradise Regained*, and its original title, *Transformation*, points to this similarity.[2]

Fred Lewis Pattee long ago asserted that the allegory "reveals the soul of Henry James"; "*he* was Benvolio."[3]   Edel agrees with Pattee: James "led always the double life of Benvolio: he courted Europe [the Countess] and he never forgot America [Scholastica]." This goes together with the perceptive comment that James's Benvolio, like his namesake in *Romeo and Juliet*, tries to keep the peace between two opposed factions.[4]   Tintner perpetuates the view that James is his own subject, saying that the tale makes it clear that "there is no real choice between the Countess and Scholastica and James was to allow each to refresh him throughout his creative life" (TBW 57). We believe this view distorts the tale by relying too simply on the autobiographical factor and thus doing less than justice to the artistic imagination, which is, as Keats says, chameleon-like. To be sure, there is a good deal of James, and of a good many other artists, in Benvolio, but the writer more immediately represented than James himself is John Milton.

Midway in his allegory James drops a palpable clue on his reader's plate: "[Benvolio] turned off a little poem in the style of Milton's 'Penseroso'" (III, 40) which, as Tintner suggests, "sends us on a treasure hunt for bits of Milton" (TBW 53); she uncovers various echoes and parallels in diction, imagery, and theme from "L'Allegro" and "Il Penseroso" and from Miltonic lore (TBW 51-57). Thus in "Benvolio" James is performing a complex act of borrowing: from Hawthorne, and also from Milton--Bunyan's Puritan contemporary--through Hawthorne.

That young Milton was very much on James's mind while he was writing "Benvolio" is supported by his review of a collection of literary essays by Professor David Masson which appeared in the *Nation* of 18 February 1875. "The best thing, perhaps, in the book," James writes, is Masson's "sketch . . . of Milton's youth." Noting that Masson "draws a very handsome portrait" of Milton, James goes on to discuss the poet at length (LC I, 1169, 1170). James had also been impressed by Eastman Johnson's painting "Milton Dictating *Paradise Lost* to His Daughters," which he saw at the 1875 Spring Exhibition of the New York Academy of Design (TBW 52). Milton serves James in "Benvolio" as Coleridge was to serve him much later in "The Coxon Fund" (1894). In the first place Benvolio is about the same age as the Milton who wrote the Horton poems--"more than twenty-five years old, but he was not yet thirty-five" (III, 23). Very specifically he is a "poet" (III, 24, 46, 55, 57, 58), and he is described as a "pretty . . . fellow" and "slim and fair, with clustering locks" (III, 23), all of which suggests the "Lady of Christ's," whom Marjorie Hope Nicolson describes as "fair in complexion and slender in build."[5] As James indicates in a quotation from Masson's description, the young Milton is "an auburn-haired youth, beautiful as the Apollo of a northern clime" (LC I, 1171).

More fundamental than the verbal and imagistic links are the struggles between Benvolio's "studious aspirations" and his "worldly habits" (III, 47)--"compounded of many anomalies; I may say more exactly that he was a tissue of absolute contradictions" (III, 24)--that correspond to Milton's warring impulses to high seriousness and to conviviality, to his alternations between, for example, Horton and poetry on the one hand, and his Latin Secretaryship to the Council of State and his polemical labours on the other. Even though Milton the poet condemned Eve for her craving to quit innocence for experience, it was the same man who played a part in the world of public affairs and politics, who could not "praise a fugitive and cloister'd vertue, unexercis'd & unbreath'd, that never sallies out and sees her adversary."[6] It is possible to see in the tale's long third paragraph that dwells on the antinomies within Benvolio (III, 24-26) a reflection of the Cavalier-Puritan split not only within the young Milton--who by the age of twenty-one "no longer cut his hair short in Puritan fashion, but let it fall loosely to his collar, covering his ears, like a Cavalier"[7]--but also within the England of the Civil War. Milton seems to have veered from Puritan to Cavalier and back to Puritan again; the Countess thinks of Scholastica as "a little underhand, hypocritical Puritan" (III, 50).

It is true that James's own life and habits were marked by a similar ambivalence, but the text of "Benvolio" keeps sending us back to Milton's life. On the visit to Italy, "the great palace through whose galleries [Benvolio and the Countess] had just been strolling" (III, 53), even though in James's tale it is within view of the Apennines, is reminiscent of the Palazzo Barberini in Rome, where Milton was entertained "with truly Roman magnificence" on a notable occasion and, incidentally, where James himself often visited when one floor of the palace was occupied by William Wetmore Story, whose biography James wrote (1903). Milton, Parker tells us, visited the Casa Barberini to pay his respects to Pope Urban VIII's nephew, Cardinal Francesco Barberini, "the soul of courtesy," "and was granted an audience of flattering length."[8] James strikes a sardonic note, of the sort with which his tale abounds, when he brings us a reflection of Milton's meeting with the cardinal: "Benvolio found himself dragged away . . . to take a pinch from the snuff-box of an epicurean cardinal" (III, 52). It is on this visit that Benvolio has "a choking sensation and a sudden, overwhelming desire to return to his own country" (III, 53); it was in Italy, if not in the Barberini Palace itself, that Milton tells us he had a similar call: "As I was preparing to pass over also into Sicily and Greece, I was restrained by the melancholy tidings from England of the civil war: for I thought it base, that I should be travelling at my ease, even for the improvement of my mind abroad, while my fellow-citizens were fighting for their liberty at home."[9]

As between Mirth and Melancholy, society and study, politics and poetry, jollity and meditation, Benvolio seems as torn as does David Garrick caught between two striking female figures in Reynolds's painting, "Garrick between Tragedy and Comedy." Although he really wants and needs the "two women at once" (III, 46) because they "complement" (III, 30) each other, in the end-- after much vacillation--Benvolio loses both Scholastica, who sails to the Antipodes, and the Countess, whom he "suddenly . . . ceased to visit" (III, 58); "'For a constancy I prefer *this*!' And he tapped his poetic brow. He never saw the Countess again" (III, 59). At this point the narrator regrets he is not telling a fairy tale because, if he were, "I should be at liberty" to relate a different ending in which Benvolio "led an extremely fretful and unproductive life, until one day he sailed for the Antipodes and brought Scholastica home. After this he began to produce again; only, many people said, his poetry had become dismally dull" (III, 59). This so-called fairy tale ending is much closer, in James's opinion, than the other to Milton's life, as we see from his review of Masson's essays, where James says that Milton "was what would be called nowadays a very high-toned young man--what even in some circles would be termed a prig." In the same review James concedes that "the danger" that Milton's "seriousness," "solemnity," and "respectability" "might operate as a blight" on his "poetic faculty was not averted by the interposition of the sense of humor" (LC I, 1171). A year later, in 1876, in commenting on a French essayist's assessment of *Paradise Lost* as "a false, grotesque, tiresome poem" that "nevertheless . . . is immortal," James says that even among English speakers "it has been for some time tacitly admitted that with regard to 'Paradise Lost' some of the cargo must be thrown overboard to save the ship" (LC II, 808-09).

The tale's last paragraphs pick up on the ambivalence that we remarked on in the opening sentences by presenting us with the two different endings. The nub of the tale is that, ironically, it is the alternative ending, which the reader is invited to dismiss as a fairy tale ending and therefore untrue, that is the real ending. Benvolio is Milton, and it is through the device of the supposedly fantastical ending that James delivers his surreptitious, surprising, and indeed subversive judgement of Milton the poet. By choosing Scholastica as his sole comfort, Benvolio (alias Milton) is able to write again, but a good deal of his later poetry, James suggests, is dull stuff. The irony is at once patent, and yet so indirect and discreet that even attentive readers have been confused. James employs this elaborately ironical method--which matches the facetious, tongue-in-cheek style--so that his irreverence will be oblique, because Milton is after all England's greatest poet after Shakespeare and James was by nature and nurture cautious, politic, conservative, and respectful. But, properly understood, the final effect is iconoclastic nevertheless.

It may be that the tale is an elaborate, roundabout rejoinder to Masson. Although James is careful to pay his respects to him-- he "writes particularly well about Milton"--the tale seems to be a reaction to Masson's drift: "it is on the pervading *consistency* of [Milton's] character that Professor Masson dwells, while he attempts to reconcile his austerity, his rigidity, . . . his want of humor with his possession of supreme poetic genius" (LC I, 1170); James's Milton (Benvolio) is, in contrast, "a tissue of . . . contradictions" (III, 24), like James himself with his ambivalence.

For his irreverent view of Milton's later poetry, James would have the comfort of some support from no less an authority than Samuel Johnson: "*Paradise Lost* is one of the books which the reader admires and lays down, and forgets to take up again."[10] It is interesting to notice that in 1913 James found Sargent's portrait of him growing "more and more like Sir Joshua's Dr. Johnson," and "a perceptive friend reinforced me a couple of sittings later by breaking out irrepressibly with the same judgment" (LL II, 318-19).   It was a likeness that James must have found far from mortifying.

Although James never wrote anything like "Benvolio" again, he could not have been altogether displeased with his *jeu d'esprit* because he revised it for its reappearance in *The Madonna of the Future* in 1879.[11]

"CRAWFORD'S CONSISTENCY" (*Scribner's Monthly*, August 1876)

This unusually weak tale is about Crawford's strange courtships and marriage. "Good-looking, gallant, amiable," aged twenty-seven, with "the tastes of a scholar" (III, 62) and "fastidious" (III, 75), he becomes engaged to a young woman who is good-looking, but with "no more intelligence than a snowy-fleeced lamb," though a "shrewd . . . politician" (III, 65), and then, after being unceremoniously dropped by her family and her, he recovers, only to marry a woman notable not only for her "unloveliness," but also for "coarseness, vulgarity, ignorance, vanity, and, beneath all, something as hard and arid as dusty bricks" (III, 79, 80). Both women are attracted to him, "the most propitious victim to matrimony" (III, 63), perhaps by his "good manners" and "gaiety" (III, 61), and certainly by his "property" and "income" (III, 62); he is "not a man of genius" (III, 62), but how is it that he falls for them?   More puzzling still is the "outward composure" (III, 72) and "equanimity" (III, 85) which he maintains throughout his vicissitudes and mistreatment, except for brief moments such as when he "turned away his head" from facing his situation put to him by his friend the narrator, who is visiting him in hospital after his wife has "pushed him down the steps" and thus broken his leg (III, 85).

Perhaps he is immediately attracted to the coarse woman because he is rebounding from Elizabeth Ingram's airs and apparent graces, but we are offered no explanation. Even his friend, a medical doctor, says, "I do not pretend to understand his conduct. I was only witness of it, and I relate what I saw. I do not pretend to speak of his motives" (III, 73). "United in friendship" with Crawford (III, 60), having "as a physician" "every excuse for taking what are called materialistic views of human conduct" (III, 76), and capable, moreover, of sardonic mockery, as when he speaks of Crawford's affections as "mystic depths" (III, 67), the narrator might be expected to provide some explanation or at least a theory, but he does not, and, if he is at sea, how much more must the reader be? It is another James story about predatory or exploitative women--often wives--but even in a tale as early as "A Landscape Painter" we are made to understand why as well as how Locksley meets his misfortune; Crawford remains a mystery. When his friend calls the Ingrams "blind brutes!" Crawford "turned away" (III, 72), as he did in hospital; his composure is bought at the price of avoiding unpleasant truths, and this is as close as we get to an explanation of his conduct.

We find too that James invents a far-fetched pretext--a matter of distant cousinship--to justify the narrator's very unlikely presence at "the most extraordinary scene of which I have ever been witness" (III, 70), when the Ingrams tell Crawford abruptly that his engagement is broken (III, 67-72). We have seen technical weakness of this kind in "The Story of a Masterpiece" (1868) and "Gabrielle de Bergerac" (1869), but those are very early stories. In 1876 it seems like a regression. The melodramatic ironies at the end are also blemishes, being manipulations to enforce too "poetic" a justice: Crawford's property almost evaporates with the collapse of a bank (III, 81), and smallpox destroys Elizabeth Ingram's beauty, causing her new fiancé to back off and post back to Alabama (III, 84).

In a letter to his father of 11 April 1876 James does say that the "pretensions" of "Crawford's Consistency" and also of "The Ghostly Rental" (which he had sent recently to *Scribner's*) were "small," though the former was "much the best"[12] of the two (L II, 39). He did not reprint it, however. Perhaps one explanation for this tale--written when James was on the threshold of greatness-- and especially for its shortcomings, is that the donnée came from James's father. In the same letter of 11 April 1876, James wrote: "You gave me [an account of the life of a friend, Webster] three years ago. I had had it in my mind ever since, and had thoughts of using it for a longer story; but then I decided it was too lugubrious to be spun out. As it is, however, you will probably think I have

been brutally curt" (L II, 39).[13] Writing the tale may in a sense
have been an act of mere filial piety, reinforced by an uneasy
conscience at leaving his homeland. Three years earlier James had
written to his mother from Rome: "Thank [Father] meanwhile
greatly for his story of *Mr. Webster*. It is admirable material, and
excellently presented: I have transcribed it in my notebook with
religious care, and think that some day something will come of it.
It would require much thinking out. But it is a first class theme" (L
I, 357). "Religious" may be significant here. James was touched
by the "admirable anxiety with which thought could be taken [by
his father], even though 'amateurishly,' in my professional interest"
(A 401), especially as he at least sometimes had been inclined to
find in his father's "schemes of importances" an "implied snub" to
his own projects (A 339). We believe that James found his father's
story too fully developed and complete to be amenable to his own
creative imagination. If Aziz is right in his belief that "Crawford's
Consistency" was "sketched out during James's stay in New York"
in 1875 (III, 13), then it may be significant too that his father's
story had to wait for its working out until this place that James
found uncongenial and this period comparatively barren of
inspiration.

   Another reason for the tale's weakness is perhaps that the
pathetic story about Webster fitted in so easily with the myth of the
Innocent, which obviously so deeply moved James, that he was not
sufficiently critical of it.   There are clear manifestations of the
theme in its most simplistic terms: Crawford's typical expression is
"a sort of intelligent innocence--the look of an absent-minded
seraph. He knew, if you insisted upon it, about the corruptions of
this base world; but, left to himself, he never thought of them";
being a "man of books, a student, a philosopher" (III, 61), he is
easily trapped by "the most sordid reality" (III, 75). It is one of the
weakest and least interesting tales in the canon.

"THE GHOSTLY RENTAL" (*Scribner's Monthly*, September
1876)

   This tale has been neglected, presumably because it is
thought of as a pot-boiler. Grounds for this view might be that,
because it is a ghost story, it is merely sensational; that James
never reissued it; and that it appeared in a journal that James is said

not to have held in the highest esteem. The last argument is a very uncertain basis; if the earlier tales published in *Scribner's*--"Adina" and "Crawford's Consistency"--are not among James's best, "Four Meetings," which was to appear in *Scribner's* in the following year, 1877, is, as all agree, a very fine and important tale.

Although we shall certainly not argue that "The Ghostly Rental" deserves to be as highly thought of as "Four Meetings," we do not see it as a pot-boiler. It must have been of the greatest importance to James, exorcising as it does his inmost feelings of guilt at leaving his homeland to live in Europe. It was not reissued because it is not wholly successful artistically, but also perhaps because its real import is somewhat private and personal.[14]

"Benvolio" followed one kind of allegory associated with Hawthorne, and "The Ghostly Rental" follows another that is in the vein of, for example, "Legends of the Province House" in *Twice-Told Tales*. Commentators have been puzzled, one supposes, by the strangeness of the ingredients of "The Ghostly Rental"--ghosts, clairvoyance, and a mysterious conflagration at the end--or they have wondered why a tale with such "small pretensions would acquire such a priority with [James] so soon after his arrival in Paris," especially as it had so "little in common with the semi-international stories [he] had lately been sending home for publication" (III, 13, 9). But it was precisely James's move from New York to Paris that was the occasion of the tale and gave it its point. In a different and less obvious sense, this too is an international tale: having surrendered to the "embrace of Europe" (EL, 506), he felt the need to come to terms with the America that he might seem to have abandoned but which he still loved and admired. In doing this, James in the tale ranges widely through many aspects and phases of American history, even theological disputes. It is the ambivalence implicit in James's situation that gives the tale a personal poignancy that many readers have missed, partly because he did not want to flaunt or exploit his personal feelings. What we ultimately derive from the tale is the tone of the relation between an emancipated young American artist and the now somewhat uncongenial social and religious American climate in which he has attained his maturity. The tale places more obvious emphasis on America than on the artist as a young man, but James, the cunning artist, has placed himself at the very centre of the picture, disguised as the unobtrusive narrator. (With "Benvolio" and now this tale, James shows he knows there is far more to narration than a choice between first- and third-person narrators.) Disguise is, as we shall see, at the very heart of the tale.

The narrator, whose name we never learn, was once a student at the Divinity School at Harvard, to which he had "taken a fancy" (III, 86); James had himself briefly been a law student at Harvard and, largely through his brother William, had had contacts with the Divinity Hall (A 411, 432). The narrator had been under the influence of William Ellery Channing, but now, perhaps by way of Plotinus and St. Augustine, it is Pascal that he identifies with.[15] Another sign that the narrator has distanced himself from New England is that he mentions that even the roofs of New England houses are altogether different from French roofs (III, 87); his point of vantage, like James's, has moved from America to Europe.

What the Gallicised narrator shows us in his retrospect is a stack of puzzle pieces, some of the most conspicuous of which are "Dr. Channing," "the old [Harvard] Divinity School," "Plotinus and St. Augustine" (III, 86), "an old, one-horse chaise" (III, 89), "Andrew Jackson" (III, 90), "Hoffman's [sic] tales" (III, 91), "Mount Auburn cemetery" (III, 92), "Miss Deborah" (III, 96), "Jonathan Edwards and Dr. Hopkins" (III, 101), and "Pascal's *Thoughts*" (III, 102). They are a pretty motley lot; how are they related to the pattern of the tale?

The narrator tells us that Captain Diamond reminds him of "the portraits of Andrew Jackson" (III, 90). The centre-piece in the puzzle to which all the others are related is Old Hickory, whose virtues, solidity, durability, and toughness the very name Diamond recalls. Diamond, who states with quiet pride that he has "seen service" (III 95), possesses many of the qualities of the victor of New Orleans and shares with the traditional image of Jackson a martial bearing, rugged features, an appearance of stoicism and endurance, and appurtenances--such as Diamond's blue military cloak (III, 93, 99), like that associated with Jackson.[16] The regular payment of the quarterly rental, together with Diamond's fiscal attitude and probity, may reflect Jackson's doggedness in his passages of "strife and struggle," and Diamond's devoted black servant calls to mind the fact that Jackson was the owner of some slaves who were apparently firmly attached to him.[17]

One might have expected that Lincoln would be the central figure James would choose for his allegory, especially when one remembers James's moving account, written more than thirty years after "The Ghostly Rental," of the news arriving "like a great earth-shudder," and James himself having "fairly to go in shame of its being my birthday," when "the figure-head" that "we . . .ourselves" had chosen was assassinated (A 490-91). But in 1876 Lincoln was no doubt still too recent a figure, too closely associated with the North, to serve Jackson's function in the tale. Jackson was the last great hero acclaimed before the house became divided. All Americans could look to him as the apotheosis of their own qualities.

Moreover, James would have felt strong personal links--and "The Ghostly Rental," despite appearances, must be regarded as something like an allegory, but an allegory with distinctly personal meanings--with Jackson, whose most trusted Cabinet member, Vice-President, and anointed successor was Martin Van Buren. Late in life James recalls his youthful pride in "the fact that our uncle, our aunt's husband, was a son of Mr. Martin Van Buren, and that *he* was the President[.] This at least led the imagination on"; James's Aunt Ellen, his father's youngest sister, was the first wife of Smith Van Buren (A 9-10, 602n), son of the President and brother of "Prince" John Van Buren, whose pathetically unfulfilled career could have been associated in James's mind with the rise and passing of the Jacksonian age.[18]

James's portrayal of Captain Diamond is in terms of a portrait or etching: "He had a crop of grizzled hair, as stiff as a brush, a lean, pale, smooth-shaven face, and an eye of intense brilliancy, surmounted with thick brows" (III, 90). "The lines in his face were as rigid as if they had been hacked out of a block by a clumsy wood-carver. His eyes were flamboyant, his nose terrific, his mouth implacable" (III, 93). One is tempted to entertain the notion that, when the eleven-year-old Henry and his father visited Brady's studio for the portrait that appears in Edel's biography (EL opposite 178), the young James saw on display and was fascinated by the Brady portrait of Jackson taken a decade earlier. We suggest it is significant that in "A Passionate Pilgrim," which James says is "in the highest degree documentary for myself" (LC II, 1206), Clement Searle, like his author intensely interested in the past as it affected him and his family, should be reminded at Lockley Park, his ancestral home in England, of "a china vase that used to stand on the parlour mantelshelf while I was a boy [in America], with the portrait of General Jackson painted on one side and a bunch of flowers on the other" (II, 63).[19]

"The Ghostly Rental" was completed and published in 1876, the centennial year of the Declaration of Independence; thus the year was a time doubly appropriate for James's reflections on

America and what it meant to him. The action of the tale, which culminates in Diamond's death, takes place "thirty years ago" (III, 87); Jackson participated in the Revolution as a boy, and died in 1845. Diamond mentions to the narrator that he has been receiving rental for "these twenty years" (III, 101), which would take the story back from the 1840s to the 1820s, when Jackson stormed on to the national political scene and was elected to the Presidency in what was one of the greatest turning points in American history. "A knightly personage, . . . prejudiced, narrow, mistaken upon many points, but vigorously a gentleman in his sense of honor and in his natural straightforward courtesies"; these are not the words of James's narrator describing Diamond but of Josiah Quincy, Jr., of Boston, no friend of Jackson's, recalling Old Hickory many years after his death. This attitude is not unlike that of the narrator of the tale toward Diamond and what he represents.

President Jackson battled against powerful sectional and financial interests throughout his administration. This "strife and struggle" became particularly prominent when Jackson faced down South Carolina's unilateral attempt to nullify the protective tariff and when he dismantled Nicholas Biddle's United States Bank. Diamond's stormy relation with his daughter reproduces something of this conflict. His daughter's deception and its blazing aftermath, the destruction of the haunted house, have their prototypes in the collapse of the movement Jackson started and in the subsequent North-South conflagration. After Jackson's departure for the Hermitage--where, profoundly moved by a sermon, he joined the local Presbyterian church[20]--Jacksonian democracy was severely weakened during the "Whig Counterreformation" and all but destroyed during the Civil War.[21] The tale is James's tribute to Jackson and the qualities he represented, the pristine American virtues that James feared had perhaps been consumed in the disasters of 1861-65. This pathos suffuses the tale.

"The Ghostly Rental" may be read as a kind of elegy, Captain Diamond being the ghostly personification of an almost dead-and-gone era of American history. The narrator first encounters him at the house which he describes as "simply haunted" and "spiritually blighted" (III, 88). He twice meets Diamond in Cambridge's Mount Auburn cemetery, of which it has been said that there is "Some choice New England stock in that little plot of ground." [22] In haunting this cemetery, Diamond represents the great families such as the Lowells and, particularly, William Ellery Channing, whose memorial is a conspicuous monument there. "This is a very comfortable place" (III, 94), Diamond says to the narrator in the first of a series of *double entendres*. But this compound ghost is very different from the Gothic apparition of the sensational-traditional kind--his own daughter's "ghost"--that Diamond believes he sees and from which he receives the rent every quarter. This latter is spurious--no ghost, but the very lively and beautiful flesh-and-blood daughter he has been hoodwinked into believing he killed. It is in large part his Calvinist conscience, his sense of guilt and sin--he, like James's grandfather, the legendary William of Albany, has "the rugged Presbyterian manner"[23]--that induces the state of mind that leads him to see the ghost, and this conscience is transmitted to his daughter, as we realize when she, in her turn, imagines she has killed her father and believes that she sees *his* ghost; she, like him, regards the visitation as "the punishment of my long folly!" (III, 111).

Although James's Captain Diamond speaks acidly of "Jonathan Edwards and Dr. Hopkins chopping logic" (III, 101), both he and they are products of the same Calvinist tradition. Edwards, the great colonial Puritan divine, was the author of probably the most famous sermon preached in America, "Sinners in the Hands of an Angry God," a "God that holds you over the pit of hell, much as one holds a spider, or some loathsome insect over the fire."[24] Elsewhere Edwards forcefully asserts the doctrine of original sin. His most significant work, however, is *Freedom of the Will*, in which, by tracing all acts of the will back ultimately to the Creator, Edwards in a brilliant exercise of logic argues that in fact there is no such thing as freedom of the will.

By 1858, a century after the appearance of *Freedom of the Will*, Oliver Wendell Holmes, recognizing the triumph of Unitarianism and its offspring Transcendentalism, argued that, in the breakdown of "The Wonderful One-Hoss Shay," "a system of logic [such as Edwards's], however perfect, must collapse if its premises are false":

> End of the wonderful one-hoss shay.
> Logic is logic. That's all I say.[25]

James seems to suggest, however, that Holmes's interment of Calvinism is premature, for in "The Ghostly Rental" the "old, one-horse chaise" still functions; the narrator watches it wheel "creakingly away" (III, 89)--thirty years earlier (1845) than the assumed present of the narrative (1875). Calvinism still shares James's stage with Unitarianism and Transcendentalism, if only as a ghost, but Samuel Hopkins, Jonathan Edwards's friend and disciple, had long since adjusted Edwards's teachings "to the growing humanitarian temper of the times."[26] A young member of Hopkins's congregation, William Ellery Channing, greatly influenced by Hopkins's teachings, went on to graduate from Harvard Divinity School--described with gentle irony in James's tale as "that detached and tranquil home of mild casuistry" (III, 86)--and to become leader of the Unitarian movement in America. Rebelling against the doctrine of human depravity, he, although a scion of the Puritan-Calvinist tradition, "breathed into theology a humane spirit."[27] Channing, of whom James's narrator "had been an admiring reader" (III, 86), thus prepared the way for Emersonian Transcendentalism, with its emphasis on self-reliance and the divinity of man. It may at first appear anomalous, but the Transcendentalists have been described as "children of the Puritan past who, having been emancipated by Unitarianism from New England's original Calvinism, found a new religious expression."[28] Transcendentalism, according to R.B. Nye and J.E. Morpurgo, "was at bottom a manifestation in philosophy and religion of the same optimistic, individualistic, egalitarian spirit that produced Jacksonian democracy."[29]   There are, then, firm grounds for presenting Calvinism, Jacksonian democracy, Unitarianism, and Transcendentalism all as folds in the single American cloth.

The narrator has distanced himself from Channing, whom James later identified with New England (see A 140), as well as from Jackson. No Puritan, and no longer even a Unitarian or Transcendentalist, James does not see his ghost, Diamond, filtered through a sense of guilt and sin. The undertones are, instead, indebtedness, acknowledgement, and also sorrow and nostalgia because of the distance in outlook and ethos that has opened between him and Diamond--between James and America. Captain Diamond is, admittedly, a very solid compound ghost: he lays his hand on the narrator's arm (III, 103), and at the end of the tale he dies (III, 113). He seems nonetheless to be ghostly in a real sense. Early in 1875, while James was trying in vain to feel at home in New York--"*hideous* is the most amiable word I can find to apply to it"--he wrote to a friend that he had "been out tonight among some people who were telling ghost stories, and heard for the first time a young woman maintain that she had seen a ghost with her own eyes. . . . But I see ghosts all the while over here; I live among

'em: the ghosts of the old world and the old things I left *là bas*" (L
I, 470-71). What is more natural than that James, safely back *là
bas* and in a reflective mood, would be visited by the ghosts of the
new world and the old things he had left over *there?* Captain
Diamond belongs among those ghosts, the ghosts of James's
mother country. Seeing "The Ghostly Rental" in relation to
James's own life gives it a new dimension and meaning; carefully
read, it reflects his feelings at his life's crisis.

It is interesting to speculate on why James refers to
Hoffmann (III, 91) instead of Hawthorne, who, James elsewhere
says, "belonged to the race of magicians" (LC I, 308), and who
was a master at conjuring up the sort of ghost that Diamond is.
We believe the answer is simply that Hawthorne was American.
Indeed, Hawthorne could easily have been associated in James's
mind with Jackson. Hawthorne's biographers suggest that Old
Hickory's great victory at New Orleans "had doubtless appealed
particularly to the boy's imagination and patriotism" and
contributed to Hawthorne's becoming a lifelong Democrat.[30]
When Jackson, then President, visited Salem in 1833, Hawthorne,
according to his sister, "walked out to the boundary of the town to
meet him, . . . and found only a few men and boys collected, not
enough, without the assistance that he rendered, to welcome the
General with a good cheer."[31] Hawthorne is, in a sense, a figure in
the tale's scenario. Although in "The Ghostly Rental" James is
borrowing Hawthorne's literary mode and technique, he cannot
invoke him precisely because he is a prominent part of the America
that James, like his surrogate the narrator, is deliberately distancing
himself from. For James felt as close to Hawthorne as to Jackson
and the Puritan tradition, but there must be separation too; the note
of admiration is also ever so slightly patronizing. Hawthorne, says
James in 1872, is "the last pure American"; although he is
"unsophisticated," "there is something extremely pleasing in [his]
simplicity," and the finest touch from the point of view of one who
has "The Ghostly Rental" in mind is that Hawthorne "was deaf to
the Parisian harmonies" (LC I, 313, 309); he is too American to be
associated with Paris or Europe. Hence Diamond has to be a
figure not from Hawthorne but from Hoffmann, who, if not
French, was at least European.

In brief, the narrator in "The Ghostly Rental" has first been
drawn to the Puritan ethos of both Jackson and the Harvard
Divinity School, but then he is drawn philosophically, by way of
Plotinus and St. Augustine, to Pascal, in a way analogous to the

manner in which James, though attached to his native land, has been drawn away to Paris.

In the cemetery scene, when asked his name by Diamond, James's narrator, instead of answering him plainly, hands him "a small volume of Pascal's *Thoughts*, on the fly-leaf of which were written my name and address. . . . 'Pray keep this little book,' I said. 'It is one I am very fond of, and it will tell you something about me'" (III, 102). Indirectly, the narrator thus identifies himself with Pascal, who, distancing himself from struggle and conflict such as that of the Age of Jackson, serenely observes that "there are . . . a great number of truths, both of faith and of morality, which seem contradictory, and which all hold good together in a wonderful system. The source of all heresies is the exclusion of some of these truths. . . . And it generally happens that, unable to conceive the connection of two opposite truths, and believing that the admission of one involves the exclusion of the other, [heretics] adhere to the one [and] exclude the other."[32] In Paris in 1876, James might from that distance have agreed with Pascal: in opening his heart to Europe, he was not closing it to America.

The ambivalence in James's narrator, and in James himself, is what is typical of the artist--perhaps all artists. James is ambivalent about everything--even about his beloved Italy--not because he is undecided but because he sees all round his subject and tries to tell as much of the complex and contradictory truths about it as possible. But why does James wrap up the inward meaning of his tale in such a phantasmagoric, Hoffmannesque fashion that it is almost hidden? The answer is partly that, as William Blake explained, this method "rouzes the faculties to act,"[33] but also that James was sensitive to the imputation of unfilial and unpatriotic attitudes; he is writing a sort of apologia. In fact his departure *was* motivated by his criticism of America. In 1875 he had expressed this obliquely in fiction: he has Rowland Mallet say, "It's a wretched business . . . this practical quarrel of ours with our own country" (N 71-80, 187), but it was not until three years after "The Ghostly Rental" (and his emigration) that, in his book on Hawthorne, James speaks out in his own person, in public, and causes something of a stir in doing so (see EL 247). Yet even then, in 1879, he speaks with some mitigation, and on general not personal grounds: "to the present day it is a considerable discomfort in the United States not to be 'in business'"; "fifty years ago [in Hawthorne's youth], greatly more than now, the literary man [in America] must have lacked the comfort and inspiration of belonging to a class" (LC I, 342). Toward the end of his life he admitted something of this sense of alienation in his 1869 self: "Nothing of the smallest interest, by any perception of mine, as I suppose I should still blush to recall, had taken place in America since the War" (A 559). Within a year of his death, explaining to his nephew--again somewhat apologetically--why he was giving up his U.S. and taking on British citizenship, James points out that he would soon have been domiciled "uninterruptedly in England for forty years" (L IV, 760), and yet he felt gratitude and loyalty toward America throughout his life. Always there was an ambivalence. "The Ghostly Rental" reflects this even in its title: for the word "ghostly," a standard American dictionary of 1878 gives the meanings of "spiritual" and "relating to the soul" before the meaning of "pertaining to apparitions." Also, among those for "rent," one finds "a compensation or return, in the nature of an acknowledgment for the possession of a corporeal inheritance."[34]

This ambivalence is even further compounded when James tells William in the summer of 1876, soon after completing "The Ghostly Rental," that his "last layer of resistance to a long-encroaching weariness and satiety with the French mind and its utterance has fallen from me like a garment" (L II, 58); two months later he is asking a friend to write him "something 'loose and gossipy' about New York--a city for which I have retained a sneaking affection" (L II, 68). Soon he would make a new European start in London.

A superficial reading suggests that the tale belongs to the "gothic" genre, but in the end we see that the pageant of wonders and sensational events is insubstantial and has altogether faded: the ghost Diamond thought he saw was his lively daughter; the ghost seen by the daughter is a hallucination; even the pronouncements of the deformed Deborah--who, seated "between a bird-cage and a flower-pot" (III, 96), seems at first to have a lot in common with her Old Testament namesake and even with the decayed Cumaean Sibyl described in Petronius Arbiter's *Satyricon* as "hanging in a cage"[35]--are in the end seen to be merely mistaken local gossip, and she perhaps a tame, updated version of a Salem witch.[36] The final conflagration consumes the house, and together with it all the apparatus of the tall tale. What we are left with is the reality of James's ambivalent feeling toward America: he feels for her as he felt for one of his aunts, in whom he found "the American past of a preponderant unthinkable queerness"; but "the pleasure of finding

[that] past," he says, is "rich and strange" (A 74).

How Andrew Jackson, another image of the richness and strangeness of that past, haunted James's imagination is shown in his description of Lafayette Square, "contiguous to the Executive Mansion" in Washington, D.C., which "could create a rich sense of the past by the use of scarce other witchcraft than its command of that pleasant perspective and its possession of the most prodigious of all Presidential effigies, Andrew Jackson, as archaic as a Ninevite king, prancing and rocking through the ages. If that atmosphere . . . was even a quarter of a century since as a liquor of bitter-sweet taste, overflowing its cup, what was the ineffable mixture now [in 1905], with all the elements further distilled . . .? One circled about the place as for meeting the ghosts, and one paused, under the same impulse, before the high palings of the White House drive, as if wondering at haunted ground. There the ghosts stood in their public array, spectral enough and clarified" (AS 355). Witchcraft, ghosts, archaic, and bitter-sweet; it is the mixture as in "The Ghostly Rental," but presented thirty years later.

Even more remarkable perhaps is the fact that on 26 September 1870, some five years before he wrote "The Ghostly Rental," James set out in a letter what amounts to a prospectus for the tale: "I know that if I ever go abroad for a long residence, I shall at best be haunted and wracked, whenever I hear an American sound, by the fantasy of thankless ignorance and neglect of my native land--and I wish in self defence to make up a little list of accomplished devotions and emotions, which may somewhat abbreviate that sentimental purgatory" (L I, 246).

It should be clear that, if "The Ghostly Rental" has been received by his readers with something less than enthusiasm, and even with a critical blankness, it was for James something very personal and important, even perhaps therapeutic; by--as it were--settling old scores of indebtedness and alienation, it allowed him to address himself again to Europe with fresh energy and zest, and to enter into the fields of his fame and greatness.

Chapter VII

FAME 1877-79

After a year in Paris, James transferred to London, and almost immediately he felt at home--so much so that he was soon entertaining ambitious projects. The fiction that he was now to write did not make him rich, but it did make him famous. With the appearance of "Daisy Miller," his first publication in England, he was able to tell Howells, "My fame indeed seems to do very well everywhere," but the "pecuniary equivalent [is] almost grotesquely small" (L II, 243).[1] As recently as January 1876, in a letter to his mother from Paris, he had been concerned to rebut an apparent charge of extravagance (L II, 18-19), but by the end of 1878 he was at least supporting himself comfortably and was financially quite independent.

London, independence, and fame brought James a tremendous access of confidence; *Confidence* was the title of his novel that began appearing in 1879. He had become strikingly experimental, as we have seen in, for example, "Eugene Pickering," "Benvolio," and "The Ghostly Rental," but now he was not only trying new forms--he was later to say, "'Kinds' are the very life of literature" (LC II, 1131)--and publishing in English journals, but also tackling larger projects. By 1878 he was ready to embark on *The Portrait of a Lady*, by far his most ambitious work to date and his first great novel, which began to be published serially in 1880. It is clear that his virtual emigration from America and arrival in Europe as an expatriate at the end of 1875 had excited and stimulated him--"I take possession of the old world--I inhale it" (L I, 484)--and had advanced his art.

"FOUR MEETINGS" (*Scribner's Monthly*, November 1877; 1879; [1883]; [1885]; 1909)

"Four Meetings" was probably written in London (see III, 14), but this short tale is the first and the best of the fruits of James's year in Paris. Its importance is in the strength of its theme and the treatment. On the surface it is the simple tale of Caroline Spencer, an earnest teacher, not very young--"she must have been close upon thirty"--who has "the native American passion . . . for the picturesque," has "waited and waited" and is "always adding a little" to the "something" she has "laid . . . by" so that she can visit Europe: "'I think I can do it within ten years,' she [said] very soberly" (III, 115-118). Three years later she does get as far as Le Havre, but there she is met and cruelly exploited by a cousin, a Parisianized American art student, who virtually robs her of her savings. After "about thirteen hours in Europe" (III, 128) she is on her way back to America, and, when the narrator sees her again five years later, she is more "waiting-maid" (III, 136) than hostess to her now deceased cousin's "wife," who passes herself off as a French countess, cynically indulging herself with Parisian refinements by battening and contemptuously imposing on the timorous small-town New England civility and goodwill of Caroline. The pathos of the Innocent is again in tandem with the international theme, but now the source of the corruption is a Europeanized American--a foreshadowing perhaps of Gilbert Osmond in *The Portrait*--and the victim is not an almost impossibly idealized heroine, like Euphemia de Mauves, but the credible, delicately sketched Caroline Spencer.

The Europeanized cousin, "ugly, vulgar, pretentious, dishonest" (III, 127), is given to us rather plainly and quickly (in a work of these small dimensions some such shorthand is perhaps unavoidable), but the restrained irony of some of the narrator's observation of the exploiter is both diverting and effective: "I perceived the object of Miss Spencer's compassion. . . . He was dining too attentively to notice me at first" (III, 126). Caroline is a convincing compound of American virtues and the limitations one might expect "in the depths of New England" (III, 114), at Grimwinter, the unlikely name of the small town, which James changed to North Verona in the New York Edition: she is "a thin-stemmed, mild-hued flower of Puritanism" (III, 120).

Caroline is by no means a ninny or a nonentity: she can recite correctly the verses by Byron that the narrator had tried unsuccessfully to quote (III, 116); she has read "a great deal" about Italy, "not only . . . Byron; I have read histories and guide-books" (III, 118); she has an "eagerness" that is real though "suppressed" (III, 117) and "the native American passion . . . for the picturesque" (III, 118), which reminds one of "Travelling Companions" and "Adina." On board ship she was "perpetually . . . looking at the eastward horizon" (III, 119), and when she arrived at Le Havre she was "extremely observant. . . . She noticed everything" (III, 122). One of the touches James added for the New York Edition was that "her lips had a certain mild decision" (III, 374). She is, however, an easy prey to her unscrupulous cousin and, later, to his accomplice the "Countess," who "appealed successfully to her eager but most innocent imagination" (III, 127). But if that were all there was to it, the tale would be simply an adult adaptation of the story of Red Riding Hood.

The structure too looks as perfectly straightforward as the title implies: there are merely four meetings between the narrator and Caroline--the first in Grimwinter, two on the same day three years later in Le Havre (one before and one just after she has been fleeced), and the fourth, in Grimwinter again, about five years after Le Havre. The symmetry is simple and the parabola perfect. But there is much more to it. The drama is intensified and enacted on an additional plane because of the role created by James for the narrator. It is a role distinctly new in James's tales. The generally nameless narrator had gradually become more important--perfunctorily functional in "A Landscape Painter," and not much more than a friend and formal contrast in "My Friend Bingham," "Crawford's Consistency," and "A Passionate Pilgrim," where, however, he begins to be a sort of yardstick and moral assessor, as he is in "The Madonna of the Future" and "Professor Fargo." Now, by a technical tour de force, the narrator, while still apparently only an observer, moves to the centre of the action. This structure is one form of James's irony at the expense of the reader because the latter's attention is first fixed in one direction, and then has to find a new direction and focus. The nameless narrator of "Four Meetings" is involved in the action in a way that we might not at first notice; he is the forerunner of Winterbourne in "Daisy Miller," his immediate successor, and eventually, for example, of Marlow in "Heart of Darkness" by Conrad, James's admirer and disciple.

This aspect of the plot unfolds from the attitude of the narrator to Caroline in the very first scene. One of "two gentlemen from New York," both "lately returned from Europe," he is complacently conscious of being an "attraction" to the ladies at a tea-party in rural New England. Apparently a little put out at finding most of the young ladies interested in his companion, who unlike him has the advantage of being well known to them, he is drawn to Caroline because she stands apart (III, 114). He jokes with his hostess about flirting with Caroline, but that this is more than a jest is shown in his pleasure at making a great impression on her by being able to say of almost every one of the European places in the photographs he is commissioned to show to her that he "had seen it several times." Her "reticence" at first puzzles him, but he is clearly gratified to see "there was a faint flush in each of her cheeks. She was waving her little fan to and fro" (III, 115) because she is "delicately agitated" (III, 118). He tries to deepen the impression on her by quoting Byron, but looks a little foolish when Caroline modestly bests him at this; nevertheless, he patronizes her with compliments, saying "she was perfectly equipped for visiting Switzerland and Italy" (III, 116). An obvious minor irony is that, although Italy "is the place which--in particular--I have thought of going to" (III, 117), the few hours she does have in Europe are spent on one of the less picturesque edges of France. To make the meaning clearer, in the New York Edition James has the narrator, when he is speaking of being "a great traveller" (III, 115), say, "I was somehow particularly admonished not to swagger" (III, 374). But of course, though in an admittedly discreet way, that is just what he is doing. The scene ends with a final boast and a challenge: "I am going back there," and "I shall look out for you" (III, 118). He would be the one ultimately responsible for Caroline's misfortune.

The narrator is telling the story "some seventeen years" (III, 114) after this first scene, but it is clear, even in the first (1877) version, that he is a Jamesian protagonist in being sensitive and morally aware of his errancy in this first scene; certainly when he recognizes her two years later at Le Havre he shows awareness of some responsibility because he tells her, "I feel as if it were for me to give you a formal reception here--an official welcome. I talked to you so much about Europe" (III, 120).

An understanding of these undercurrents will explain what Roger Seamon has seen as the narrator's irritability in the fourth meeting.[2] His vehement denunciation of the "Countess" in that last scene matches what he has said of the cousin--she is "coarse, common, affected, dishonest" (III, 392)--because she is a sort of extension of the cousin, who probably was her husband, but we shall understand the narrator's irritation more fully when we see that the Countess's relation to Mr. Mixter--a naive young local--in the last scene is not altogether unlike his own to Caroline in the first.

An interesting way of demonstrating James's intention here is to compare the 1877 version with that of 1909. In the first version Mixter has "clasped his arms round his knees and was watching [the Countess's] demonstrative graces in solemn fascination" (III, 136); in the New York Edition James has transferred both "solemn" and "fascination" from Mixter in the last scene to Caroline in the first (see "solemnity" and "I'm just fascinated"--III, 374). Both terms are applicable to both characters in their respective situations, but in 1909 James seems to have been intent on making Mixter somewhat more, and Caroline somewhat less, ridiculous. In all versions there is a clear connection between Caroline's "small, tremulous ecstasy" and Mixter's "ecstasy of contemplation" (III, 117, 136). Another slight but significant change made in the first scene is to give greater prominence to what Caroline does with her fan: in the 1877 version the last sentence of this scene reads, "And she went away, looking delicately agitated and moving her little straw fan" (III, 118), which becomes "And she left me, fluttering all expressively her little straw fan" (III, 377), thus showing more clearly Caroline's emotional response to the narrator and the responsibility he should feel for involving her in the imbroglio. This change too makes it easier for the reader to see why and how the narrator would be aware of a correspondence between the Countess and himself, and therefore between the unscrupulous cousin and himself. One might say that he sees the Countess as a reflection of himself, though somewhat magnified and distorted. His venial condescension in the first scene is reflected in her patent and blatant exploitation not only of Mixter but of Caroline and North Verona (Grimwinter) as well in the last scene. When, in Mixter's presence, the Countess boasts contemptuously to the narrator in French (which she is teaching Mixter but which he cannot follow) that Mixter "adores me" (III, 136), we recall the narrator's exhibitionistic posing and poor Caroline's agitation, looking at him "askance" and with her "sidelong gaze" (III, 115, 116), and her "faint flush" and "blushing" (III, 115, 116, 117) in the first scene.

Does James clearly show us in the 1877 version that the narrator does in fact see the reflection? He is presented as a man of cultivation and conscience, capable of moral insight and self-criticism. We can sense this when he approaches Caroline's house for the fourth meeting: "I hesitated abruptly to present myself. . . . Gently, but gravely and timidly, I advanced to the doorstep" (III, 129)--statements that survive both the revisions and indicate a pronounced difference from his attitude at the time of the tea-party eight years before. When the Countess hails him as a bird of her own sophisticated feather--"I knew it so soon as I looked at you" (III, 134)--we feel the penetrating irony involved and sense his mortification. His horrified fascination suggests that he is deeply but obscurely disturbed, and his vehemence in castigating her--in his narrative, not in her hearing!--is a sign that he feels himself painfully implicated, though he cannot admit, and indeed has to suppress, an awareness that the Countess's behaviour is a reflection of his own.

When Caroline seems to appeal to him to tell her the truth that she suspects about the Countess, it makes the narrator "extremely uncomfortable. I could not tell her," so he acts out a lie and tries "suddenly . . . to show a high consideration" for the Countess, as if she were genuine. "But I got up; I couldn't stay longer" (III, 136). James revises this passage extensively for the New York Edition and has the narrator call this "a retreat in good order and with all the forms of courtesy" (III, 394). His confusion seems to stem from more than compassion for Caroline, seems indeed to come from a sense of personal failure and humiliation, and from something like remorse. If he has not attained full self-knowledge, he is at least ashamed at his avoidance of it, which is the next best thing.[3]

James's ironic indirection in having a character who is ostensibly only an observer and narrator but in reality the main protagonist is not quite new in "Four Meetings"; it had appeared in *Roderick Hudson* (1875) over two years earlier. As James himself puts it in his Preface (1907) to that novel: "The centre of interest throughout 'Roderick' is in Rowland Mallet's consciousness, and the drama is the very drama of that consciousness. . . . [The] whole was to be the sum of what 'happened' to him . . .; but as what happened to him was above all to feel certain things happening to others . . . the beauty of the constructional game was to preserve in everything its especial value for *him*" (LC II, 1050). But in fact James was not fully in control of this method when he wrote *Roderick Hudson* because he meant Roderick, not Rowland, to be the centre. In "Four Meetings" two years later, James had more fully focused his material and mastered his method.

An experience of self-revelation comes to characters in some of the great novels in the canon of English literature: to Jane Austen's Emma after she has deplored and felt superior to Mrs. Elton,[4] to Conrad's Lord Jim when he is confronted by Brown, though in this case too the protagonist's realization is not made explicit but is left to be inferred, as is the narrator's in "Four Meetings." For Emma and Jim, as for Milton's Samson, the encounter with a reflection of the self leads to knowledge which is a condition of full moral stature. In "The Beast in the Jungle," written a quarter of a century later, James gives a fuller and in the end a more explicit and tragic treatment of the process. He has achieved a new form for "'subjective' adventure" (LC II, 1170), which brings him in practice to the concept of the fine central intelligence that he has been approaching for some time. Until now the fineness has been sometimes in a protagonist, but generally in an observer; now James has broken down the distinction between narrator and protagonist, and the narrator has become a protagonist whose experience may be even more dramatic than that of the ostensible hero, as Marlow's is more immediate to us than Kurtz's. When we find a character, "finely aware and richly responsible," who experiences "plenty of bewilderment" (LC II, 1088, 1090), we have the distinctive situation in James's mature art.

"THÉODOLINDE" (*Lippincott's Magazine*, May 1878; 1885 as "Rose-Agathe")

This very short tale is about a simple but artfully prolonged case of cross-purposes. The narrator thinks his friend Sanguinetti is planning to carry off the handsome wife of a Parisian hair-dresser, whose shop is within sight of the narrator's apartment, but all the while his friend, a collector of "pretty things," "gimcracks and knickknacks" (III, 144, 143), is negotiating for the blonde "effigy of the coiffeur's window" (III, 153), which he dotes on obsessively and eventually instals in his apartment. It is matter for farce.

Difficult questions arise, however. Aziz says that James obviously did not think much of the story because he submitted it to "a second-rate American magazine" (III, 16), but the facts are that "Daisy Miller" had been first submitted to and declined by the very magazine, *Lippincott's*, that published "Théodolinde," and that James revised the tale, re-titling it "Rose-Agathe," for *Stories*

Revived (1885).

The narrator--again unnamed--starts with a long, detailed, evocative, and fascinated description of the sights, odours, and sounds of "a Parisian thoroughfare" (III, 138-41), which might correspond with James's own current or very recent impressions of a "mixture of every sort of queer old Parisian amenity and reference" (A 214), but, although James was no doubt possessing or repossessing himself of Paris when he wrote the tale, this does not go far as a justification of so slight and light a tale written by an artist who is about to produce masterpieces.

The point is made that both the narrator and Sanguinetti are Americans--though the latter's strange obsession is apparently derived from an Italian grandfather who was an image-vendor (III, 143)--but this does not seem to be significant, except that it explains why, having "a stranger's alertness" (III, 138), the narrator is so attentive to empirical experience and makes possible his facetious comment that he too might "become equally perverted" by "the Parisian tone" (III, 149). It seems that James is still conscious of and playing up to an American readership and prejudice.

It may be that in this tale James is exploring his instrument, the narrator, because it shows that the narrator can be a conscientious observer, describing and relating what he sees with the best will in the world, and yet he can discover that he has been building on an hypothesis that is far wide of the truth. In a simple and crudely comic way the tale is analogous to the disturbing and tragic masterpiece, "The Beast in the Jungle" (1903). Like "Maud-Evelyn" (1900), but on a superficial, merely literal plane, "Théodolinde" demonstrates the tendency and ability of the human mind and imagination to fabricate fantastic and often fallacious constructs.

"DAISY MILLER: A STUDY" (*Cornhill Magazine*, June-July 1878; [1878]; 1879; [1883]; 1909; [1915])

This was the first of James's tales to be published in England, and it is his first *nouvelle*, perhaps his favourite form: in the Preface to *The Lesson of the Master* he waxes lyrical about "the beautiful and blest *nouvelle*" (LC II, 1227). Among the many merits of the tale is its architectonic structure. None of the scenes is set in Geneva, but Winterbourne, the central intelligence, studies there, and its presence is powerfully felt throughout as a citadel of European protocol, though this is enforced, ironically enough, by none more strictly than the expatriate Americans: social proprieties and forms of courtship are "stiff," which is a nodal term (III, 186, 189, 190, 196), and Geneva is of course spectrally presided over by the figure of Calvin. In Rome, the setting for the second half of the tale, Genevan proprieties are reinforced by shades of Papal and Imperial authority, and it is there that the pathetically unorganized, unformulated American "sense of freedom" (III, 173), associated with "innocence" (III, 161, 166, 175, 177, 184, 192, 195, 201-- where it occurs three times) and embodied by Daisy, is pitted against this adamantine power. There is no doubt where our sympathies lie.

The unpretentious heroine's name is Annie P. Miller; her familiar name associates her with all that is "natural" (III, 169), universal, and perennial, though her action is no stronger than a flower. The "[child] of nature and of freedom" (LC II, 1270) is deplored and virtually disowned by her expatriate countrywomen as "common" (III, 165, 169, 174) and has on her side only her own ignorant but engaging vitality and courage, feebly supported by the unauthoritative forms of distant Schenectady, New York, where her father stays, running a "big business" (III, 159). He leaves Daisy's travels in Europe to her mother, who is a passive nonentity, and her nine-year-old brother, who is amusingly undisciplined and assertive. Even representatives of New York and New England society seem to range themselves with Genevan rigidities--James's father once described Calvin as "a sort of model Bostonian"[5]--and this is a significant and rich complication of James's international theme.

The characters and action are arranged in relation to the two poles of Geneva and Schenectady: Daisy's mother is in contrast to Mrs. Walker and Mrs. Costello; Randolph, Daisy's free-ranging young brother, is at a hotel where "Polish boys [walk] about, held by the hand, with their governors" (III, 155). This polarity is dramatized in the friction in the mind and conscience of Winterbourne, a Europeanized American; the oppositions are much more effective than they were in "Mme. de Mauves," where the characters were either idealized or stereotyped and the conflict melodramatic rather than internal and convincing.

The "Genevese mind", given support and force by a sort of "German earnestness" and "narrowness and intolerance" (LC II, 185-86)--qualities soon to be given prominence in *Confidence* (see

TMW 68)--is epitomized in Mrs. Costello, social arbiter even though an invalid, who holds court sitting, significantly, "on a little portable stool at the base of one of the great pilasters" of St. Peter's, attended by "a dozen of the American colonists in Rome" (III, 193-94). Rome and St. Peter's have already appeared prominently in James's fiction. The ways in which James uses famous places and monuments as dramatic presences show the benefits of his sentimental tourism and also the progress of his artistic skill.[6] The historic reverberations that were contrived with ingenuity in "Travelling Companions" are now, in "Daisy Miller," being orchestrated with dramatic force. Like the narrator in "Four Meetings," but with a less questionable motive, Winterbourne tells Daisy the "history of Bonivard," which goes "into one ear and out of the other" (III, 175)--Daisy is different from Caroline Spencer-- but, ironically, it was she who in the first place wanted so "dreadfully" to visit "that old castle," the Chateau de Chillon (III, 162), quite oblivious of the free spirit that was extinguished there, as hers is to be in Rome.[7] Toward the end, Winterbourne comes upon Daisy and her Italian escort, Giovanelli--the couple that respectable society will not receive--when she is seeing "the Colosseum by moonlight" and in fact catching the Roman fever that will kill her (III, 199); the irony is patent and poignant when Daisy says of Winterbourne, "He looks at us as one of the old lions or tigers may have looked at the Christian martyrs" (III, 198). She is a different kind of martyr. James is squeezing every drop from the Roman orange.

Less obvious but not less judicious is the new and convincing balance James strikes in the international theme. Whereas infamy tended in the earlier stories to be located in the European upper-class (Clement Searle's English cousin, M. de Mauves, or the Vicomte de Treuil) and virtue to be monopolized by Americans adventuring at their peril in Europe, now the evil is less melodramatic but more tragic, being rooted in this instance in the unfeeling stiffness of the American colony in Rome, though Mrs. Costello and Mrs. Walker are not by nature malicious or cynical and indeed seem to have Daisy's best interests at heart. Moreover, an ironic light, quite absent in the case, for example, of Euphemia de Mauves, plays about Daisy, for whom our sympathy and admiration are aroused, so the justice is more even-handed and compelling. Daisy's appendages, her brother Randolph and her mother, are even ridiculous in their ignorance and gaucherie. They ironically illustrate the severe limitations of Daisy's culture and reinforce the gentle comedy of Daisy's innocence as well as the tragic pathos of her fate.

James uses Daisy's brother Randolph to satirize the blinkered self-regard and complacency of some Americans: "American men are the best," he says (III, 156). James might even be making fun of his earlier international tales. Mrs. Miller is absurdly naive, ignorant, lacking in curiosity and taste, and utterly unconscious of the rocks on which Daisy's slender craft will founder: "We only want to see the principal [castles]. We visited several in England" (III, 170).

It is not only that James is more even-handed but also that he hits on characteristics that struck readers, especially European readers perhaps, as typically American. To a European, Randolph's independence would be indiscipline and impertinence, and Daisy would seem uncouth, or at least ungracious, when she deplores "those dreadful old men that explain about the pictures and things" (III, 182), or is so frank in "*persiflage*" (III, 175), and so brazenly open about her volitions: "Don't you want to take me out in a boat?" she says to Winterbourne (III, 171). But the characters are American in the very tones of their voices, whereas the speech of Clement Searle, Theobald, and Eugene Pickering was not distinct from that of the Europeans. Consider the compactness, frankness, and dryness of Randolph's one-liner: he says that the ship the City of Richmond was "the best place I've seen. . . . Only it was turned the wrong way" (III, 179). When Winterbourne says politely that he would have liked to call on Daisy sooner in Rome but that he has "only just stepped out of the train," Daisy's disconcerting rejoinder is, "You must have stayed in the train a good while after it stopped!" (III, 181). This is indeed American tactlessness!

In this regard, a letter James wrote to Howells on 24 October 1876, not long before he left Paris for his final domiciliary perch in London, marks an important change in his art that allows one to see that he was ending one phase of his career and beginning another. Howells had argued for a different end for *The American*, wanting a marriage in the end between the American Newman and the French noblewoman, and James answers: "The whole point of the *dénouement* was, in the conception of the tale, in his losing her. . . . My subject was: an American letting the insolent foreigner go, out of his good nature, after the insolent foreigner had wronged him and *he* had held him in his power. To show the good nature I must show the wrong and the wrong is of course that the American is cheated out of Mme de Cintré." (L II, 70). James might have gone on to say, as he did in the Preface to *The American*, that the work is a romance.   James seems to have turned the crucial corner from romance to realism in his international tales when he wrote "Four Meetings" and "Daisy Miller".[8]   Again it is in his tales that James conducts his experiments and makes his advances.

Even if they were wrong, it is significant that James and Howells both thought that *Lippincott's Magazine* had declined "Daisy Miller" because "it was seen to be presenting an unfavourable image of American girlhood" (III, 16); in fact the satire is mild and tolerant and clearly overridden by the author's approval and affection, which is to be distinguished from the attitude of Winterbourne. The portrait of Daisy shows some of the qualities in her that James *in propria persona* felt in his large New York cousinage, the Emmet families; if they belonged to a somewhat more sophisticated society than Daisy does, they nevertheless had, in their "singularly natural way" (A 25), some of what we see in Daisy, who says, "If I didn't introduce my gentlemen friends to mother . . . I shouldn't think I was natural" (III, 169). As James explained to Mrs. Lynn Linton in 1880, "Poor little Daisy Miller was, as I understand her, above all things *innocent*" (L II, 303).[9]   In this respect one could say of James's presentation of Daisy what James said about Thackeray's of Becky Sharp: the "satire . . . always goes hand in hand with a certain tender, sympathetic comprehension of her, with the thoroughly human tone which belongs to perfect insight" (LC II, 191); two years later, in 1875, James commented on "how humanly, how generously" George Eliot exhibits the ladies of the "ridiculous" and "disagreeable" Dodson family (LC II, 56).   James not only borrowed from but successfully emulated writers he admired.

In "Daisy Miller" James brings Americanness and Innocence together very convincingly. Daisy's innocence is quite different from Euphemia de Mauves's, and different again from that of the later exemplars of innocent young womanhood, Isabel Archer and Milly Theale. She does not have their intelligence, education, or cultivated sensibility, and because of this she is all the more vulnerable and evokes all the more pathos. European readers could be moved by her even while they were entertaining somewhat superior and patronizing attitudes to the naive and immodest American girl, thus flattering themselves and having their preconceptions confirmed by a writer who was himself a good

American. James no doubt amused himself as well as his readers with this play on national traits, but the strength of the tale derives from the deeper sources of James's imagination that sprang from a conception of Innocence betrayed. As we move from "Four Meetings" to "Daisy Miller," we cross the unmarked boundary between pathos and tragedy and reach the deep waters that will be plumbed later, in James's greatest fiction. As James said to Howells in a letter written about a year before "Daisy Miller" appeared: "I suspect it is the tragedies in life that arrest my attention . . . and say more to my imagination" (L II, 105).

It is in such mundane-sounding matters as technique and method, however, that "Daisy Miller" has perhaps its highest merit and its deepest interest for the student of James's career. And here we turn from Daisy to Winterbourne. He is not the narrator but the centre of consciousness and a participant, and thus subject to the reader's scrutiny. Winterbourne is an American too, but, unlike Daisy, he has "imagination and . . . sensibility" (III, 173), or at least the cultivation that comes from education and a knowledge of Europe; he has been absorbed into Europe's artificial and structured society. In this way he is a lapsed American, "dishabituated to the American tone" (III, 161), which means that he has almost lost his innocence, but not quite, for he can still at their first meeting respond to Daisy's American quality: he realizes that hers "was not . . . what would have been called an immodest glance, for the young girl's eyes were singularly honest and fresh" (III, 158).

Winterbourne's "old attachment for the little metropolis of Calvinism" (III, 155) goes together with his innate characteristics, which are hinted at by his name rather less obtrusively than was the character of the New England town by the name "Grimwinter" in "Four Meetings." Though susceptible to Daisy's charm, he is emotionally inhibited and timid; this reinforces his Genevan wariness, and from the outset we find him wondering "whether he had gone too far" (III, 157) and, with barely adequate cause, he tentatively decides "he must advance farther, rather than retreat" (III, 157).

How far and how quickly James has come in fitting the means of a narrator to the ends of his art is shown by a comparison of Winterbourne and his function with the unnamed and rather featureless narrator and his ineffectual role in "Crawford's Consistency," published two years earlier. The latter is merely an observer and, though he has sympathy, is scarcely involved in

Crawford's misfortunes; indeed he does not even understand how they come about. Winterbourne is different. From the beginning he is "amused, perplexed, and decidedly charmed" (III, 161), and what he sees and feels fuels an urgent, unceasing, and never resolved debate in his mind and conscience; in this he is like Longmore in "Mme. de Mauves." He is very much involved, even to the point of wondering whether he is in love with Daisy and should court her. On the one hand, he thinks Daisy is merely a "flirt"--the word recurs frequently (III, 162, 183, 186, 190, 200)-- "a designing, an audacious, an unscrupulous young person" (III, 161), but then, as we have seen, he thinks again and again that she is as "innocent" as she is beautiful. And, when Winterbourne does "advance farther" and says, "I should much rather go to Chillon with you" than stay to look after Randolph (III, 162-63), he is taking up a position that entails responsibilities. At Vevey, in the first half of the tale, he defends Daisy against his aunt Mrs. Costello's acerbic comments (III, 164-66), and in Rome, where he is in somewhat hesitant pursuit of Daisy, he is really on the spot.

It is interesting to follow in some detail Winterbourne's feelings and inner struggle in Rome through several pages (III, 183-88). In spite of the admonition of Mrs. Walker, he allows Daisy to conscript him to take her to the Pincio, a very public promenade, so that she can meet Giovanelli. Winterbourne, as usual, is complaisant. Still he resents the Italian as a rival, although he has not, despite some encouragement, declared his affection for Daisy and therefore has no claim to assert, and it is this jealousy that partly explains why Winterbourne is highly critical of Giovanelli and thus of Daisy too: "Winterbourne felt a superior indignation at his own lovely fellow-countrywoman's not knowing the difference between a spurious gentleman and a real one" (III, 183). He is soon wondering whether Daisy is guilty of "extreme cynicism": it is impossible to regard her as a "well-conducted young lady; she was wanting in a certain indispensable delicacy." The countermovement sets in before the end of the paragraph, however: "But Daisy, on this occasion, continued to present herself as an inscrutable combination of audacity and innocence" (III, 184).

Patrolling the Pincio in her carriage in the supervisory function that she has arrogated to herself, Mrs. Walker beckons to Winterbourne. Amenable and docile again, he detaches himself from Daisy and Giovanelli and joins Mrs. Walker; although he objects to Mrs. Walker's tactic of ordering Daisy away from

Giovanelli, he does not block it and is in fact the bearer of the summons to Daisy. In the end he merely looks on as Daisy openly and at great length defies Mrs. Walker. His attempt to be neutral and evade his responsibility is not successful, because Daisy embroils him: she turns to him and appeals to him for judgement. He "hesitated greatly" but finally suggests that Daisy "should get into the carriage" (III, 186) and submit to Mrs. Walker and conventional respectability. Thus, when it comes to the test, Winterbourne fails Daisy. This is underlined when his attempt to join Daisy is stopped by Mrs. Walker's declaration "that if he refused her this favour [of remaining with her] she would never speak to him again"; when he tries to explain to Daisy that he must accede to Mrs. Walker's "imperious claim upon his society," she "only shook his hand, hardly looking at him" (III, 186). Seeing Daisy and Giovanelli close together under a parasol, he "lingered a moment, then he began to walk. But he walked--not towards the couple with the parasol; towards the residence of his aunt, Mrs. Costello" (III, 188). In poor Winterbourne's oscillating between Geneva and his own timid spontaneous feelings, James effectively dramatizes his dilemma and his impotence.

James intensifies the drama. Excluded from "respectable" society and by Winterbourne's desertion virtually confined to the company of Giovanelli, whom she must meet outdoors, Daisy is on the path to the Colosseum by moonlight and to her death, but Winterbourne still does nothing to help her. That she is drawn to him is shown by the message she sends him from her deathbed. It is true that he "went often to ask for news of her" (III, 200), but this is too little too late. She dies, leaving him with feelings of guilt and remorse. When he bitterly reproaches Giovanelli for taking Daisy to "that fatal place" (III, 201), he is in part trying to comfort himself, trying to minimize the "mistake" (III, 202) he realizes he has made. He is being rather hard on himself, but it was a dereliction or failure of courage and conviction in an intelligent and sympathetic young man who, like Henry James (one is tempted to say), is by temperament cautious and circumspect, heedful of authority and convention; it is the cynical Giovanelli who is most culpable: when he decides he stands no chance with her, he does not prevent the headstrong girl from risking the dread Roman fever.

Winterbourne is an advance on the narrator in "Four Meetings" because the shortcomings in the latter's conduct are clearly visible in the first scene, whereas Winterbourne's position and views have at first no such obvious flaws. In fact the reader will probably tend at first, in the Vevey scenes, to endorse his judgement that Daisy is "a pretty American flirt" (III, 162). Winterbourne makes his discovery gradually, and, as his view changes, so will that of the reader, who will therefore pass through an analogous experience; we begin to see the truth of Quentin Anderson's perception: James "is . . . aware of the arc which separates the reader and himself. . . . He seeks to diminish that arc, so that the end of the story takes place at the moment when your position coincides with his."[10] Thus the reader is drawn into the action, following the centre of consciousness, which serves one of the important purposes of the chorus in classical drama. By 1878, with "Daisy Miller: A Study," James had forged a technique that would serve him throughout his greatest work.

According to Aziz, James wrote "Daisy Miller" "in the early months of 1878" (III, 15). It is not surprising therefore that a little earlier, in a letter to Howells of 30 March 1877, we should hear--when he is referring to his next novel, *The Europeans*--not the ironic self-deprecating note of the past, but a new and exuberant confidence: "You shall have the brightest possible sun-spot for the four-number tale of 1878. It shall fairly put your readers eyes out. The idea of doing what you propose much pleases me; and I agree to squeeze my buxom muse, as you happily call her, into a hundred of your pages" (L II, 105). Writing in a soberly prophetic vein to his brother William from London on 28 January 1878, when he was perhaps already at work on "Daisy Miller," James said: "If I keep along here patiently for a certain time I rather think I shall become a (sufficiently) great man. I have got back to work with great zest after my autumnal loafings, and mean to do some this year which will make a mark. I am, as you suppose, weary of writing articles about places, and mere potboilers of all kinds; but shall probably, after the next six months, be able to forswear it altogether, and give myself up seriously to 'creative' writing. Then, and not till then, my real career will begin" (L II, 150-51).

"LONGSTAFF'S MARRIAGE" (*Scribner's Monthly*, August 1878; 1879; [1883])

This tale occupies a strange place in the story of James's development. It is one of his less successful tales, and yet it was published just after a masterpiece. Since it was probably written in London, one of the "by-products of the Parisian year," and *before* "Daisy Miller" (III, 14,16), this was partly because of the accident of Scribner's dilatoriness. Our study would be neater if "Longstaff's Marriage" had been written before "Four Meetings" because it has little of the merit that we expatiated on in that tale.

Starting with "Forty years ago," the tale is a romance. Diana Belfield, who has some of the divine qualities and the beauty "foreshadowed in her name" (III, 203), is in a "situation . . . so strange and romantic that one's old landmarks of propriety were quite obliterated" (III, 215). In other words, as James was to put it in the Preface to *The American,* there is an attempt "to cut the cable" that is attached to "the balloon of experience" (LC II, 1064). An apparently dying man has a strange, childishly romantic desire to marry the beautiful, vigorous, and "wakeful huntress" (III, 203), and the once "fiercely virginal" huntress (III, 204), now in her turn dying, has the converse and morbid wish to marry the now fully recovered but not-so-young man. He is more amenable than she had been, and she has her way, only to die the next day.

Not only does the plot sound unpromising, but the tale does not carry forward any of James's interesting recent experiments in narration; it is told in the conventional omniscient third-person. It is at first difficult to see why James should have considered it worth revising once and reprinting twice. He did tell William, to whom he was sometimes defensive and self-deprecating, that it "had seemed but a poor affair" (L II, 216), but he may have been referring to the unenthusiastic reception of the tale. Edel sees links between the tale and James's reaction to Minny Temple's death, suggesting that, after Diana rejects his proposal, Longstaff recovers because he no longer feels threatened, just as James was paradoxically relieved when the cousin he loved "had permanently been converted into a statue" (EL 111). Edel is probably right in feeling that Longstaff reflects some of James's timidity in his relations with women. Minny's death did seem to leave him strangely relieved, apparently absolved from his commitment to courtship, but it did also have a far-reaching and saddening effect on his life; however, when Edel also links the strange see-saw pattern involving Longstaff and Diana (EL 109) with James's saying after Minny's death, "I can't put away the thought that just as I am beginning life, she has ended it" (L I, 228), one should remember that this pattern in James's work dates back at least to "De Grey: A Romance" (1868), published almost three years before Minny died.

Longstaff suggests that his miraculous recovery after his rebuff by Diana was due to "wounded pride" (III, 224), but it may well have been because he felt safe once she was inaccessible. If so, James must have been indulging in conscious irony when he named him Longstaff, and it seems that it is at this point that we are offered the lever that will resolve the enigma that the tale presents. The psychosexual irony is given extra force if Longstaff's name also reminds one of the redoubtable bowman who is prominent in the largest cycle of ballads in English--Robin Hood's henchman, Little John. This suddenly makes clear why it is that this narrative, conventional in form, is constantly enlivened by "sportive commentary" (III, 222). James is playing in a fanciful manner with traditional material. There are more signs of this in the reference to "something . . . read of in poetry and fable" (III, 224), in the statement: "It will be like a story" (III, 212), and perhaps in the mention of "old-fashioned comedy" (III, 215). There is frequent whimsical, sub-ironic exaggeration or emphasis, as, for example, in "[Diana] had . . . a trick of carrying her long parasol always folded . . . across her shoulder, in the fashion of a soldier's musket on a march" (III, 203). This detail is touched on again (III, 209), like a motif in a cartoon. In ballads this sort of queer detail repeated has the effect of making comedy piquant or tragedy poignant; in James's tale the effect is consistently towards dehydrating pathos, making scenes intrinsically tragic almost ridiculous, as when Diana, seated in a chair next to the bed of the desperately ill Longstaff, is said to be resting "in maidenly majesty" (III, 217). When Longstaff's valet takes snuff "with a melancholy gesture, like a perplexed diplomatist" (III, 218), it is almost *opéra bouffe*.

James's main borrowing for "Longstaff's Marriage" is not from the Robin Hood cycle, however, but from a perhaps even more popular ballad--heard with great pleasure, for instance, by Samuel Pepys on 2 January 1665/6--"Barbara Allen's Cruelty."[11] Diana Belfield is like Barbara Allen in more than the number of syllables in her name. She has a number of admirers, and it is her cruelty to them, her "fiercely virginal" attitude (III, 204), that links her with the ballad, where Barbara addresses her company as "virgins all." She also, of course, takes after the goddess--Jonson's "Queen and Huntress, chaste and fair"--with whom she shares her name. Before following further the likenesses between the tale and the ballad, we should examine the classical myths that James has, as it were, mounted on the back of the ballad.

James constantly, and somewhat ironically, likens his heroine to the goddess Diana. Her surname, Belfield, perhaps echoes the appellation *Nemorensis* ("of the grove"), given the goddess in her most famous cult, at Ariccia, overlooking Lake Nemi in the Alban Hills, a neighbourhood well known to James; Ariccia appears as Lariccia in "Adina" (II, 352), where its associations become important; in "Roman Neighbourhoods," a travel-piece written a few years before "Longstaff's Marriage," James describes the area as haunted by "the ghosts of classic nymphs and naiads" that "beckon me with irresistible arms," and as being pervaded by "vague pagan influences."[12] Instead of the goddess's large company of female admirers (or Barbara Allen's numerous "virgins"), James's Diana has only one, her kinswoman, Agatha Gosling--in revision, Josling, and thus a little less obviously ridiculous--who is "the most judicious and most devoted of companions" (III, 203), having "an almost Quakerish purity and dignity; a bristling dragon could not have been a better safeguard" (III, 204). James's "goddess" is well protected.

In the ballad there is a hint that Barbara's state is pathological in the slowness of her response to the appeal of the dying young man, and in the unfeeling bluntness of her comment, "Young man, I think y'are dying"; at this point the young man "turned his face unto the wall," just as Longstaff "turned away" when Diana utters in his hearing the equally brutal comment, "Suppose, after all, he should get well?" (III, 218). Again like Barbara, the classical Diana is rather strangely inconsistent, both savagely chaste and resolutely passionate: she caused Actaeon to be torn apart by his dogs because he happened to glimpse her nakedness, but then, in some versions of the Endymion myth, which is mentioned in James's tale (III, 204), it is she who falls in love with the sleeping shepherd prince, and it is Diana-Artemis who persuades Aesculapius to revive the dead Hippolytus so that she may take him with her to her grove at Ariccia. At least one version of the ballad emphasizes the imbalance in Barbara by suggesting she is revenging herself on the young man because she feels she has been "slighted" by him.[13] James amplifies these implications. That his Diana's feelings are confused is shown near the beginning when, despite her apparently implacable attitude, she evinces at least a slight interest in Longstaff (III, 207). That there is an unresolved conflict within her appears not least when she is most vehement, capricious, and bitter in response to Longstaff's timid advance (III, 218, 219). Also the devoted and understanding Agatha is upset, presumably because she realizes that Diana's behaviour is harming her own best interest and is inconsistent with her deepest feelings. After two years, Diana makes her great turnabout and then herself becomes an unhappy suitor.

The most obvious signs of James's borrowing are to be seen in the plain outline of the plot of the ballad. Like the young man, Longstaff sends his manservant to appeal to the cold woman to come to him. Diana's situation is very nearly that of Barbara, who cries,

> My love has died for me to-day,
> I'll die for him to-morrow.

As is usual in his borrowings, James modifies the plot, making Longstaff recover, so that instead of being simply mourned he can actually be pursued by the lady. This intensifies the strangeness and the dramatic irony and also makes for more symmetry, a feature discernible as early as, for instance, in "Poor Richard," but becoming increasingly important to James. He was drawn to the pattern of reciprocal inversion--a sort of psychological Boyle's Law--that reached its most conspicuous application in *The Sacred Fount* (1901).

James's persistence with "Longstaff's Marriage" may be explained by the value he attached to the sort of harmony and completeness that he felt symmetry gave to artistic form, and also by the fun he obviously had in changing the mode of the piece from something close to tragedy in the ballad into the ironic and almost comic tale; the ingenuity in the adaptation is something like what we commented on in "A Tragedy of Error" and "A Light Man," and, as in these tales, if the reader does not see the relation between James's tale and the "source," the tale loses much of its point.

James seems sometimes to have asked too much of his reader. Perhaps in "Longstaff's Marriage" he was carried too far by the influence of Francis J. Child, the great authority on Chaucer and the ballads, whom James knew well when at Harvard Law School and who has been mentioned in our commentaries on "A Tragedy of Error" and "Poor Richard." In a letter James describes a story as one "such . . . as F.J. Child likes to tell" (L I, 206); in fact, Child became a much-loved friend of two generations of the James family.

As for symmetry, we saw how it heightened the pathos and

irony in "Four Meetings," and later it is effective in the hourglass shape of *The Ambassadors* (1903), but, unless it is delicately handled, an imposed symmetry can become too complete and procrustean for the realism associated with the sort of short story that "Longstaff's Marriage" seems at first to be; sometimes the symmetry is achieved--as perhaps in "Broken Wings" (1900) and "Fordham Castle" (1904)--at too great a sacrifice of what James in the Preface to *The Portrait of a Lady* was to call "felt life" (LC II, 1074).

"AN INTERNATIONAL EPISODE" (*Cornhill Magazine*, December 1878-January 1879; [1879]; 1879; [1883]; 1902; 1908)

The obvious symmetries in this tale are in the two balancing parts--the first, in which two upper-class Englishmen visit America, and the second, in which two American sisters visit England--and in the similarities and differences that unite and distinguish the two pairs, and the individuals within each pair. Lord Lambeth is provided with an older, more intelligent, and wittier companion in Percy Beaumont, and Bessie Alden with an older sister, Mrs. Westgate, not more intelligent than she, but worldly-wise, "satirical," "wicked and critical" (III, 270, 271), as garrulous as Jane Austen's Miss Bates, delivering herself of a similar torrent of disjointed observation and chat, but more shrewdly and with a sardonic humour. In the second part at least, she is not as "silly" as James makes out to a critical correspondent, and she is a great success as a comic sketch of a wry American "way of taking things" (L II, 222).

The relation between this *nouvelle* and its more famous predecessor is interesting. In letters James describes "An International Episode" as a "counterpart" or "*pendant*" to "Daisy Miller" (L II, 180, 183). But these terms alone might over-emphasize the similarity. It is the differences that are more significant: the dominant note of "Daisy Miller" is tragic pathos; its successor is a comic study of manners. Many motifs are similar-- the "innocent" girl, the contrast between liberty on the one side and, on the other, conventions such as those involved with "*precedence*" (III, 280): "At Newport he could do as he liked; but here [in London] it is another affair" (III, 263)--but all is transposed into another key and mode. Other aspects that appeared in earlier international tales appear again: the young Bessie's expectations of England, derived from "the poets and

historians," her "ejaculations and rhapsodies," and her fondness for
the "picturesque" (III, 258), such as her dream of living in a castle
(III, 287), all might remind us of Brooke ("Travelling
Companions"), Clement Searle ("A Passionate Pilgrim"), Euphemia
de Mauves, and Caroline Spencer ("Four Meetings"). Bessie's
many "disappointments" (III, 276) turn not to irreversible tragedy
but to the acquisition of experience and wisdom--to comedy.
James allows Daisy to be a little ridiculous in the early Vevey
scenes, but not in Rome; Bessie is made the object of gentle fun
throughout, on account of her Bostonian earnestness in writing
down "all the curious facts she hears, in a little book she keeps for
the purpose" (III, 286), and of her relentless and somewhat
priggish cross-examination of Lord Lambeth on his "hereditary"
privileges (III, 255), though this is also touching; it reminds one of
Isabel Archer's dissatisfaction with Lord Warburton (*The Portrait
of a Lady*, Chap. IX) and of the growing importance in James of an
"ideal of conduct" (III, 277) and "first principles" (III, 280); there
is also some fun at the expense of--but ultimately involving no
disrespect to--her "innocent little Boston" (III, 261).

Bessie does not meet Daisy's fate because she has an older
sister to advise her, and also because her imagination fosters a self-
awareness which allows her to see and make fun of herself: "I think
there is nothing so charming as an old ruinous garden" (III, 269);
and she does have "a fund of scepticism" (III, 273). In portraying
her, James shows that not all young American women are Daisy
Millers.

Because "Longstaff's Marriage" is a romance, it starts with
"Forty years ago" (III, 203), but being a topical comedy "An
International Episode" begins: "Four years ago" (III, 228). The
two Englishmen land in New York on their first visit to the New
World. James manages this skilfully by describing aspects of the
big city and Newport, the resort of its wealthy citizens, that would
strike the European visitors. There is no deep emotion involved,
only the curiosity of transatlantic travellers; this gives James the
opportunity to use his exceptional powers of observation and
evocation, of finding "pleasure in the differences" (III, 244), and
also his chameleon-like sympathy (which does not exclude a
tincture of satire), to present the strangers' "desultory observation
of the idiosyncrasies" of, for instance, the architecture, "exotic
odours," the square--"that queer place without palings" that "was
not much like Belgrave Square"--and "American citizens doing
homage to an hotel-clerk" (III, 230-31). Because Beaumont is

very perceptive, the observations move from new sights such as a young man's "wonderful cream-coloured garments and a hat with a blue ribbon," the "elevator . . . shooting upward in its vertical socket" that "presently projected them into the seventh horizontal compartment of the edifice," and "the uproar of the street . . . infinitely far below" (III, 233), to American attitudes and behaviour: the vitality, the "hospitality"--one of the most often repeated notes (see, e.g., III, 231, 236, 246, 252)--the businessman who has no time for social life, and then on to intellectual or aesthetic culture (a topic James recurs to often, as we have seen in his Preface to *The Reverberator*). American women are a prime topic--how addicted to shopping (III, 251) and how "clever" they are (III, 239), how they "don't mind contradicting you" (III, 256)-- and especially young American women. The two upper-class Englishmen coolly debate whether or not they are "fast" (III, 254), the question that Winterbourne agonizes over in "Daisy Miller." Toward the end it is still very much a question for Lambeth's mother, the Duchess of Bayswater, whether Bessie's remarks are "very artless or very audacious" (III, 287). Poor Daisy's shadow falls across the scene, but not ominously: the two American sisters are aware of too much, too confidently in control of affairs, to be easy victims. They will not be imposed upon or even "patronized" (III, 271).[14]

On his American tour twenty-five years after writing "An International Episode," James would read a paper on "The Question of Our Speech" at the Bryn Mawr Commencement of 1905. We began to see his interest in regional speech emerging in "Daisy Miller"; now he has a black saying "He goes out dis way in de mo'ning" (III, 232) and his English gentlemen using fashionable slang: "rum"--as in "rum-looking"--appears frequently (III, 229, 268), "jolly" even more often (III, 241, 242, 247, 252, 255, 268, 272), and "capital," descriptive of a person or place (III, 231, 234), among other locutions such as "I say" (III, 229), on which score James was criticized by Mrs. F.H. Hill. His reply is interesting (L II, 219-22), especially for his denying the imputation that in "the two English ladies [the Duchess and her daughter Lady Pimlico], I meant to make a resumé of my view of English manners" (L II, 221).

In the first half of the tale, apart from some mild humour at their expense--and at the expense of their American hosts also-- James presents the two Englishmen quite sympathetically: "They were extremely good-natured young men." Then he adds that, "in a sort of inarticulate, accidentally dissimulative fashion, they were highly appreciative" (III, 229), which shows remarkable understanding and tolerance of Englishmen's apparent phlegm; Lambeth's "intellectual repose" is scarcely stupidity (III, 248), though it could be very irritating to Americans. However, in the second half the balance tips fairly markedly in favour of the two American women, especially in comparison with the two high-born Englishwomen, whose visit is clearly an attempt to try to interfere in the courtship of Bessie by their son and brother, Lord Lambeth. This infringement of personal freedom and independence James was too American to present as other than outrageous or absurd; our sympathies veer sharply to the American sisters, and we support Mrs. Westgate's protest against one of the milder manifestations of the English class system. Even English hospitality seems to amount to no more than giving the visitors "a great deal of attention" (III, 271).

Taking account of the national chauvinism in the heyday of imperialism, we should not be surprised that some English readers who applauded "Daisy Miller" felt somewhat upset at having their patriotic pride and complacency disturbed in "An International Episode." The reviewer for the *Atlantic* agreed with them about the tendency of the tale but enjoyed their discomfiture: he gibed mildly at "Mr. James's premature admirers in England" and was pleased at the "refined practical joke" James had played on his English readers (III, 512). As we have seen, James, writing to his mother, reported that "many of my friends here [in London] (as I partly know and partly suspect) take it [the second half of the tale] ill of me as against my 'British entertainers.' It seems to me myself that I have been very delicate; but I shall keep off dangerous ground in future" (L II, 212-13).

There is no doubt that the tale is the work of a disinterested artist who bases his comedy on the preconceptions each nation cherishes about the other--John Bullish as well as "Yankee prejudice" (III, 275)--whether it is a naive notion about the English coastline that Bessie has gathered from the "scenery in Kingsley's novels" (III, 247) or Lord Lambeth's idea that "you Americans were always dancing" (III, 248). We are told that "it is . . . beneath the dignity of our historic muse to enumerate the trivial objects and incidents which this simple young lady . . . found so entertaining" (III, 260), but the muse is being disingenuous because the strength of the tale is precisely in the way that a vast aggregation of "trivial objects and incidents" is brought into a picture in which the patterns made by the writer give them all meaning and--for both sides of the Atlantic--a comic and salutary effect. In James's great works the pointed and witty cut and thrust of social comedy, often with some ironic satire, is a vein that offsets the moving and pathetic drama.

Chapter VIII

END OF A PHASE

The period of his first great successes, 1878-79, takes us up to the point where James starts on his first great novel. *The Portrait of a Lady* began to appear in the *Cornhill Magazine* in October 1880, and it ran until November 1881. There were other events at this time that were to change his life. In 1881 he visited America for the first time since 1875. That James himself felt that he was entering a new phase is suggested by the way in which he reviewed his life and situation in his American Journals at the end of 1881 (N 213-28). Then his mother died early in 1882, and before the end of that year his father's illness and death caused him to return to America again. With these family ties broken, he found himself confirmed in his feeling that London--or at least England--was his proper domicile. He was now financially independent and firmly rooted in his own place.

In view of these disruptions it is not surprising that James wrote little between *The Portrait* and "The Siege of London," which appeared in January 1883. After "Daisy Miller" and "An International Episode," however, there were three tales--"The Pension Beaurepas," "The Diary of a Man of Fifty," and "A Bundle of Letters"--all of which appeared in 1879, and we must also take account of "The Point of View" (1882), which is a sort of pendant to James's work of 1879.

"THE PENSION BEAUREPAS" (*Atlantic Monthly*, April 1879, 1881, [1883], 1908)

The tale opens with a declaration that James's plan is to "follow in the footsteps" of Stendhal and Balzac (III, 290). He had never before acknowledged indebtedness so explicitly, and yet his borrowing here is less direct and specific than often before; there does not seem to be any detail derived from *La Chartreuse de Parme* or *Le Père Goriot* as there was, for example, from *Hamlet* in "Master Eustace."

"The Pension Beaurepas" has several points of interest. In the Preface to *The Reverberator* James confesses his inability in his early work to do much with the American man, who was "thinkable only as the American 'business-man,'" before whom "I was absolutely and irredeemably helpless, with no fibre of my intelligence responding to his mystery" (LC II, 1203). Two years before "Beaurepas" James had made Christopher Newman (*The American*) a businessman, but we do not see him functioning in that capacity, and moreover he has vigour, intelligence, imaginative enterprise, and as much youth as James could possibly attribute to a man so successful. In "Beaurepas" James has found a solution to his problem in presenting Mr. Ruck, but the solution is not capable of much extension or development: he is the American businessman on a reluctant European tour, escorting his wife and daughter, like Mr. Evans in "Travelling Companions." He has his dry humour and a "little dry laugh" (III, 296), but little interest in foreign travel, especially as his affairs at home are struggling in a recession. His two women, voracious shoppers, keep piling up bills with no regard for his difficulties. He is a comically pathetic figure, oppressed by the assertive American Female, a common figure in James. In "An International Episode" Mrs. Westgate says, "An American woman who respects herself . . . must buy something every day of her life. If she cannot do it herself, she must send out some member of her family for the purpose" (III, 251); James had noted this earlier when, in "Newport" (1870), he wrote of the "diurnal necessity" of the conscientious American woman to "buy something" (AS 487).

Mrs. Ruck and Sophy are not very interesting, though it is possible to see the daughter as a somewhat unsympathetic Daisy Miller: she is indulged, gets her own way, and is unconscious of history and the complexities of society in Europe. Indeed the discussion of European mountains (III, 299) might remind one specifically of that of the "mountain" and perhaps that of "old castles" in "Daisy Miller" (III, 158, 162).

Aurora Church is a contrast to Sophy, and a much more significant character. She is an American who, ever since she was very young, has been kept in Europe by her earnest, socially and intellectually pretentious mother for her education, and now, perhaps partly in defiance of her mother but also because she yearns for the reputed freedom of America, she longs to return to the States. What is most interesting in Aurora is that, as she says, she has "to pretend to be very innocent, but I am not very innocent" (III, 319); she is "less submissive to her mother than she has to pretend to be" and is therefore "a sly thing" (III, 313). The question arises--though in a somewhat hyperbolic, jocular vein-- whether she is a "hypocrite" (III, 326). She says it is her mother's fault because she "has so perverted my mind that when I try to be natural I am necessarily immodest" (III, 329). She is perceptive and engagingly frank, but it is just possible to see her as a foreshadowing of the sinister Gilbert Osmond, another unsatisfactorily Europeanized American. Aurora represents a new and dramatic dimension in James's portrait of Americans; it is significant that she should appear again in "The Point of View" (1882).

The narrator is a writer, a sophisticated American observer in Geneva, and--like earlier Jamesian protagonists such as Brooke ("Travelling Companions") and Searle ("A Passionate Pilgrim")-- one who appreciates the "picturesque" (III, 292), though James does not turn this to obvious dramatic account as he did in those earlier tales. The narrator makes no discovery and suffers no major revolution, but he is sensitive and catholic enough to be fascinated instead of disconcerted by Aurora.

In "The Pension Beaurepas," as in two of the next three tales, James is gliding on a current that is flowing smoothly and broadly after "Daisy Miller." James himself wrote, "Though I have my head full of urgent ideas for other tales [and no doubt also for *The Portrait*], I have allowed myself to be diverted for the present into some other work," such as articles for the *North American Review* (L II, 215). One must not accept a writer's judgements on his own work without question, but one can accept James's statement that "Beaurepas" is "a mere pretext"; he goes on to explain: "I am pledged to write a long novel . . . and am obliged to delay it only because I can't literally afford it. . . . I have always to keep the pot a-boiling" (L II, 243). "Beaurepas" does not need much apology, however; it is a competent and creditable tale, though not written at the pitch James was now capable of.

"THE DIARY OF A MAN OF FIFTY" (*Harper's New Monthly Magazine* and *Macmillan's Magazine*, July 1879, 1879, [1880])

Before the success of *The Portrait*, where Isabel is the centre of consciousness in the way in which Winterbourne is in "Daisy Miller," James reverts to a diary, and then attempts the epistolary form.

"The Diary of a Man of Fifty" is evidence of James's growing attraction to symmetry: a middle-aged man, a bachelor and soldier, meets in Florence a young Englishman, Stanmer, who is paying attention to the beautiful wellborn daughter of a woman, now dead, who was once courted by himself. He has always believed that the mother, whom he threw over, was a "perfect coquette" and "dangerous" (III, 346), and, seeing a perfect "analogy" (III, 340, 346) between his case and the young man's, he attempts to separate the young lovers because he takes "a paternal interest" (III, 350) in the young man, who is frequently described as "young," "poor," even "little" (III, 350), as an "Englishman," and as his "companion" (III, 339, 340, 341), which suggests that the diarist has an almost morbid interest in him as a compatriot and even as a son. We soon realize that this is a more interesting case of the sort of error we saw in "Théodolinde." In the diarist's last, brief, remorseful entry, he too realizes he has been wrong in both cases, impoverishing his own life and almost ruining the now dead woman's as well, but fortunately not the young couple's, because Stanmer has defied the warning, saying, "*A fig for analogies*" (III, 359).

This is the sort of discovery that the diary form lends itself to most dramatically, but the weakness here is that the reader becomes aware of the diarist's error too soon, partly through the young woman's saying twice that her mother described the old bachelor as "a great original" (III, 343, 344), thereby suggesting her genuine affection for him and putting the analogy in question. Because we see the direction and the moral so early, the tale is rather like a cumbersome machine lumbering to its predictable ending. Both this and the reader's lack of sympathy with the protagonist, the diarist, are shortcomings that James avoided in "The Beast in the Jungle" (1903), where, with a different narrative method, the whole process of avoidance and self-discovery in John Marcher engages our sympathy and the complex situation is handled with consummate skill, bespeaking perhaps James's poignant awareness of qualities in himself of remoteness, coldness, even an egotistic blindness in the face of the affection and need of others. "The Diary of a Man of Fifty" was written long before James had the apparent suicide of Constance Fenimore Woolson to reflect on,[1] and yet some of this kind of feeling seems to inform the tale. James's affections were unfulfilled in life for the sake of his art, or perhaps the truth was that art offered his sensitive soul an escape from what Yeats calls "the fury and the mire of human veins."

"A BUNDLE OF LETTERS" (*Parisian*, December 1879, 1880)

"A Bundle" consists of nine letters written by six people in Paris; four are by Miranda Hope, a young American woman, to her mother in Bangor, Maine. In her second letter she reports her move from a hotel to a boarding-house; this might remind us again of Balzac's *Le Père Goriot*. Miranda--her name suggests an ironic contrast to Shakespeare's heroine with her imaginative response to a "brave new world"--is, says Violet Ray, a "most extraordinary specimen of artless Yankeeism" (ECT IV, 438), which is a little unkind for this variation of Daisy Miller, who is however something of a rattle-pate and somewhat devious, though in an amusing and venial way: she writes to her mother that her object in Paris is to gain "a general idea of French conversation" (ECT IV, 431) and "information" (ECT IV, 429), but she is mainly interested in the attentions of young men. Though she sends frequent coquettish messages to her hometown beau, she apparently has some sort of little affair (different from Miranda's with Ferdinand!) with a young Frenchman at the boarding-house, which no sooner reaches a certain undisclosed point than she flees, giving the German professor the occasion to call her behaviour "licentious" (ECT IV, 463). But Miranda's attitudes and antics are not interesting enough to provide a central interest.

Violet Ray, a young American with an ironic wit--she describes herself as "agreeably disappointed" (ECT IV, 437)--has intelligence and penetration, and might remind one of Aurora Church ("The Pension Beaurepas"), though she is not in the latter's dilemma. Perhaps the most interesting letter is written by Louis Leverett to his friend Harvard Trement in Boston. Leverett, "always looking out for experiences, for sensations" (ECT IV, 439) and another Jamesian American very susceptible to Europe, very different from Miranda, is an intelligent, well-read aesthete with many of the enthusiasms of James himself--Gautier, Matthew Arnold, Balzac (ECT IV, 440, 441)--and has an eye for feminine charm, but Evelyn Vane, the young Englishwoman whom he finds "delightfully picturesque" (ECT IV, 444), refers to him in her arrogantly philistine way as "a dreadful little man who is always sitting over the fire, and talking about the colour of the sky" (ECT IV, 454), which suggests that, again like James, his eloquent raptures are private and undeclared and that he thus avoids romantic involvement. Leverett is an amusing and slightly effeminate parodic portrait of James himself. Like Aurora Church ("The Pension Beaurepas") he is to reappear in "The Point of View."

What is surprising is that James, who was by 1879 very familiar with Europe and more "at home" in London (see L II, 134, 143, 217, 261) than in even New York or Boston, should still be relying on types in portraying the young Frenchman as the familiar Lothario and the German professor as stereotypically pedantic and chauvinistic. Part of the explanation may be in Edel's report that James, prevented by a blizzard from leaving Paris for Florence, "sat snugly in his hotel" and wrote this "light tale of American and European manners" "in a single sitting" (EL 249). It is a lightweight and not very satisfactorily crafted tale, written, it seems, for his friend Theodore Child to publish in the *Parisian* (see EL 249).

"THE POINT OF VIEW" (privately printed, 1882, 1883)

This tale is interesting for many reasons. It revives Aurora Church from "The Pension Beaurepas" and Louis Leverett from "A Bundle of Letters"; it resumes the epistolary mode of the latter tale, making a more satisfactorily unified whole; it repeats, amplifies, and rounds off what James had said about America in *Hawthorne* (1879).

There had been some indignation in the United States at his book on Hawthorne. Howells remarked that James "will be in some quarters promptly attainted of high treason"; he himself felt that James had laid too much stress on American provincialism.[2] The passage in James's book that probably provoked most comment was the one in which he listed all that was so important to a novelist and yet "absent from the texture of American life" in Hawthorne's time, and clearly also in 1879:

> No State, in the European sense of the word,
> and indeed barely a specific national name. No
> sovereign, no court, no personal loyalty, no
> aristocracy, no church, no clergy, no army, no
> diplomatic service, no country gentlemen, no

palaces, no castles, nor manors, nor old country-
houses, nor parsonages, nor thatched cottages nor
ivied ruins; no cathedrals, nor abbeys, nor little
Norman churches; no great Universities nor public
schools--no Oxford, nor Eton, nor Harrow; no
literature, no novels, no museums, no pictures, no
political society, no sporting class--no Epsom nor
Ascot! (LC I, 351-52)

The letter in "The Point of View" written by M. Gustave
Lejaune, of the French Academy, makes some of the same points in
complaining about the "platitude of unbalanced [American]
democracy intensified by the platitude of the spirit of commerce";
in the same spirit of exuberant hyperbole that is in the *Hawthorne*
passage, Lejaune fires off a similar fusillade of gibes: "no amenities,
no preliminaries, no manners" (ECT IV, 504), "no *salons*, no
society, no conversation," "no imagination, no sensibility, no desire
for the convent." The country itself has "no features, no objects,
no details" (ECT IV, 505); "no architecture . . ., no art, no
literature, no theatre"; "no form, no matter, no style, no general
ideas" (ECT IV, 506), and so on, in a Shandean Niagara of jocular
taunts. But Louis Leverett makes some of the same points more
soberly: "There is no form here. . . . I feel so undraped, so
uncurtained, so uncushioned" (ECT IV, 500). We know from his
journal entries that James himself had these feelings. Nevertheless,
in "The Point of View" James is replying to those who took
offence at *Hawthorne*: he is not flatly or humourlessly repeating
the high-spirited statements of 1879, but, through the variety of
opinions expressed about America in the letters in "The Point of
View," he is indicating that there are many valid opinions on the
subject and that this is one of them. It is his way of echoing
Galileo's "But it does nevertheless move."

For those who could understand, James was showing that
he was not a politician but an artist, and that like Walt Whitman,
though in a very different way, he could "contain multitudes."
Some years later James was to say in his Preface to *The Portrait of
a Lady*: "The house of fiction has . . . not one window, but a
million" (LC II, 1075). For James the task of the artist was to
convey as much as possible of the whole large and infinitely
variegated truth, which typically consists of many often
contradictory smaller truths that must all be accommodated by the
mind and imagination to give the work of art impressive order and

a beautiful pattern through their diversity. Thus James meant very seriously what he wrote in a letter of March 1879: "Nothing is my *last word* about anything" (L II, 221).

"The Point of View" allowed James to present seven diverse views of America, but, although there is some semblance of a formal ending--Aurora Church, who writes the first, writes also the last of the letters, in which she reports a surprising reversal in her mother's attitude to America--the epistolary form did not allow enough scope for his shaping imagination to create the order and pattern that should ideally emerge from the diversity of letters. This is a limitation inherent in the epistolary mode, and James never returned to it. Even the cognate method, in which a tale is told by one or more narrators, was rarely used by James in his final phase. The method he generally adopted was the one involving centres of consciousness because this allowed the material to be more thoroughly shaped and to be supplemented by the author's own creative genius.

Chapter IX

TOWARDS *THE PORTRAIT OF A LADY*

The Portrait of a Lady was the decisive and culminating achievement of James's early period. In January 1878 he was probably already projecting the novel when he wrote that "after the next six months" he would be able to devote himself to "'creative' writing" and that "then, and not till then, my real career will begin" and "I rather think I shall become a (sufficiently) great man" (L II, 151). Although by July at least he had already--but only just-- "begun" the novel (L II, 179), a year later, in June 1879, he was still referring to the novel "which I am waiting to write, and which, begun sometime since, has remained an aching fragment" (L II, 244). However, his career had been gathering to a greatness for over a decade, and before the end of 1880 *The Portrait* had been launched and its greatness was patent.

Our main purpose in this chapter is to follow James's progress through the early tales towards *The Portrait*, but we shall first discuss, though somewhat cursorily, the five novels that James wrote in the 1870s to show how different they are from the great novel that marked the end of his apprenticeship and also to help give substance to our argument that James carried out in the early tales rather than in the early novels the significant experiments that were to bear fruit in *The Portrait*.

Not much need be said about the first novel, *Watch and Ward* (1871). It is a rather flaccid tale about a 29-year-old man's adoption of a young, tragically orphaned twelve-year-old girl and their eventual marriage. The narrative is filled out with obvious formal contrasts, does not altogether avoid mawkishness and melodrama, and is so full of stereotypes that many critics have claimed a great number of sources for the novel, such as novels by Oliver Wendell Holmes, George Sand's *La Mare au Diable*, the

Pygmalion myth,[1] Jane Austen's *Mansfield Park*, and, especially, Charlotte M. Yonge's *The Heir of Redclyffe*, which James, in the revised edition of 1878, goes out of his way to have the young orphan read aloud to her guardian--her "twentieth perusal of the classic tale"--whose falling asleep after a dozen pages provides evidence that the author of *Watch and Ward* is not without a sense of humour.[2] Since James singled out *The Heir of Redclyffe* for mention as one of the best of "these semi-developed" but "charming" novels that "almost legitimate themselves by the force of genius" (LC I, 826), we are tempted to view *Watch and Ward* as James's effort to develop fully the situation of Yonge's novel; both are stories involving guardians, orphans, sets of good and bad cousins, marriages, and attacks of fever crucial to the plot.

Watch and Ward, moreover, seems almost to be the wish-fulfilment of a man conscious of an inadequate sex drive. It is not informed with any of James's real interests and is developed so conventionally that it is devoid of technical interest. The novel might have found a vital centre if, for example, the young girl, Nora, had been in some sense a forerunner of Maisie (*What Maisie Knew*, 1897), a centre of consciousness, in whom the process of self-discovery had been made dramatic, but "Guest's Confession" (1872) was not yet written, and we get not much more from Nora than "If I'm wiser now, I've learnt wisdom at my cost" (N 71-80, 160). It is not surprising that James virtually disowned the novel. It is a singularly flabby multiple "borrowing" in which James appears to be at every step of the way writing to a formula.

Roderick Hudson (1875) is a very different affair, and it was the earliest novel to find its way into the New York Edition. James brought into it material from subjects very important to him, such as Italy, art, and the provincialism of New England. One feels some of the reverberations of what had been achieved in, for instance, "At Isella" (1871), "The Madonna of the Future" (1873), and "The Last of the Valerii" (1874), and in making Rowland Mallet a centre of consciousness and of moral scruples he is developing the art that went to the depiction of Longmore in "Mme. de Mauves" (1874). But that he still had not realized the full potential of this method James himself admitted in the Preface of the New York Edition of *Roderick Hudson*: "The centre of interest throughout 'Roderick' is in Rowland Mallet's consciousness" (LC II, 1050), whereas the obvious intention of the young James in writing the novel was to put Roderick and his failure as an artist at the centre.

James could hardly have written *Roderick Hudson* without being conscious of Hawthorne's Roman novel, *The Marble Faun*, and we suggest that he borrowed as well from the English Romantic poets Keats and Shelley, whose works he knew and admired. Both Keats's "Lamia" and Shelley's "Alastor" offer parallels to the threesome of Roderick Hudson, Rowland Mallet, and Christina Light. Keats's Lamia, a lovely vampire--something like the imagination or even like art itself--with no evil intent makes a dead set at, seduces, and brings disaster to Lycius, the artist manqué, but it is Apollonius, Lycius's "trusty guide / And good instructor" (lines 375-76), who, in exorcising Lamia through his "cold philosophy" (line 230), actually brings about his death. James's Christina Light, like Lamia, is described as "a phantasm, a vapor, an illusion," and (in the revised version of *Roderick Hudson*) as a "vampire." Roderick, seemingly a version of Lycius, on realizing that he has lost Christina declares that his inspiration "is dead." Rowland, who has "sprung from a rigid Puritan stock," is a kind of Apollonius in that he is instrumental in banishing Christina (see N 71-80, 172, 229, 355, 363-65).[3]

More significant perhaps is the similarity between the novel and Shelley's "Alastor." In "Alastor" there are two protagonists: the sorrowing Wordsworthian narrator and the visionary poet whose dream vision leads him to ignore the sanctions of human love in a vain quest for a reunion with the lovely dream figure, who is something like a muse, uniting the reason, the imagination, and the senses. Finally, the visionary poet, in despair, meets his death on a "grey precipice," "the edge" of a "vast mountain" (lines 573, 571), bitterly mourned by the narrator, who has earlier seemed to blame him for ignoring his human obligations. It is difficult to ignore the connection of Rowland Mallet, "trudging . . . over half Switzerland" carrying "a volume of Wordsworth in his pocket," with the Wordsworthian narrator of "Alastor." The temptation to see in the dead Roderick Hudson, "at the bottom of the cliff," something of the lost poet of "Alastor" is similarly compelling: "He had fallen from a great height, but he was singularly little disfigured." Mary Garland, Roderick's neglected fiancée, may be considered James's version of the faithful but ignored "Arab maiden" (line 129) of "Alastor," and, finally, Christina Light, something like the "veiled maid" (line 151) in "Alastor," has ceased to exist for Roderick long before his plunge to his death (see N 71-80, 468, 509).

But how seriously can we take Shelley's visionary as a poet

and Roderick as a sculptor? That both desert their calling to pursue seductive female figures provides drama, of course; Keats, Shelley, and now James are all developing, somewhat ambivalently, the Wordsworthian idea that the artist who withdraws into the Palace of Art, "Housed in a dream, at distance from the Kind!" ("Elegiac Stanzas," line 54), may desert not only his art but his human responsibilities as well. What makes this especially interesting for us is that in *Roderick Hudson* James seems to have borrowed from Keats and Shelley, but in borrowing he follows his patterns too uncritically; he does not really take possession of what he borrows, nor does he make his story convincing. There might even be some truth in saying that, in 1875, he could still be somewhat indiscriminate in his borrowing. In *The Portrait* it would be different.

In *The American* (1877) James used a large canvas to expatiate on the genial irony that had earlier been felt, for instance, in "Mme. de Mauves" (1874). In the opening sentences he has Christopher Newman, whose name proclaims his representative status, "reclining at his ease" with "his legs outstretched" in the Louvre. Robert Emmet Long has noticed that "Guest's Confession" (1872) anticipates the novel in that Crawford foreshadows the "type" of Newman and the narrator "destroys an incriminating document rather than . . . use it for coercive purposes,"[4] just as Newman does. But with Newman's courtship and his conflict with the woman's aristocratic French family, the novel is soon weighed down, its virtues compromised by international stereotypes, in particular the hidebound arrogance of the French family--only slightly less extravagant and immoral than that of the French family in "Mme. de Mauves"--which leads James to sentimental melodrama in the dénouement. As James says in his Preface to *The American*: "The great house of Bellegarde . . . would, I now feel, given the circumstances . . . have comported itself in a manner as different as possible from the manner to which my narrative commits it" (LC II, 1065); even though *The American* is a romance, an aspect that James gives great prominence to in the Preface, this does not allow one to condone the crudity of the stereotypes. Moreover, there are no notable technical advances in *The American*: the narrator makes us too aware of Newman's often amusing limitations to be able to use him as a centre of consciousness that can absorb and carry the reader along in profound sympathy.

There is still no technical experimentation in *The*

Europeans (1878) but a much more equitable and convincing poise between the American and the European parties in this short novel. There is detached amusement at the expense of the Americans that does not exclude affection and even some admiration. This is not altogether unlike the treatment of Newman in *The American*, but the Europeans are new: there is spontaneity and sincerity in Felix that has a positive moral value, and the degree of corruption in his sister Eugenia, the Baroness, is well within the bounds of familiar human weakness and quite different from that of the French family in *The American*. It is as if James had learnt, in "Four Meetings" (1877) and "Daisy Miller" (1878), to rely on a less simple moral scheme, to portray the more heinous faults as well as the virtues of Americans and also the virtues and the charms of Europeans as well as their corruption. The virtuosity with which James plays on these combinations and contrasts gives *The Europeans* its comedy and charm, and it heightens our sense of James's discernment and even-handedness.

It is difficult to give an enthusiastic account of *Confidence* (1879), like "Longstaff's Marriage" a weak performance in between such impressive achievements as "Daisy Miller," *The Europeans, The Portrait*, and, a little later, *Washington Square*. The novel does not rise from any of James's familiar sources of inspiration-- Italy, art, the international comedy of manners--and we do not see any significant relationship between it and the tales he wrote about this time. It may be that it has its origin in more purely intellectual concepts and contrasts. James was inclined to see as antipathetic to art and the highest civilization a theoretical logic, an emphasis on consistency, and an austerity belonging to the exact sciences that he associated with the German mind. William had insisted to Henry, the lover of French culture and Italy, that German literature was more "classical and cosmopolitan" than either English or French,[5] a proposition that Henry obviously resisted. Moreover, in Paris in 1876 James had seen a good deal of C. S. Peirce, a colleague and friend of William's, who was a logician and physicist and whose work was much admired in Germany. In *Confidence* these Germanic qualities seem to be represented by Gordon Wright, who, when he is introduced to the reader, is "living in Germany" (N 71-80, 1051). Tintner suggests that there is some reflection of Peirce in Winterbourne ("Daisy Miller," 1878), and some of the associated ideas seem to be at play in *The Europeans* (1878) where James has Eugenia say that "one's reason is dismally flat. It's a bed with a mattress removed" (N 71-80, 1033).

Confidence Gordon Wright, with his "honest and serious visage" (N 71-80, 1087), is in contrast to Bernard, whose French-sounding surname, Longueville, might evoke some of the poetic fancy and fun of *Love's Labour's Lost* and who in at least one important respect is like James himself in having "a nature which seemed at several points to contradict itself" (N 71-80, 1042). Perhaps it is not too fanciful to suggest that James is contrasting two approaches to life, the French and the German, his own and William's.

It is difficult to quarrel with Leon Edel's verdict that *Confidence* is James's worst novel. He suggests that "its plot is like an old eighteenth century comedy."[6] The novel's two pairs of lovers, we are tempted to add, bear some slight resemblance to the various sets of lovers in *Love's Labour's Lost, Much Ado about Nothing, Two Gentlemen of Verona,* and *The Taming of the Shrew.* (James's original note specifies the name of one of the two central female characters as "Bianca"; the name as eventually applied to the other young woman is "Blanche.") As finally written, the story is--perhaps as a result of James's failure of nerve or his need for "that which is bread"--a complete turnaround from the "violence" (James's word) of the original dénouement sketched in his notebook, in which James has one of his two young men forbid his friend to marry the heroine, because, although married to another, "he himself has been *always* in love with her." Later he reveals that "he is free--that his wife is dead . . . . It is left to be supposed . . . that he has himself been the means of his wife's death." The heroine "guesses the horrible truth" and "flings herself . . . into a religious life." The hero "is left with" his friend "and with the latter's terrible secret" (N 8). Susan Coolidge, writing in *The Literary World* (April 10, 1880), unerringly detects the lurid melodrama that underlies the jumble of James's comedy, in which both couples apparently live happily ever after: "In real life," Coolidge writes, "such an imbroglio would have terminated in murder or the mad-house."[7] This deliberate matching of various opposites in such a patently contrived intellectual structure perhaps accounts for the failure of the novel, which has little in common with *The Portrait.*

All James's successes in the tales and novels he wrote in the fifteen years between 1864 and 1879 lead to *The Portrait,* which is the chest in which the sweets compacted lie. To trace James's "step by step evolution" through the tales written between 1864 and 1879 that led up to *The Portrait* we have somewhat arbitrarily chosen eight routes, some of which run close together and at times coincide. For convenience we use these headings: Borrowings, Romance and Realism, Even-handedness in the International Theme, Innocence, Methods of Narration, Moral Dilemmas, Discovery, and Tone. The differences between the total effect of *The Portrait* and the early novels are no doubt too numerous and complex to be captured completely, but some clarification can be achieved by this sort of analysis.

In James's borrowings we find a fairly clear progression. It is concisely described by Adeline Tintner as an advance from "a one-to-one" correspondence to "a freer, more subtle, and more generalized attitude" (TBW 4). In the borrowings from Chaucer in "A Tragedy of Error" (1864) and from *Hamlet* in "The Story of a Year" (1865) the likenesses are the result of something like stencilling--even if upside down--from the originals. Even in "Master Eustace" (1871) and "Guest's Confession" (1872) the borrowings are explicit and direct, though we must not ignore the intervening "A Light Man" (1869), in which the correspondences are ingenious and intricate.

In his excellent analysis of James's indebtedness to Hawthorne, Richard H. Brodhead describes his borrowings (from Mérimée's "*La Vénus d'Ille*" as well as from Hawthorne's *Our Old House* and *The Marble Faun*) in "A Passionate Pilgrim" (1871) and "The Last of the Valerii" (1874) as "more assertive,"[8] that is, less direct and docile. In "Professor Fargo" (1874), "Eugene Pickering" (1874), and "Benvolio" (1875) the borrowings are much less direct, and, in fact, so unobtrusive that they might escape notice in a first reading.

In *The Portrait* the borrowings are so general that there are no specific clues at all; indeed only a familiarity with the main features of sources such as George Eliot's *Middlemarch* and *Daniel Deronda*[9] will bring the borrowing home to the reader. What this change indicates is that, whereas in the more direct borrowing the writer has manipulated and reorganized the plot and perhaps some of the motives in the original in order to make comparatively superficial alterations, in the later, more general borrowing the source has been internalized to a greater extent and the situation of, say, Dorothea in *Middlemarch* or Gwendoline in *Daniel Deronda* is fundamentally reassessed and stated in new terms. It is now less a borrowing than it is a theft; certainly it is artistically more satisfactory and complete.

In general there is a movement from romance to realism.

James was always drawn to romance; even his last works are suffused with a romantic aura. Of course, "romance" means many things. In his Preface to *The American* James described the writing of romance as a cutting of the cable so that the balloon of the imagination is no longer tied to the earth (LC II, 1064). But this circumscription is so loose that it could apply to a great deal of fiction. By "romance" we mean here the kind of tales that James specifically called romances: "The Romance of Certain Old Clothes" (1868) and "De Grey: A Romance" (1868), in which there is an element of the supernatural or inexplicable, and tales in which the consciousness of mundane reality is suspended by a gulf in time, as in "Gabrielle de Bergerac" (1869), which is set in pre-Revolutionary France. James moved away from this kind of romance and toward, not the mundane, but the more familiar and the contemporary. This shift offered less latitude for the more obviously wonderful and sensational and moved toward a strangeness that one might call psychological and moral in "Master Eustace" (1871) and "Guest's Confession" (1872). Realism is not intrinsically superior to Romance, but James's early romances, without the weight of Hawthorne's moral fables in the same genre, are inferior in that they offer an easy escape from life. By 1878 James is writing "Daisy Miller," which he subtitles "A Study"; it is a study from life.

There was a European--especially French--movement in literature towards Realism at this time. When James emigrated to Paris in 1875, he was drawn to Flaubert and his circle, where he met Zola, among others; when he was admitted to the *cénacle* he told his friend Perry, "*Je suis lancé en plein Olympe*" (EL 185), though there may have been a touch of irony in this boast. James honoured Flaubert as an artist, but he vehemently rejected what he saw as the morbid and sordid "realism" of the art of these Frenchmen, which he felt produced only disgust and dullness. James continued his pursuit of the strange--for example, in the fantastic and sterile egotism of Gilbert Osmond and in the spell that he could cast over an intelligent young American woman.

Closely related to James's treatment of the strange in his early romances is his portrayal of foreigners, especially the French and Italians. It is not only distance in time that gives romantic licence, but also distance in space. American readers were perhaps ready, in the period just after the Civil War, before Europe became well known to them, to accept somewhat extravagant stereotypes, especially of the European upper class. This is certainly what we find not only in "Gabrielle de Bergerac" (1869), but in fiction set in contemporary Europe: "A Passionate Pilgrim" (1871), "At Isella" (1871), "The Last of the Valerii" (1874), and even works as late as "Mme. de Mauves" (1875) and *The American* (1877). James's residence in Europe (from the end of 1875) and perhaps the prospect of being published in England, as well as his greater maturity as an artist, brought into his fiction a more balanced and convincing view of Europeans vis-à-vis Americans. One notices for the first time in "Four Meetings" (1877) that the "villain," Caroline Spencer's cousin, is an American, though an American Europeanized. This is more marked in "Daisy Miller" (1878), where it is the women of the American society in Rome who ostracize Daisy and bring about the tragedy. These are the forerunners of Mme. Merle and Gilbert Osmond, the renegade Americans and arch-villains of *The Portrait*, where the Europeans, such as Mr. Bantling and Lord Warburton, though perhaps ineffectual or effete in contrast to vigorous and confident Americans (Caspar Goodwood and Henrietta), are charming and humane. Again, it is in the tales rather than in the novels that James first achieves this advance.

It is not only in the arrangement of his plots that James borrowed. Under the rubric of even-handedness we can identify a quality that he learned or at least shared with his models. We refer to his ambivalence, his ability to see all round a question and put many--sometimes opposed--points of view. He found this in Hawthorne, who was, for instance, both "conscious of hereditary sympathies" with the English and at the same time "thrown upon his national antagonism by some acrid quality in the moral atmosphere" of England.[10] Moreover, in the world in general, Hawthorne saw good and evil as inextricably mixed. Part of what James described as the "deeper psychology" that he admired in Hawthorne may be seen in Miles Coverdale's comments on "the process by which godlike benevolence has been debased into all-devouring egotism," and the fact that "from the very gate of heaven there is a by-way to the pit."[11] A similar quality is conspicuous in another of James's models, Ivan Turgenev, who was also a dear friend. James found Turgenev's talk full of "justesse" (L II, 20), and he admired the "impartial justice" (LC II, 985) in, for example, *Fathers and Sons*. It was a part of Turgenev's "meditative and forgiving irony."[12] Turgenev exclaimed in a letter written almost ten years after *Fathers and Sons*, "God only knows whether I loved [Bazarov] or hated him."[13]

What James wrote of Turgenev applies aptly to himself: "He felt and understood the opposite sides of life" (LC II, 1010). Not only their talents and temperaments but even their limitations were similar: Turgenev told James that he "had never *invented* anything or any one" (L II, 26), and Edmund Wilson agrees, saying he was "not one of the great inventors."[14]

This even-handedness is related to the theme of innocence also. In early James the Innocent appears in many forms. The first of these is the landscape-painter, Locksley (1866), who is intelligent, generous, and naive--easy prey for a sharp young woman living in a remote part of the country and eager to enjoy city life with a wealthy husband. But when we come to the "international" tales--"A Passionate Pilgrim" (1871), "Mme. de Mauves" (1874), and "Eugene Pickering" (1874), we find that the theme, with all its pathos, has become involved with international issues: the Innocent is generally a young, naive American who becomes the victim of corrupt or designing Europeans. This is in the main true of the novels *Roderick Hudson* (1875) and *The American* (1877). But in his tales James has begun to diversify and enlarge this theme. In "The Sweetheart of M. Briseux" (1873) the young and naive girl is English, and she liberates herself by her own perception and initiative; in "Professor Fargo" (1874), the innocent is an American, but not a young man; he is old enough to be the father of a young girl, and both father and daughter are exploited by an American charlatan. In "Daisy Miller" (1878) the victim is again an unsophisticated young woman, but she is not by any means a passive victim. James starts with a fairly simple stereotyped formula, but gradually diversifies the theme until it becomes a tale with many different kinds of exploitation and universal implications. Isabel is the innocent in *The Portrait*, but the story of her capture is far from simple, and her fate is one that she does not merely submit to; she accepts it. Unlike the pathetically defenceless Caroline in "Four Meetings" (1877) she remains unvanquished. James's later innocents would typically be young women--e.g., Verena (*The Bostonians*, 1885), Maisie (*What Maisie Knew*, 1897), Milly (*The Wings of the Dove*, 1902), and Maggie (*The Golden Bowl*, 1904)--and all in some degree perhaps avatars of James's loved and long-dead cousin, Minnie Temple, but they are all different and their cases very complex, involving histories, social nuances, and the "deeper psychology."

We have discussed James's experiments in narration in previous chapters, but this aspect is so important in his development that it will bear brief treatment again here. After "The Story of a Year" (1865) James tried persistently to get away from the mode of simple, omniscient third-person narration; it was too free and easy, something like--to adapt Robert Frost's witty observation about rhyme--playing tennis without a net. In any case, James wanted to come closer to inner sensations and velleities and to convey them with the immediacy that comes with first-person narration. For this reason he tried the diary form--"A Landscape-Painter" (1866), "A Light Man" (1869), and "The Diary of a Man of Fifty" (1879)-- and letters--"A Bundle of Letters" (1879) and "The Point of View" (1882)--but in their strictest form these devices preclude hints and suggestions from the author that can lead and guide the reader's reactions and give clearer shape and form to the tale. An alternative was to have a narrator tell the story from beginning to end, as in "My Friend Bingham" (1867), "A Passionate Pilgrim" (1871), "The Ghostly Rental" (1876), and "Four Meetings" (1871). This device gives scope to very subtle effects and comes much closer to what James wanted. But when James makes Winterbourne not the narrator but a centre of consciousness in "Daisy Miller" (1878), he has the best of both, or indeed of all, worlds: there is the immediacy of Winterbourne's experience, especially the intensity of his embarrassments and dilemmas, and the flexibility that allows the author with unobtrusive omniscience to represent the thoughts of other and absent characters and to offer his own comments. Thus we have the views of Winterbourne, who is an interesting character in himself, but also other perspectives, and an inclusive view which gives us the satisfaction of feeling that we have completely understood all the bearings of the action and apprehended the formal completeness of the tale. This is the method that James employed in *The Portrait*: Isabel is the centre of consciousness. It is her perceptions and awareness that we are concerned with throughout, even though there are scenes of which she has no knowledge; the reader goes through her experience with (or just ahead of) her.

James's success in getting close to and even inside a character's actual experience gives high relief to a feature of drama that Aristotle saw was most important--the moment of discovery, when the protagonist's view of his situation or of himself suddenly changes. When fully developed, the change is not merely one of physical fortune but involves moral and spiritual depths as well. In Max Austin ("A Light Man," 1869) the change is one of these deep-seated transformations, but James--through the diarist, Austin himself--gives us only glimpses of the unreformed man and only the consequences of the change, not the change itself. In "Travelling Companions," a year later, the change in the narrator is almost as complete, involving aesthetic attitudes, and deep enough to make him ready for a love relationship that will embrace both the sacred and the profane. But again the change is only perfunctorily dealt with in the tale. It is not until "Guest's Confession" (1872) that James attempts to convey the experience of the actual conversion itself, the moment when the narrator is moved to abjure blackmail and appeal to Guest's goodwill and generosity.

In *The Portrait* this discovery comes to Isabel in Chapter 42, during the long vigil in which she reviews her situation and begins to face up to unpalatable truths; her whole life changes. This kind of scene--another example is Maggie's perception when she is on the terrace at night at Fawns in Chapter 36 of *The Golden Bowl*--becomes more important and central in James's fiction not only because it makes an effective dramatic crisis--he was to realize that he must "dramatise" (LC II, 1241, 1244, 1253, 1267, 1269, 1272)--but also because, true to what he inherited from New England and admired in Hawthorne, he came more and more to deal with moral dilemmas in his protagonists and with the "deeper psychology." This sort of crisis crops up in "The Story of a Year" (1865), but Lizzie virtually avoids it; in "Poor Richard" (1867) Richard tells his lie without premeditation, almost spontaneously, and then remorse brings about a change in him. In "Mme. de Mauves" (1874), Longmore ponders his difficult situation at length, but it doesn't come to a very dramatic head or point; in "Four Meetings" (1877) there are very subtle effects, but it is only by implication that we realize that the narrator is facing his moral crisis, and in "The Diary of a Man of Fifty" (1879) it is not until the last brief entry in the diary that the protagonist suddenly grasps his tragic error and writes, "God forgive me, how the questions come crowding in!" (ECT IV, 425). Throughout the early tales we can watch James dealing with some form or other of this inner moral struggle, but it is in "Guest's Confession" (1872) that he first places it in a spotlight, though the handling of it is somewhat conventional and stagy. By the time he writes *The Portrait* he treats this key passage of discovery with consummate skill and gives it a high and dramatic definition.

The last of the aspects that we have chosen to follow

through the early tales in order to find its apogee in *The Portrait* is the most difficult to indicate, isolate, and define. We have called it "tone"; another term might be "nuance." It is not difficult to find passages that exhibit the distinctive Jamesian quality; in fact it declares itself in the opening paragraphs of *The Portrait of a Lady*,[15] which describe the scene on "the lawn of an old English country-house" owned by the American, Mr. Touchett.

There is mention of a number of details that we associate with cultivation--afternoon tea, the delightful situation, the "smooth, dense turf," the "sense of leisure," "desultory talk," the "old man sitting in a deep wicker-chair," "two younger men strolling to and fro," the "long gabled front of red brick" with its ivy and creeper, the house's history, the "privacy," and so on. The three men are presumably prominent figures in the novel; there is not the slightest suggestion that these men, though wealthy, are greedy capitalists or selfish recluses, and we shall be surprised if their behaviour is not that of cultivated gentlemen, matching the setting. In fact we are likely to surmise that they are free to try to shape their lives according to their ideal conceptions.

While all this is true, it is not the main point. Even more immediate to us than our sense of the characters is our sense of the authorial voice. The relaxed, benevolent, polished tone of this voice is an assurance not only that we are in highly civilized company but that the moral judgements that are implicit (as they always are in even the simplest narrative) will be humane. It is the manner of speech of someone who not only values the beauty and the serenity in the scene he describes but also embodies qualities that we respect. He is humane and charming as well, and "charm" is a quality that James rated very highly in his literary criticism.

In the last paragraph of his book on Hawthorne, published in 1879, James wrote, "He combined . . . the spontaneity of the imagination with a haunting care for moral problems," and all this was embodied in his "charming art" (LC I, 457. See also, e.g., LC I, 368, 409). We feel Richard H. Brodhead is wrong to say that the word "charm" becomes "a kind of traitor's kiss" in James's book.[16] In common usage "charm" does not have the virtue that James invests it with. He meant much more than having "on the surface . . . many little flowers and knots of ribbon" (LC II, 1011). The last sentence of James's first review (1866) of a novel--*Felix Holt*--by George Eliot, for whom he always had great admiration, ends by referring to "the charm which such gifts as hers . . . are sure to exercise" (LC I, 912); for James her gifts included a firm grasp of moral values. For all his veneration of Balzac, whom he saluted as "the father of us all" (LC II, 120), James felt bound in 1875 to say that, though the great French novelist was "a final authority upon human nature," he "has against him that he lacks that slight but needful thing--charm" (LC II, 68).   One might observe that a needful thing can scarcely be slight.

In the opening pages of *The Portrait*, as generally in the mature James, the humanity is closely linked with the charm. Whereas in the opening of *Roderick Hudson* (1875) one feels James attempting a little nervously or strenuously to maintain a vein of fanciful wit--when Rowland's cousin Cecilia married, he "had seemed to feel the upward sweep of the empty bough from which the golden fruit had been plucked" (N 71-80, 167)--now in *The Portrait* we are aware of no strain, only an apparently easy suavity and grace.   Part of the charm is in the gentle irony that in the first sentence describes afternoon tea as a "ceremony"; it is also a "little feast" to which an hour is "dedicated," for which "implements" are provided, and which "votaries" attend.   This is amusing, but it is more than that.   It is clear that the narrator enjoys this sort of occasion, and this is an engaging quality in him, but the comic exaggeration also demonstrates that he is aware that, in the scale of human capacity and experience, the taking of afternoon tea is relatively unimportant.   The vastness of that scale is indicated by the playful, ironic solemnity with which afternoon tea is compared, but in reality contrasted, with a religious service and its "ceremony" and "votaries."   This playfulness indicates that the narrator has a well established sense of values.   There is a place in his consciousness for things of the spirit and intellect as well as for physical comforts such as afternoon tea.

One of the young men strolling to and fro "from time to time, as he passed, looked with a certain attention at the elder man."   This is Ralph Touchett showing concern for his father.   We do not know their names yet, but we see that a young man is attending to a senior, who may be an invalid.   We notice and applaud this kindness, but the point is that the narrator remarks on it, choosing this unsensational detail, presented quite without sentimentality, and chosen from many others that might have taken its place, thus showing that he puts a value on human affection and loving-kindness.   It is another sign of the narrator's values, confirming what we have gleaned from what might be taken for a mere description of the setting.

James treats the base characters in a manner consistent with this tone. They are dealt with politely, almost with ceremony, and we see them, at first at least, somewhat obliquely, catching their baseness only in glimpses and hints. He gives no obvious handholds to enable us to grasp their real nature. Early in their acquaintanceship Mme. Merle tells Isabel, "When you have lived as long as I, you will see that every human being has his shell, and that you must take the shell into account."[17] This sounds "metaphysical" and impressive, and yet it contains within it the clues to all Mme. Merle's cynicism and treachery. Even as perceptive an observer as Ralph can at first say nothing worse of her--with only a touch of irony--than that "she does everything beautifully. She is complete."[18] James has come a long way from the melodrama of *The American*, written no more than four years earlier. Evil is now like Milton's serpent, which had a "shape" that was "pleasing" and "lovely" and speech that "glozed."[19] Isabel is a modern Eve, but her doom is far less unmistakably foretold. In *Roderick Hudson*, on the other hand, there are signs of Roderick's shortcomings and foreshadowings of his failure when we meet him in the very first chapter.

The tone is distinctively Jamesian: suave, meditative, mandarin, tolerant, ironical, amused, but also morally sensitive and sure. It has been developing throughout the period we are studying, and will be found emerging in the novels as well as the tales written between 1864 and 1879. Consider, for example, the amusement in the opening paragraphs of *The American*, the irony in "all weak-kneed lovers of the fine arts" and the hero's "profound enjoyment of his [comfortable] posture" on a divan while he stares, apparently indifferently, at "Murillo's beautiful moon-borne Madonna," or take the first paragraph of *The Europeans*, a year later, in which a bored and disconsolate foreign lady contemplates from a Boston hotel "the ineffectual refreshment of a dull, moist snow-fall," while the calendar indicates that "the blessed vernal season is already six weeks old." But if one goes back to, say, "The Story of a Year" (1865), one will find little but the rudiments of that vein. The style is not infelicitous, but it is comparatively matter-of-fact and flat: "In early May, two years ago, a young couple I wot of strolled homeward from an evening walk, a long ramble among the peaceful hills which inclosed their rustic home" (I, 20); there is a self-conscious note in "I wot of" and a suspicion of cliché in "rustic home" and even perhaps in "strolled homeward from an evening walk." In "Poor Richard" (1867) one finds, we suggest, some of the first clear hints of what was to come:

"Edmund Severn was a man of eight-and-twenty, who, having for some time combated fortune and his own inclinations as a mathematical tutor in a second-rate country-college, had, on the opening of the war, transferred his valour to a more heroic field" (I, 138); we can feel something of the ironic but humane play of the mind of the narrator.

It is clearer still in "Mme. de Mauves" (1874). Euphemia "had been placed for her education, twelve years before, in a Parisian convent, by a widowed mamma, fonder of Homburg and Nice than of letting out tucks in the frocks of a vigorously growing daughter. Here, besides various elegant accomplishments--the art of wearing a train, of composing a bouquet, of presenting a cup of tea--she acquired a certain turn of the imagination which might have passed for a sign of precocious worldliness" (II, 289). Here we are very much aware of authorial comment applying familiar satirical criticisms to trivial aims of girls' education. The target is a little too obvious to sustain much more in this vein, but we certainly feel the activity of a mind in the narration, though a less subtle activity than in *The Portrait*, where all the effects, never melodramatic, culminate in tragedy.

It is clear that James's early tales have considerable importance in his development, and this is really no more than what James himself told William, whom he took into his confidence more than anyone else, in a letter of November 1878: "I have a constant impulse to try experiments of form, in which I wish to not run the risk of wasting or gratuitously using big situations. But to these I am coming now" (L II, 193). He clearly implies that it is the experiments he has conducted in the tales that have brought him to the point where he can embark with confidence on his first master-piece. After his "step by step evolution" (LII, 194), he would now achieve the brilliance that has been so widely recognized in *The Portrait*.

NOTES AND SELECTED REFERENCES

Preface

[1] See the Introduction to our edition of *The Finer Grain* (Delmar, New York: Scholars' Facsimiles & Reprints, 1986), pp. v-xxix.

Introduction
THE YOUNG MAN AND THE EARLY TALES

[1] See, e.g., A 20, 31, 53, 57, 67, 89, 113, 135, 137, 149, 172, 185, 188, 198, 261, 262, 273, 317, 337, 339, 367, 428, 437, 456, 457, 493, 551, 557, 569. James had what Robert C. Le Clair calls a "speech defect," apparently only a stammer, which does not seem to have been very marked and which he overcame, but it may have been both a cause and an effect of shyness (*Young Henry James* [New York: Bookman Associates, 1955], p. 43).

[2] See L II, 240, and Leon Edel, *Henry James, The Conquest of London: 1870-1881* (New York: Avon Books, 1978), p. 325.

[3] Jean Strouse, *Alice James: A Biography* (Boston: Houghton Mifflin, 1984), p. 25, quoting a letter of 23 January 1874 from Mary, Henry's mother, to William, her eldest son, which must have had the effect of playing on fraternal rivalry and possible jealousy. In 1882, after the death of his wife, Henry Senior told James that, of all their children, he was "the one that has cost us the least trouble, and given us always the most delight" (JF 129).

[4] *Young Henry James*, p. 109.

[5] Strouse, *Alice James*, p. 26. In a letter of 24 July 1869, his mother apostrophizes James: "You dear reasonable over-conscientious soul!" (JF 258).

[6] Strouse, *Alice James*, p. 29.

[7] Edel says that these titles "reflect Henry's need to put himself into the forefront" (EL 17), but we suggest that, although the volumes are really autobiographies, James's original declared motive -- to publish a memoir of his brother (see A vii) -- and the titles he eventually settled on both point the other way, to his habitual diffidence, under which nevertheless flourished a Napoleonic ego. As Matthiessen says, James's is "one of the least self-centered autobiographies on record" (JF 72).

[8] *Henry James, The Master: 1901-1916* (New York: Avon Books, 1978), p. 448. James had hoped to give prominence to Alice too in his *Autobiography* but found only a "meagre provision" of her letters available (LL II, 290); like William, James believed Alice's journal constituted "a new claim for the family renown" (L III, 481).

[9] *Italian Hours* (New York: Grove Press, 1979), p. 72.

10 *Henry James, The Untried Years: 1843-1870* (New York: Avon Books, 1978), p. 198.

11 Introduction to *The Complex Fate* by Marius Bewley (London: Chatto and Windus, 1952), p. xiii.

12 Edward Nehls, ed., *D.H. Lawrence: A Composite Biography* (Madison: University of Wisconsin Press, 1957-59), II, 414.

13 Robert Emmet Long, *Henry James: The Early Novels* (Boston: Twayne Publishers, 1983), pp. 7-8.

14 Tales include short stories and nouvelles, such as "Daisy Miller," which are to be distinguished from short novels, such as *The Europeans*.

Chapter I
UNPUBLISHED TRANSLATIONS AND THE FIRST SIX TALES, 1860-67

1 Philip Grover, *Henry James and the French Novel: A Study in Inspiration* (London: Paul Elek, 1973), p. 193.

2 *The Early Development of Henry James* (Urbana: University of Illinois Press, 1965 [1930]), p. 154.

3 "*La Vénus d'Ille's*" Greek epigraph, from Lucian's dialogue "Lovers of Life, or the Disbeliever," is perhaps evidence of this. The relevant passage may be interpreted in part as "May the statue be kind and beneficent." The reference is to a nocturnally ambulant statue of the general Pellichos which is supposed to have the power to inflict and cure the ague. The sceptic Tychiadas speaks the passage as part of an ironic prayer upon hearing of its reputedly miraculous powers. We thank our colleague R.L. Fowler for tracking down the quotation. See Prosper Mérimée, *"Carmen" précédée de "La Vénus d'Ille" et de "Colomba,"* introd. Marcel Thiebaut, 2nd ed. (Monaco: Editions du Rocher, 1947), p. 117.

4 See our essay, "The Provenience of Henry James's First Tale," *Studies in Short Fiction* 24 (Winter 1987): 57-58.

5 See Le Clair, *Young Henry James*, p. 358. We shall have occasion to refer to F.J. Child again in our discussion of "Poor Richard" and "Longstaff's Marriage."

6 *Selected Essays* (London: Faber, 1951), p. 206.

7 There is another distinction. One should not assume that James borrows or steals the initial idea, situation, or *donnée* of any of his tales. It is likely that generally he had a concept of his own, and in developing this found that he was treating a theme that was analogous to that of a literary classic--*Hamlet*, St. Augustine's *Confessions*, or *The Merchant of Venice*. He would then, as it were, ride piggy-back on his model or in tandem with his master, giving the theme a new twist or direction. As Hubert says in *Watch and Ward*: "When I read a novel my imagination starts off at a gallop and leaves the narrator hidden in a cloud of dust" (N 71-80, 104). For a discussion of ways in which, to the very end of his life, James's imagination was apparently working on and re-creating the stuff of literature, history, and his own experience, see our essay, "The 'Inexhaustible Sensibility' and Henry James's 'Deathbed

Dictations,'" *Neophilologus* 77 (1993): 163-65.

8 See our essay, "Critical Responsibility in Henry James's 'The Coxon Fund' and 'The Birthplace,'" *English Studies in Canada* 8 (March 1982): 62-75.

9 See W.R. Martin, "*Hamlet* and Henry James's First Fiction," *ANQ* N.S. 2 (October 1989): 137-38.

10 *Henry James and the French Novel*, p. 10.

11 *Lost Illusions*, in Vol. 10, Honoré de Balzac in Twenty-Five Volumes (New York: Peter Fenelon Collier, 1900), p. 205.

12 "*First Love*" and "*Rudin*," introd. Lord David Cecil, trans. Alec Brown (London: Hamish Hamilton, The Novel Library, 1950), p. 213.

13 "Turgenev and the Life-Giving Drop," in *Turgenev's Literary Reminiscences*, ed. and trans. David Magarshack (n. p.: Funk & Wagnalls, Minerva Press, 1968), pp. 50-52.

14 Ivan Turgenev, *A Sportsman's Notebook*, trans. Charles and Natasha Hepburn (London: Cresset Press, 1950), p. 301.

15 "'The Lord of Burleigh' and Henry James's 'A Landscape-Painter,'" *Notes and Queries* N.S. 2 (May 1955): 220-21.

16 This satiric element is not inconsistent with the fact that James admired Tennyson and had an affection for his verse, which he "ached over in nostalgic years"; when James visited the poet, he suggested that Tennyson read his "Locksley Hall," which he did in a "deep-voiced chant" (A 515, 593). In a letter of January 1902 James refers to "The Lord of Burleigh" (L IV, 222).

17 James Kraft shows insight into Adela and makes the interesting suggestion that Ludlow is "an early version of Christopher Newman [in *The American*]," *The Early Tales of Henry James* (Carbondale, Illinois: Southern Illinois University Press, 1969), pp. 13-14.

18 One indication that James is at this early period very conscious of different modes of narration in his tales is perhaps a passage in "A Most Extraordinary Case" (1868): "If I were telling my story from Mrs. Mason's point of view . . ." (I, 235).

19 "'5 M.S. Pages': Henry James's Addition to 'A Day of Days,'" *Studies in Short Fiction* 25 (Spring 1988): 153-55.

20 See our essay, "James's 'My Friend Bingham' and Coleridge's 'Ancient Mariner,'" *English Language Notes* 25 (December 1987): 44-48.

21 Henry Fielding, *Joseph Andrews*, Bk. IV, Chap. 8.

22 See EL 75-78 and Catherine Drinker Bowen, *Yankee from Olympus: Justice Holmes and His Family* (Boston: Little, Brown, 1944), p. 224.

23 James wrote of the New England ethos as "a danger [he] after all escaped" (A 305), but he obviously knew it well and respected it highly.

24 It is remarkable that James's father, Henry Sr., often original and always on the rebound from Puritan notions, should write to an unknown correspondent "that he thought no young American should be put in the path of death [during the Civil War] until he had experienced some of the good of life -- 'until he has found some charming conjugal Elizabeth or other to whisper his devotion to, and assume the task if need be of keeping his memory green.'" Strouse, *Alice James*, p. 71.

25 *The Early Development of Henry James*, pp. 62-64.

Chapter II
THE CROP OF 1868

[1] See Oscar Wilde, *The Picture of Dorian Gray*, ed. and introd. Isobel Murray (Oxford: Oxford University Press, 1981), p. 223; "The Decay of Lying," *The Artist as Critic: The Critical Writings of Oscar Wilde*, ed. Richard Ellmann (New York: Random House, 1969), pp. 307, 320. An accidental irony, which demands to be mentioned at this point, is that in May 1914 John Singer Sargent's portrait of James, commissioned by friends to honour his seventieth birthday and exhibited at the Royal Academy, was slashed by an elderly suffragette who had never heard of Henry James but was protesting against the prices commanded by the paintings of male artists; she slashed it with a meat-cleaver, and, as James wrote to a friend, "I naturally feel very scalped and disfigured, but you will be glad to know that I seem to be pronounced curable" (L IV, 712; see EL 685-86).

[2] Cornelia Pulsifer Kelley observes that James "failed to keep Lennox as a central figure" and aptly says that "The Story of a Masterpiece" belongs to "the explanatory type of fiction that James had been writing up to this time," *The Early Development of Henry James*, p. 81.

[3] See Kelley, *The Early Development of Henry James*, p. 82.

[4] See EL 82; *The Conquest of London*, pp. 40-41; EL 429-31.

[5] "Rustle" often has connotations of richness and something like female seductiveness in James; see, for example, in this tale, also I, 241, 242, and 243; in "The Romance" (I, 216), "The Madonna of the Future" (II, 202), and *The Golden Bowl* (Harmondsworth: Penguin, 1966), pp. 129, 192, 308, 423.

[6] See the addition of "what people are supposed to live for" and "motives" (I, 485).

[7] The narrator of "The Pension Beaurepas" (1879) tells us in his opening paragraph that he "was an admirer of the *Chartreuse de Parme*" (III, 290).

[8] M.I. Finley, *The Ancient Greeks* (Harmondsworth: Penguin, 1966), p. 52.

[9] *The School of Hawthorne* (New York: Oxford University Press, 1986), p. 127.

Chapter III
FIRST CULMINATION, 1869

[1] "The Hawthorne Aspect" (part of "On Henry James"), in *The Question of Henry James: A Collection of Critical Essays*, ed. F.W. Dupee (London: Allan Wingate, 1947), p. 130.

[2] "Refurbishing James's 'A Light Man,'" *Arizona Quarterly* 42 (Winter 1986): 305-14.

Chapter IV
ADVENTURE TO EUROPE AND RETURN, 1869-72

[1] *Young Henry James*, p. 111.

[2] Quoted in Le Clair, *Young Henry James*, p. 429.

[3] Although "Travelling Companions" was not included in the New York Edition, the Preface to *The Reverberator* refers to the contents of that volume, which includes some early "international" tales, and it seems that James did have "Travelling Companions" in mind; note that Charlotte Evans stirred the narrator's curiosity because in her he found "positive, not negative maidenhood" (II, 6), and in the Preface James says of the exceptional young American women: "their negatives were converted and became in certain relations lively positives and values" (LC II, 1199).

[4] *Italian Hours*, p. 23.

[5] For James's own view of Tintoretto, see W.R. Martin, "'The Eye of Mr. Ruskin': James's Views on Venetian Artists," *The Henry James Review* 5 (Winter 1984): 107-116.

[6] Compare the couple's visit to Padua with James's; see L I, 145-146.

[7] Charlotte seems to accept Brooke's notion that she denied his profane love, assuming this figure to be the one "with unbound hair, naked, ungirdled by a great reverted mantle of Venetian purple," but, as Adeline Tintner has pointed out, informed opinion now appears to believe that Profane Love is the other, "richly clad, and full of mild dignity and repose" (II, 40; TMW 24). See also Harold E. Wethey, *The Paintings of Titian, The Mythological and Historical Paintings*, Vol.3 (London: Phaidon, 1975), pp. 20-21. Stranger still are the errors in the description of Tintoretto's *Crucifixion* in San Cassiano; see our note, "Henry James's 'Travelling Companions': Did the Master Nod?" *Notes and Queries* N.S. 34 (March 1987): 46-47.

[8] See, e.g., L I, 106, 204, 216, and for James's account of Oxford see the second half of "Two Excursions," *English Hours* (London: Oxford University Press, 1981), pp. 108-112.

[9] The narrator's description is not altogether unlike James's own, a few years later (1877), when he records seeing "numerous" examples of "the recumbent British tramp" in Green Park. *English Hours*, p. 92.

[10] A similar image appears in "Flickerbridge" (1902) (ECT XI, 340).

[11] Peter Buitenhuis (*The Grasping Imagination: The American Writings of Henry James* [Toronto: University of Toronto Press, 1970], p. 49) has pointed out that this aspect of the tale is based on two incidents in Hawthorne's English sketches ; the incidents illustrate what Hawthorne calls "this peculiar insanity [that] lies deep in the Anglo-American heart": "an unspeakable yearning towards England." The following are among the many passages in Hawthorne's sketches that the tale might bring to mind: "Common objects of English scenery," through literature and talk, "had insensibly taken their places among the images of things actually seen"; "I take leave of Oxford without even an attempt to describe it; there being no literary faculty, attainable or conceivable by me, which can avail to put it adequately, or even tolerably, upon paper." See *Our Old Home: A Series of English Sketches*, The

Centenary Edition of the Works of Nathaniel Hawthorne, Vol. V (Columbus: Ohio State University Press, 1970), pp. 15-21, 63, 191.

[12] Throughout his life James deprecated the prominence of the business mentality in the American male; see, e.g., A 278; AS 64; and James's tale "The Jolly Corner." With some satisfaction he is able to say that, after his grandfather's time, his own family "were never in a single case, I think, for two generations, guilty of a stroke of business" (A 109).

[13] Cf. Ralph Pendrel in *The Sense of the Past*; see EL 505.

[14] Apparently asked by his father to give his views on the British character, James says in March 1870: "If I knew just a little more about the English I wouldn't hesitate to offer my 'views'" (L I, 217).

[15] Adeline Tintner, who lays great stress on James's borrowings from Shakespeare, discusses in some detail "James's Hamlets" in "Master Eustace," *The Princess Casamassima*, and *The Ivory Tower* (TBW 3-19). We believe that echoes of *Hamlet* are even more pervasive in James's writing than she shows, as we saw in "The Story of a Year."

[16] It is odd that James should have used the word "cope" three times in the *Galaxy* version (II, 136, 137, 148): the presumably unconscious wordplay was removed in the revision. "Eustace" is twice remarked on as a pretty name (II, 128, 129); James was soon to have a "Euphemia" de Mauves (1874), a "Eugene" Pickering (1874), a Eugenia (*The Europeans*, 1878), and a Eunice ("The Impressions of a Cousin," 1883). "Europe" is similar, but has a different root. "Master" in the title indicates that Eustace is only a boy, but also that he is inappropriately imperious and petulant.

[17] *The Conquest of London*, pp. 39-40.

[18] For James's borrowing from *The Merchant*, see TBW 19-23.

[19] It is remarkable that James should soon have another, though very different, Crawford in "Crawford's Consistency" (1876), and that in "The Siege of London" (1883) there should be a not dissimilar Mrs. Beck and a Mr. Littlemore who is like the Crawford in "Guest's Confession," at least in owning a silver mine in the American west and in his genial relationship with Mrs. Beck. Robert Emmet Long has noticed that "Guest's Confession" foreshadows *The American* (1877) in that in both works the central figure destroys an incriminating document, and that the character of Crawford "anticipates" Christopher Newman. See *Henry James: The Early Novels*, pp. 47-48.

[20] See, for example, the extended passage beginning "I ought in justice . . ." and running to ". . . to save a deal of time in courtship" (II, 173-75).

Chapter V
RENEWAL IN EUROPE, 1872-74

[1] Henry James Senior reports that Howells had "a decided shrinking from one episode -- that in which Theobald tells of his love for, and his visit from the Titian-ic beauty, and his subsequent disgust of her worthlessness--as being risky for the magazine" (II, xxxix). Editorial sensitivity on exchanges between the sexes took many forms; see our discussion in Chapter I of the change James was persuaded by the editors of the *Galaxy* to make in "A Day of Days."

[2] When James was overseas it was apparently usual for his father to make

minor revisions in his work when seeing it through the American press. See, e.g., James's message of thanks for his father's "revision" of "Gabrielle de Bergerac" in 1869 (L I, 132).

3 The first stanza of Tennyson's poem throws an ironic light on Theobald and perhaps suggests James's title:

> Love thou thy land, with love far-brought
> From out the storied Past, and used
> Within the Present, but transfused
> Thro' future time by power of thought.

4 Robert Browning, *Poems*, ed. Donald Smalley (Boston: Houghton Mifflin, 1956), pp. 216-17.

5 It is interesting that James himself has some ambivalent feelings about Raphael at about this time. In "Florentine Notes" (1874) he writes of "the flower-like irresponsibility of Raphael's 'Madonna of the Chair'" (*Italian Hours*, p. 287). The painting is referred to again in "The Diary of a Man of Fifty" (1879), where it is admired by the diarist, whose judgement is generally at fault. Although "before Rafael's great portraits in Florence there was nothing I wouldn't have conceded to him," in a letter of November 1869 James finds himself "irresponsive" in the famous *Stanze* of the Vatican (L I, 165).

6 *The School of Hawthorne*, p.131.

7 Introduction, *The Art of the Novel* (New York: Charles Scribner's Sons, 1937), p. xvi.

8 Balzac, whom James regarded as the "father," the "master of us all" (LC II, 120, 138), provided stories for the great French illustrator Grandville's *Les animaux peints par eux-mêmes et dessinés par un autre*: "Heartaches of an English cat," "Handbook for Animals Desirous of Honors," and "Journey of an African Lion to Paris," for example. See *Bizarreries and Fantasies of Grandville,* introd. Stanley Appelbaum (New York: Dover, 1974), pp. 87-89. But Balzac was elevating animals to the human level, even if to satirize or excoriate men's behaviour, whereas James's narrator's disgust is provoked by the reversal of this process, by the reduction of human behaviour to the animal level.

9 At one point in a passage which he later deleted, James had Guy Domville crying, "But 'life'--for *me*--is evil!" *The Complete Plays of Henry James* (London: Rupert Hart-Davis, 1949), p. 515n.

10 *Henry James and the French Novel*, p. 25.

11 Cornelia Kelley suggests that, like "The Madonna," this tale too derives -- though less directly -- from Balzac's "*Le Chef d'Oeuvre Inconnu.*" See *The Early Development of Henry James*, pp. 152-53.

12 *Italian Hours*, p. 271.

13 Trans. Frances Frenaye (London: Four Square Books, 1959).

14 *James the Critic* (London: Macmillan, 1984), p. 64.

15 To be fair, one must remember that James has many interesting unprivileged characters who are presented with insight and sympathy; besides

a great number of Americans in comfortable but not especially affluent circumstances who are centres of consciousness, there are, for instance, the unnamed young woman who is a post-office clerk ("In the Cage," 1898) and Morris Gedge ("The Birthplace," 1903).

16 It is possible that James was reading Jane Austen at about this time. *Watch and Ward*, the novel that he wrote a year or two before "Mme. de Mauves," seems to be structured like *Mansfield Park*.

17 *The Early Tales of Henry James*, p. 66.

18 Kraft maintains that James's portrait of Longmore too is ironic and critical: "Longmore has no passion, no life, no art. He is the emasculated American male held up to scorn" (*The Early Tales,* p. 63). We think Kraft is reading far too much into the text. Longmore is perhaps rather like James himself, as is Winterbourne in "Daisy Miller," for whom some such criticisms are implied by James, though "scorn" will still be much too strong a term.

19 In a review published in January 1876 James writes of "a not unfounded mistrust of the Italian element in light literature. Italy has been made to supply so much of the easy picturesqueness, the crude local color of poetry and the drama, that a use of this expedient is vaguely regarded as a sort of unlawful short-cut to success" (LC I, 486).

20 See Jean-Jacques Rousseau, *Émile ou de l'éducation* (Paris: Garnier, 1964), pp. 25-26, 72, 83, 87, 119-20, 296, 417, *et passim*.

Chapter VI
AMERICAN INTERRUPTION, 1874-76

1 *The Marble Faun; or, The Romance of Monte Beni*, 2 Vols. in One (Boston: James R. Osgood, 1874), II, 71.

2 In *The Marble Faun* there is a conspicuous reference to a "grand, calm" sculptured head of Milton and to various of his poems, including *Paradise Lost* and "L'Allegro" (see I, 150-51), as well as a quotation from "Il Penseroso" (see II, 97) and many verbal echoes from the two shorter poems.

3 *The Development of the American Short Story: An Historical Survey* (1923; rpt. New York: Biblo and Tannen, 1966), pp. 199-200.

4 *The Conquest of London*, pp. 193, 191. Another famous Benvolio is the sceptical courtier in Marlowe's *Doctor Faustus* who falls victim to Faustus's conjuring tricks.

5 *John Milton: A Reader's Guide to His Poetry* (New York: Farrar, Straus, 1963), p. 12.

6 *The Works of John Milton*, Columbia University Edition, Frank Allen Patterson, general ed., Vol. IV (New York: Columbia University Press, 1931), p. 311.

7 William Riley Parker, *Milton: A Biography* (Oxford: Clarendon Press, 1968), I, 70.

8 *Milton: A Biography* I, 177.

9 George Burnett, trans.; Moses Hadas, rev., *Joannis Miltoni Angli Pro Populo Anglicano Defensio Secunda*, in *The Works of John Milton*, Columbia University Edition, Frank Allen Patterson, general ed., Vol. VIII (New York:

Columbia University Press, 1933), p. 125.

10 "Milton," in *Lives of the English Poets*, Vol. I (London: Henry Frowde, Oxford University Press, 1906), p. 132.

11 For a slightly more extended form of our discussion of "Benvolio" see our "Henry James's 'Benvolio' and Milton," *Studies in Short Fiction* 27 (Spring 1990): 260-63.

12 Aziz (III, 11) gives this as "better."

13 For his father's story, see III, 11n-12n, JF 123-25, or A 402-04.

14 The argument that follows appeared in slightly different form in our essay, "Captain Diamond and Old Hickory: Realities and Ambivalence in Henry James's 'The Ghostly Rental,'" *Studies in Short Fiction* 26 (Winter 1989): 1-9.

15 In 1868 William James showed sympathetic insight into Channing's "moral culture," and in the letter that discloses this he says he is surprised to find "many of the elements of a Pascal in me." *The Letters of William James*, ed. Henry James [William's son] (Boston: Atlantic Monthly Press, 1920), I, 132-33.

16 See Marquis James, *The Life of Andrew Jackson--Part One: The Border Captain* (Indianapolis: Bobbs-Merrill, 1933), pp. 216, 219. For a discussion of the importance of Andrew Jackson in the tale and of the significance of the tale in James's life, see our essay cited above.

17 See Arthur M. Schlesinger, Jr., *The Age of Jackson* (New York: Book Find Club, 1945), p. 523, and Marquis James, *The Life of Andrew Jackson--Part Two: Portrait of a President* (Indianapolis: Bobbs-Merrill, 1937), pp. 499-500.

18 See Schlesinger, *The Age of Jackson*, pp. 482-83.

19 Adeline Tintner thinks that James's portrait, in "The Solution" (1889), of an American ambassador of the period of pristine virtue, "like a sitting Cicero" (ECT VII, 400), suggests, among others, Andrew Jackson and his bust by Powers (TMW 40).

20 See Marquis James, *Portrait of a President*, p. 443, and James Parton, *The Life of Andrew Jackson* (New York: Mason, 1863), pp. 451-54.

21 Schlesinger, *Age of Jackson*, pp. 267-81.

22 Edwin M. Bacon, *Boston: A Guide Book*, rev. ed. (Boston: Ginn, 1907), p. 108.

23 Edel, *The Untried Years*, p. 21.

24 Jonathan Edwards, *Basic Writings*, ed. Ola E. Winslow (New York: New American Library, 1966), p. 159.

25 Sculley Bradley, Richmond Croom Beatty, and E. Hudson Long, eds., *The American Tradition in Literature*, rev. ed. (New York: Norton, 1961), I, 1406n, 1409.

26 *Encyclopaedia Britannica*, 1965, XI, 684.

27 *Dictionary of American Biography*, Vol. II, Part 2, p. 6.

28 Perry Miller, ed., *The American Transcendentalists* (Garden City, New York: Doubleday, 1957), p. ix.

29 *A History of the United States* (The Pelican History of the World) (Harmondsworth: Penguin, 1955), II, 396.

30 See Randall Stewart, *Nathaniel Hawthorne* (New Haven: Yale University

Press, 1948), p. 20.

[31] James R. Mellow, *Nathaniel Hawthorne in His Times* (Boston: Houghton Mifflin, 1980), p. 46.

[32] *Pascal's Pensées*, introd. T.S. Eliot (New York: Dutton, 1958), p. 258.

[33] *The Letters of William Blake*, ed. Geoffrey Keynes, 3rd ed. (Oxford: Clarendon Press, 1980), p. 8.

[34] See Noah Webster, *An American Dictionary of the English Language* (Springfield: G. & C. Merriam, 1878).

[35] *Petronius*, trans. Michael Heseltine; Seneca, *Apocolocyntosis*, trans. W.H.D. Rouse (Loeb Classical Library) (London: Heinemann, 1961), p. 87.

[36] It is tempting to see in James's Deborah also something of the redoubtable Lady Deborah Moody, daughter of the Earl of Lincoln, described by Governor John Winthrop as "a wise and anciently religious woman," who, "being taken with the error of denying baptism to infants," in 1643 left the Salem church and found refuge with Peter Stuyvesant on Long Island. Lady Deborah's name was closely associated with Swampscott, fondly recalled by James as a "scene of fermentation" in "the summer of '66" (A 494, 497). See Harriet Sylvester Tapley, "Women of Massachusetts (1620-1689)," *Commonwealth History of Massachusetts*, ed. Albert Bushnell Hart (1927; rpt. New York: Russell & Russell, 1966), I, 311-12; *Winthrop's Journal: "History of New England*," ed. James Kendall Hosmer (1908; rpt. New York: Barnes & Noble, 1966), II, 126; James Duncan Phillips, *Salem in the Seventeenth Century* (Boston: Houghton Mifflin, 1933), p. 130.

Chapter VII
FAME 1877-79

[1] The name of James's brave but naive heroine became a byword for the young American woman travelling abroad; the *nouvelle* even features--clearly, though its title is not given--in another of James's tales, "Pandora" (1884) (see ECT V, 361, 363).

[2] See Seamon, "Henry James's 'Four Meetings': A Study in Irritability and Condescension," *Studies in Short Fiction* 15 (Spring 1978): 155-63.

[3] For an earlier statement of this argument, see W.R. Martin, "The Narrator's 'Retreat' in James's 'Four Meetings,'" *Studies in Short Fiction* 17 (Fall 1980): 497-99.

[4] See W.R. Martin, "*Emma*: A Definition of Virtue," *English Studies in Africa* 3 (March 1960): 21-30.

[5] Edel, *The Untried Years*, p. 192.

[6] See "Travelling Companions," "The Last of the Valerii," "Adina," *Roderick Hudson*, and James's next tale, "Longstaff's Marriage." St. Peter's is often a place for the discovery of one's real self or of deep truth. Both Rome and St. Peter's become important presences in *The Portrait*. In "The Solution" (1889-90) the fact that the narrator treats St. Peter's merely as "a public promenade," and on its "solemn fields of marble" (ECT VII, 365-66) prepares to make game of the innocent Wilmerding, makes his callousness all the more deplorable.

[7] See our essay, "Hemingway and James: 'A Canary for One' and 'Daisy

Miller,'" *Studies in Short Fiction* 22 (Fall 1985): 469-71.

[8] In this he may have been influenced by Howells; in a review of Howells's *A Foregone Conclusion* in January 1875, James wrote that "not the least charm of [Howells's] charming heroines" is that "they have been American women in the scientific sense of the term" (LC I, 494); in other words, they were "studies." Howells's Florida Vervain is a plant as indigenous to America as Daisy, though less common.

[9] In her discussion of the tale Adeline Tintner draws attention to the piquant irony of Daisy's innocence being juxtaposed with Velazquez's "Innocent X" (III, 194) (see TMW 63-68).

[10] Introduction to *Henry James: Selected Short Stories*, rev. ed. (New York: Holt, Rinehart and Winston, 1957), pp. vi-vii.

[11] Several versions of this ballad are recorded. One that would have been readily accessible to James was in Bishop Percy's *Reliques of Ancient English Poetry*, with Memoir and Critical Dissertation by the Rev. George Gilfillan (Edinburgh: James Nichol, 1858), III, 102-04. For a full discussion of the borrowing, see our essay, "Henry James's 'Longstaff's Marriage' and 'Barbara Allan'", *A.L.R.: American Literary Realism 1870-1910*, 24, 2 (Winter 1992): 81-87.

[12] *Italian Hours*, p. 179. James's (and his characters') favourite guide, Murray's, notes that Aricia (the modern Ariccia) "was supposed to have been founded by Hippolytus, who was worshipped under the name of Virbius, in conjunction with Diana, in the neighbouring grove," and that "the lake of Nemi" is "the Lacus Nemorensis of the ancients." See *A Handbook of Rome and its Environs*, 8th ed. (London: John Murray, 1867), pp. 399, 402.

[13] *The English and Scottish Popular Ballads*, Vol. II, ed. Francis J. Child (New York: Cooper Square Publishers, 1962 [1882]), p. 277.

[14] James has other and richer gifts than Théophile Gautier's, which were for the "pictorial" and the "picturesque," but he certainly has Gautier's ability to capture "those happiest hours . . . when we have strolled forth into a foreign town . . . and lost ourselves deliciously in the fathomless sense of local difference and mystery"; in "An International Episode" he has, like Gautier, "achieved the remarkable feat of suppressing the sense of familiarity and winning back . . . a certain freshness of impression" (LC II, 366, 363-64, 365). For James's possible borrowings from Alexis de Tocqueville in "An International Episode," see TBW 167-71.

Chapter VIII
END OF A PHASE

[1] It has been suggested that James felt she killed herself on account of unrequited love of him (see EL 391).

[2] Edel, *The Conquest of London*, p. 389.

Chapter IX
TOWARDS *THE PORTRAIT OF A LADY*

[1] See Buitenhuis, *The Grasping Imagination*, pp. 57-58.

[2] Henry James, *Watch and Ward* (New York: Grove Press, 1959), p. 70. James apparently found the name for his heroine of *The Bostonians*, Verena, in Yonge's novel. See, e.g., *The Heir of Redclyffe* (London: Collins, n.d.), p. 576.

[3] See also the revised version: Henry James, *Roderick Hudson* (Boston: Houghton Mifflin, 1917), p. 226.

[4] *Henry James: The Early Novels*, pp. 47-48.

[5] Edel, *Henry James, The Untried Years*, p. 292.

[6] *The Conquest of London*, p. 385.

[7] Henry James, *Confidence*, ed. Herbert Ruhm (New York: Grosset & Dunlap, 1962), p. 226.

[8] *The School of Hawthorne*, p. 129.

[9] See, e.g., F.R. Leavis, *The Great Tradition* (Harmondsworth: Penguin, 1962 [1948]), p. 141.

[10] *Our Old Home*, p. 4.

[11] *The Blithedale Romance* (New York: W.W. Norton, 1958), pp. 93, 247.

[12] John Hayward, Editorial Note, *A Sportsman's Notebook* (London: Cresset Press, 1950), p. viii.

[13] Quoted in Isaiah Berlin's "Fathers and Children," the Romanes Lecture 1970, printed in Turgenev, *Fathers and Sons*, trans. Rosemary Edmonds (Harmondsworth: Penguin, 1975), p. 39.

[14] "Turgenev and the Life-Giving Drop," p. 49.

[15] (Boston: Houghton, Mifflin, 1881), pp. 1-3.

[16] *The School of Hawthorne*, p. 135.

[17] *The Portrait*, p. 175.

[18] *The Portrait*, p. 153.

[19] *Paradise Lost*, IX, 503-4, 549.

WORKS CITED

Allott, Miriam. "'The Lord of Burleigh' and Henry James's 'A
　　Landscape Painter.'" *Notes and Queries*, N.S.2 (May 1955): 220-21.
Anderson, Quentin, ed. and introd. *Henry James: Selected Short Stories.*
　　Rev. ed. New York: Holt, Rinehart and Winston, 1957.
Appelbaum, Stanley, introd. *Bizarreries and Fantasies of Grandville.*
　　New York: Dover, 1974.
Auden, W.H., ed. *The American Scene.* By Henry James. New York:
　　Charles Scribner's Sons, 1946.
Aziz, Maqbool, ed. *The Tales of Henry James.* 3 vols.+. Oxford:
　　Clarendon Press, 1973-84--.
Bacon, Edwin M. *Boston: A Guide Book.* Rev. ed. Boston: Ginn, 1907.
Balzac, Honoré de. *Lost Illusions. Honoré de Balzac in Twenty-Five
　　Volumes.* Vol. 10. New York: Peter Fenelon Collier, 1900.
Beatty, Richmond Croom. See "Bradley, Sculley."
Berlin, Isaiah. "Fathers and Children" (1970 Romanes Lecture). In *Fathers
　　and Sons.* By Ivan Turgenev. Trans. Rosemary Edmonds.
　　Harmondsworth: Penguin, 1975.
Bewley, Marius. *The Complex Fate.* Introd. F.R. Leavis. London:
　　Chatto and Windus, 1952.
Blackmur, Richard P., introd. *The Art of the Novel.* By Henry
　　James. New York: Charles Scribner's Sons, 1937.
Blake, William. *The Letters of William Blake.* Ed. Geoffrey Keynes.
　　3rd ed. Oxford: Clarendon Press, 1980.
Bowen, Catherine Drinker. *Yankee from Olympus: Justice Holmes and His
　　Family.* Boston: Little, Brown, 1944.
Bradley, Sculley, Richmond Croom Beatty, and E. Hudson Long, eds.
　　The American Tradition in Literature. Rev. ed. Vol. 1.
　　New York: Norton, 1961.
Brodhead, Richard H. *The School of Hawthorne.* New York: Oxford
　　University Press, 1986.
Browning, Robert. *Poems.* Ed. Donald Smalley. Boston: Houghton
　　Mifflin, 1956.
Buitenhuis, Peter. *The Grasping Imagination: The American Writings
　　of Henry James.* Toronto: University of Toronto Press, 1970.
"Channing, William Ellery." *Dictionary of American Biography.*
Child, Francis James, ed. *The English and Scottish Popular Ballads.* 5 vols.

in 3. 1882-98. New York: Cooper Square Publishers, 1962.
Dupee, F.W., ed. *The Question of Henry James: A Collection of
Critical Essays*. London: Allan Wingate, 1947.
Edel, Leon. *Henry James: A Life*. New York: Harper & Row, 1985.
_____. *Henry James, The Conquest of London: 1870-1881*. New
York: Avon Books, 1978.
_____. *Henry James, The Master: 1901-1916*. New York: Avon
Books, 1978.
_____. *Henry James, The Untried Years: 1843-1870*. New York:
Avon Books, 1978.
Edwards, Jonathan. *Basic Writings*. Ed. Ola E. Winslow. New York:
New American Library, 1966.
Eliot, T.S. "The Hawthorne Aspect" (part of "On Henry James"). In
The Question of Henry James: A Collection of Critical Essays.
Ed. F.W. Dupee. London: Allan Wingate, 1947.
_____. *Selected Essays*. London: Faber, 1951.
Fielding, Henry. *Joseph Andrews and Shamela*. Ed. and introd.
Martin C. Battestin. Boston: Houghton Mifflin, 1961.
Finley, M.I. *The Ancient Greeks*. Harmondsworth: Penguin, 1966.
Gérard, Jean-Ignace-Isidore. See "Grandville."
Grandville [Jean-Ignace-Isidore Gérard]. *Bizarreries and Fantasies of
Grandville*. Introd. Stanley Applebaum. New York: Dover, 1974.
Grover, Philip. *Henry James and the French Novel: A Study in
Inspiration*. London: Paul Elek, 1973.
A Handbook of Rome and Its Environs ("Murray"). 8th ed. London: John
Murray, 1867.
Hart, Albert Bushnell, ed. *Commonwealth History of Massachusetts*. 4
vols. 1927. New York: Russell & Russell, 1966.
Hawthorne, Nathaniel. *The Blithedale Romance*. New York: W.W.
Norton, 1958.
_____. *The Marble Faun; or, The Romance of Monte Beni*. 2 vols in one.
Boston: James R. Osgood, 1874.
_____. *Our Old Home: A Series of English Sketches*. Centenary
Edition of the Works of Nathaniel Hawthorne. Vol. 5. Columbus:
Ohio State University Press, 1970.
Hayward, John, ed. *A Sportsman's Notebook*. By Ivan Turgenev. Trans.
Charles and Natasha Hepburn. London: Cresset Press, 1950.
"Hopkins, Samuel." *Encyclopaedia Britannica*, 1965 ed.
James, Henry. *The American Scene*. Ed. W.H. Auden. New York: Charles
Scribner's Sons, 1946.
_____. *The Art of the Novel*. Introd. Richard P. Blackmur. New York:
Charles Scribner's Sons, 1937.
_____. *Autobiography*. Ed. Frederick W. Dupee. Princeton: Princeton
University Press, 1983.
_____. *The Complete Notebooks*. Ed. Leon Edel and Lyall H. Powers.
Oxford: Oxford University Press, 1987.
_____. *The Complete Plays of Henry James*. London: Rupert Hart-Davis,
1949.
_____. *The Complete Tales of Henry James*. Ed. Leon Edel. 12 vols.
Philadelphia: J.B. Lippincott, 1961-64.
_____. *Confidence*. Ed. Herbert Ruhm. New York: Grosset & Dunlap,
1962.
_____. *English Hours*. London: Oxford University Press, 1981.

_____. *The Finer Grain*. Ed. and introd. W.R.Martin and Warren U. Ober. Delmar, New York: Scholars' Facsimiles and Reprints, 1986.
_____. *The Golden Bowl*. Harmondsworth: Penguin, 1966.
_____. *Italian Hours*. New York: Grove Press, 1979.
_____. *Letters*. Ed. Leon Edel. 4 vols. Cambridge, Mass.: Harvard University Press, 1974-84.
_____. *The Letters of Henry James*. Ed. Percy Lubbock. 2 vols. New York: Charles Scribner's Sons, 1920.
_____. *Literary Criticism: Essays on Literature; American Writers; English Writers*. Ed. Leon Edel and Mark Wilson. New York: Library of America, 1984.
_____. *Literary Criticism: French Writers; Other European Writers; The Prefaces to the New York Edition*. Ed. Leon Edel and Mark Wilson. New York: Library of America, 1984.
_____. *Novels 1871-1880*. Ed. William T. Stafford. New York: Library of America, 1983.
_____. *The Portrait of a Lady*. Boston: Houghton Mifflin, 1881.
_____. *Roderick Hudson*. Boston: Houghton Mifflin, 1917.
_____. *Selected Short Stories*. Ed. and introd. Quentin Anderson. Rev. ed. New York: Holt, Rinehart and Winston, 1957.
_____. *The Tales of Henry James*. Ed. Maqbool Aziz. 3 vols.+. Oxford: Clarendon Press, 1973-84--.
_____. *Watch and Ward*. New York: Grove Press, 1959.
James, Henry [William's son], ed. *The Letters of William James*. 2 vols. Boston: Atlantic Monthly Press, 1920.
James, Marquis. *The Life of Andrew Jackson--Part One: The Border Captain; Part Two: Portrait of a President*. Indianapolis: Bobbs-Merrill, 1933, 1937.
James, William. *The Letters of William James*. Ed. Henry James [William's son]. 2 vols. Boston: Atlantic Monthly Press, 1920.
Johnson, Samuel. *Lives of the English Poets*. Vol. 1. London: Henry Frowde, Oxford University Press, 1906.
Jones, Vivien. *James the Critic*. London: Macmillan, 1984.
Kelley, Cornelia Pulsifer. *The Early Development of Henry James*. Urbana: University of Illinois Press, 1965.
Keynes, Geoffrey, ed. *The Letters of William Blake*. 3rd ed. Oxford: Clarendon Press, 1980.
Kraft, James. *The Early Tales of Henry James*. Carbondale, Illinois: Southern Illinois University Press, 1969.
Leavis, F.R., introd. *The Complex Fate*. By Marius Bewley. London: Chatto and Windus, 1952.
_____. *The Great Tradition*. 1948. Harmondsworth: Penguin, 1962.
Le Clair, Robert C. *Young Henry James*. New York: Bookman Associates, 1955.
Levi, Carlo. *Christ Stopped at Eboli*. Trans. Frances Frenaye. London: Four Square Books, 1959.
Long, E. Hudson. See "Bradley, Sculley."
Long, Robert Emmet. *Henry James: The Early Novels*. Boston: Twayne Publishers, 1983.
Martin, W.R. "*Emma*: A Definition of Virtue." *English Studies in Africa*, 3 (March 1960): 21-30.
_____. "'The Eye of Mr. Ruskin': James's Views on Venetian Artists." *The Henry James Review*, 5 (Winter 1984): 107-16.
_____. "*Hamlet* and Henry James's First Fiction." *ANQ: A Quarterly*

Journal of Short Articles, Notes, and Reviews, N.S.2 (1989): 137-38.
_____. "The Narrator's 'Retreat' in James's 'Four Meetings.'" *Studies in Short Fiction*, 17 (1980): 497-99.
Martin, W.R., and Warren U. Ober. "Captain Diamond and Old Hickory: Realities and Ambivalence in Henry James's 'The Ghostly Rental.'" *Studies in Short Fiction*, 26 (1989): 1-9.
_____. "Critical Responsibility in Henry James's 'The Coxon Fund' and 'The Birthplace.'" *English Studies in Canada*, 8 (March 1982): 62-75.
_____. "'5 M.S. Pages': Henry James's Additions to 'A Day of Days.'" *Studies in Short Fiction*, 25 (1988): 153-55.
_____. "Hemingway and James: 'A Canary for One' and 'Daisy Miller.'" *Studies in Short Fiction*, 22 (1985): 469-71.
_____. "Henry James's 'Benvolio' and Milton." *Studies in Short Fiction*, 27 (1990): 260-63.
_____. "Henry James's 'Longstaff's Marriage' and 'Barbara Allan.'" *American Literary Realism 1870-1910*, 24 (1992): 81-87.
_____. "Henry James's 'Travelling Companions': Did the Master Nod?" *Notes and Queries*, N.S.34 (March 1987): 46-47.
_____. "James's 'My Friend Bingham' and Coleridge's 'Ancient Mariner.'" *English Language Notes*, 25 (1987): 44-48.
_____. "The Provenience of Henry James's First Tale." *Studies in Short Fiction*, 24 (1987): 57-58.
_____. "Refurbishing James's 'A Light Man.'" *The Arizona Quarterly*, 42 (1986): 305-14.
_____, ed. and introd. *The Finer Grain.* By Henry James. Delmar, New York: Scholars' Facsimiles and Reprints, 1986.
Matthiessen, F.O. *The James Family.* New York: Alfred A. Knopf, 1947.
Mellow, James R. *Nathaniel Hawthorne in His Times.* Boston: Houghton Mifflin, 1980.
Mérimée, Prosper. *"Carmen précédée de "La Vénus d'Ille" et de "Colomba."* Introd. Marcel Thiebaut. 2nd ed. Monaco: Editions du Rocher, 1947.
Miller, Perry, ed. *The American Transcendentalists.* Garden City, New York: Doubleday, 1957.
Milton, John. *The Works of John Milton.* Gen ed. Frank Allen Patterson. Columbia University Edition. 18 vols. with 2-vol. index. New York: Columbia University Press, 1931-40.
Morpurgo, J.E. See "Nye, R.B."
"Murray". *A Handbook of Rome and Its Environs.* 8th ed. London: John Murray, 1867.
Nehls, Edward, ed. *D.H. Lawrence: A Composite Biography.* 3 vols. Madison: University of Wisconsin Press, 1957-59.
Nicolson, Marjorie Hope. *John Milton: A Reader's Guide to His Poetry.* New York: Farrar, Straus, 1963.
Nye, R.B., and J.E. Morpurgo. *A History of the United States.* 2 vols. Harmondsworth: Penguin, 1955.
Ober, Warren U. See "Martin, W.R., and Warren U. Ober."
Parker, William Riley. *Milton: A Biography.* 2 vols. Oxford: Clarendon Press, 1968.
Parton, James. *The Life of Andrew Jackson.* New York: Mason, 1863.
Pascal, Blaise. *Pascal's Pensées.* Introd. T.S. Eliot. New York: Dutton, 1958.

Pattee, Fred Lewis. *The Development of the American Short Story: An Historical Survey*. 1923. New York: Biblo and Tannen, 1966.

Percy, Thomas. *Reliques of Ancient English Poetry*, with Memoir and Critical Dissertation by the Rev. George Gilfillan. 3 vols. Edinburgh: James Nichol, 1858.

Petronius. Trans. Michael Heseltine. *Seneca: Apocolocyntosis*. Trans. W.H.D. Rouse. Loeb Classical Library. London: Heinemann, 1961.

Phillips, James Duncan. *Salem in the Seventeenth Century*. Boston: Houghton Mifflin, 1933.

Rousseau, Jean-Jacques. *Émile ou de l'éducation*. Paris: Garnier, 1964.

Ruhm, Herbert, ed. *Confidence*. By Henry James. New York: Grosset & Dunlap, 1962.

Schlesinger, Arthur M., Jr. *The Age of Jackson*. New York: Book Find Club, 1945.

Seamon, Roger. "Henry James's 'Four Meetings': A Study in Irritability and Condescension." *Studies in Short Fiction*, 15 (Spring 1978): 155-63.

Smalley, Donald, ed. *Robert Browning: Poems*. Boston: Houghton Mifflin, 1956.

Stafford, William T., ed. *Henry James: Novels 1871-1880*. New York: Library of America, 1983.

Stewart, Randall. *Nathaniel Hawthorne*. New Haven: Yale University Press, 1948.

Strouse, Jean. *Alice James: A Biography*. Boston: Houghton Mifflin, 1984.

Tapley, Harriet Sylvester. "Women of Massachusetts (1620-1689)." In vol. 1 of *Commonwealth History of Massachusetts*. Ed. Albert Bushnell Hart. 4 vols. 1927. New York: Russell & Russell, 1966.

Tintner, Adeline R. *The Book World of Henry James: Appropriating the Classics*. Ann Arbor, Michigan: UMI Research Press, 1987.

_____. *The Museum World of Henry James*. Ann Arbor, Michigan: UMI Research Press, 1986.

Turgenev, Ivan. *Fathers and Sons*. Trans. Rosemary Edmonds. Harmondsworth: Penguin, 1975.

_____. *"First Love" and "Rudin."* Introd. Lord David Cecil. Trans. Alec Brown. London: Hamish Hamilton, The Novel Library, 1950.

_____. *A Sportsman's Notebook*. Ed. John Hayward. Trans. Charles and Natasha Hepburn. London: Cresset Press, 1950.

_____. *Turgenev's Literary Reminiscences*. Ed. and trans. David Magarshack. N.p.: Funk & Wagnalls, Minerva Press, 1968.

Webster, Noah. *An American Dictionary of the English Language*. Springfield: G. & C. Merriam, 1878.

Wethey, Harold E. *The Paintings of Titian: The Mythological and Historical Paintings*. Vol. 3. London: Phaidon, 1975.

Wilde, Oscar. *The Artist as Critic: The Critical Writings of Oscar Wilde*. Ed. Richard Ellmann. New York: Random House, 1969.

_____. *The Picture of Dorian Gray*. Ed. and introd. Isobel Murray. Oxford: Oxford University Press, 1981.

Wilson, Edmund. "Turgenev and the Life-Giving Drop." In *Turgenev's Literary Reminiscences*. Ed. and trans. David Magarshack. N.p.: Funk & Wagnalls, Minerva Press, 1968.

Winslow, Ola E. *Jonathan Edwards: Basic Writings*. New York: New American Library, 1966.

Winthrop, John. *Winthrop's Journal: "History of New England."* Ed. James Kendall Hosmer. 2 vols. 1908. New York: Barnes & Noble,

1966.
Yonge, Charlotte M. *The Heir of Redclyffe*. London: Collins, n.d.

INDEX

Emma (Austen) 139, 153, 192
Emmets, the (James's "cousinage")
144
England 55, 57, 58, 64-71, 84, 118,
156-57, 159, 187-88, 188
"Enlèvement de la Redoute, L'"
(Mérimée) 12
Euripides 13
Europe 3-5, 11, 27, 31, 39, 46, 52,
55, 57-60, 69, 72, 80, 81, 84,
86, 106, 111, 116, 123, 134,
142, 145, 164, 171, 176, 188
Everett, Edward 32

Fables (La Fontaine) (translated by
James) 46
Fathers and Sons (Turgenev) 175
Felix Holt (Eliot) 29, 38, 179-80
Feuillet, Octave 7, 97
Flaubert, Gustave 174
Foregone Conclusion, A (Howells)
193
Fort Wagner 16
Fowler, R. L. 184
Franklin, Benjamin 27, 28
"Franklin's Tale, The" (Chaucer)
14-16
Frazer, Sir James G. 106
Freedom of the Will (Edwards) 127
French Revolution 47, 49, 174
Frost, Robert 177

Gainsborough, Thomas 66
Galaxy, The, 14, 24, 31, 39, 42, 45,
50, 71, 74, 96, 103, 112, 114,
188
Galerie d'Apollon 3
Garrick, David 118
*Garrick between Tragedy and
Comedy* (Reynolds) 118
Gautier, Théophile 163, 193
Genesis 18
Geneva 1, 141-42, 145, 147
Germany 171
Gettysburg 32
Giotto 63

Godkin, E. L. 31
Goethe, Johann Wolfgang von 54
Golden Bough, The (Frazer) 106
Grandville (J. I. I. Grandville) 189
Gray, John Chipman 26
Great Tradition, The (Leavis) 194
Grover, Philip 17, 89

Hamlet (Shakespeare) ix, xii, 12, 16,
18-19, 66, 74, 76, 160, 173,
184-85, 185, 188
Harper's New Monthly Magazine,
161
Harvard University 6, 14, 124, 128,
129, 152
Haus, Illona ix
Hawthorne, Nathaniel 3, 13, 14, 22,
26-27, 32, 35, 36, 40, 54, 60,
66, 92, 95, 103, 115-16, 129,
130, 164-65, 169, 173, 174,
175, 178, 179, 187-88, 190, 194
"Heart of Darkness" (Conrad) 104,
135, 139
Heir of Redclyffe, The (Yonge) 168,
194
Hemingway, Ernest ix, 192-93
*Henry James: The Conquest of
London* (Edel) 183, 188, 190,
193, 194
Henry James: A Life (Edel) vii
Henry James: The Master (Edel) 183
Henry James: The Untried Years
(Edel) 184, 191, 192, 194
Henry V, King (Shakespeare) xi
Herodotus 39
Hill, Mrs. F. H. xiv, 155
Hippolytus (Euripides) 13
"History of Lieutenant Ergunov, The"
(Turgenev) 19
Hoffmann, E. T. A. 124, 129, 130
Holmes, Oliver Wendell 127, 167
Holmes, Oliver Wendell, Jr. 26
Hooper, Clover 4, 69
Hopkins, Samuel 124, 127-28
Horace 51
House of the Seven Gables, The

Wilson, Edmund 19
Wilson, Mark vii-viii
Winter's Tale, The (Shakespeare) 36
Winthrop, Governor John 192
Wonder-Book, A (Hawthorne) 115
"Wonderful One-Hoss Shay, The"
  (Holmes) 127
Woolson, Constance Fenimore 162-
  63, 193

Wordsworth, William 25, 93, 169

Yeats, W. B. 84, 105, 163
Yonge, Charlotte M. 168, 194
"Young Goodman Brown"
  (Hawthorne) 14, 36
Young Henry James (Le Clair) 183

Zola, Émile 174